God in South Africa: The challenge of the gospel

Albert Nolan

GOD IN SOUTH AFRICA
The challenge of the gospel

David Philip: Cape Town & Johannesburg
Wm. B. Eerdmans: Grand Rapids, Mich.
Mambo Press: Gweru
CIIR: London

First published 1988 in southern Africa by David Philip, Publisher (Pty) Ltd, 217 Werdmuller Centre, Claremont 7700, South Africa

Published 1988 in Zimbabwe by Mambo Press, P O Box 779, Gweru

Published 1988 in the United Kingdom by Catholic Institute for International Relations, 22 Coleman Fields, London N1 7AF

Published 1988 in the United States of America by Wm. B. Eerdmans Publishing Co., 255 Jefferson Ave. SE, Grand Rapids, Michigan 49503

ISBN 0-86486-076-5 (David Philip)
ISBN 1-85287-014-1 (CIIR, cased)
ISBN 1-85287-010-9 (CIIR, paper)
ISBN 0-8028-0413-6 (Wm. B. Eerdmans)

British Library Cataloguing in Publication Data:

Nolan, Albert

God in South Africa.

1. South Africa. Society. Role of Christian Church
I. Title
261. 1′0968
ISBN 1-85287-014-1 Hdbk
ISBN 1-85287-010-9 Pbk

Library of Congress Cataloging-in-Publication Data:

Nolan, Albert, 1934–
God in South Africa: the challenge of the gospel/ Albert Nolan.
p. cm.
Bibliography: p. 230
Includes index.
ISBN 0-8028-0413-6
1. Theology, Doctrinal -- South Africa. 2. Christianity and culture.
I. Title.
BT30.S5N65 1988
230′.0968 -- dc19 88-21737
CIP

Printed by Clyson Printers (Pty) Ltd, Maitland, Cape, South Africa

Contents

I hear it said all the day long:
'Where is your God?'

Psalm 42: 3

Foreword

When one looks back at the history of the Christian faith, one is amazed at the resourcefulness of the Church. It is both amazing and exciting to see the Church's ability to produce its rare but timely insights of dissent in human affairs. Jesus of Nazareth represented such a phenomenon in his lifetime. Through his resurrected life, numerous others have stood as beacons of witness to what he called the narrow path, which few will find.

Through this volume, Father Albert Nolan must be given a place among those beacons. He throws a beam of light on the narrow path for all to see. Some will be blinded by the brilliance of the light, and instead see darkness! Some will see and know that this is the narrow path which is hard and painful to follow. They will choose to close their eyes to avoid seeing it. Yet others will see it and trust the Spirit to give them the courage to follow this path. Wherever we stand on this, and whatever we do, we shall have little reason to say we did not know.

The champions of Christian truth in the Church, who have always remained a minority, have their counterpart in 'secular' champions of social justice. The ideology of power in the world has developed a dichotomy between the 'sacred' and the 'secular'. In this scheme of things, religious faith has no say in 'secular' affairs, except to bless secular authorities and dutifully bury their victims. In the South Africa of the 1980s, we have just woken to the realisation that this division between the 'sacred' and the 'secular' is a big lie. The faithful live their life, not in the bliss of heaven, but in the harsh realities of world history, of national security and economic growth. The lives of the people we are called to minister to are ordered by the political and economic relationships that the rulers of this world design. We have become painfully aware that this is our lot in the very world that the God of 'sacred' life created for our enjoyment. The struggle for the control of that enjoyment is the struggle for faithful stewardship over creation. To use the popular slogan of Christian activists: the Church is a site of struggle.

What Albert Nolan is doing here is to establish, once and for all, that the classical battle of 'Christian soldiers' against sin and this world is the battle against a sinful situation for the creation of a new world anticipated in a new and more just society.

In the last couple of years I have developed the opinion that South Africa will definitely be transformed if three things can happen *together*: an unrelenting popular movement of resistance; co-ordinated international pressure upon the government of South Africa; and religious legitimation for change.

This last is important because religion is a central feature of South African life. Traditionally it has been used to legitimate the subjugation of the majority of South Africans. There needs to be a different message emanating from theology to expose the lie that identifies organised and violent dehumanisation with God's will for our people.

The three components are clearly interrelated. In fact their division is a matter of practical application. Albert Nolan's work belongs to the third component, theology. In that regard he speaks directly to my own concerns, as the following story will tell.

I first encountered this diminutive giant in his tiny book, *Biblical Spirituality*, several years ago when I was writing a position paper with the title, 'God, My God, Our God, Their God'. My paper was an attempt to wrestle with the fact that unavoidably I, as a black South African, share a creator God with white South Africans who are the source of generations of grief in my country. The study was an apologetic to settle for my perplexed mind the conflict about being both black and a convinced Christian in South Africa. What do I mean when I say I believe in God? Who or what is this God? Is it the same God that my forebears believed in before the advent of the Europeans and 'their' Christian faith in this part of the world? Can it be the same God who created in God's image all human beings of all races, languages and countries. The God whose image is fully revealed in Jesus Christ? Is the God of *'Die Stem'* and of *'Nkosi Sikelela'* one and the same God?

These questions have continued to haunt me in my own pilgrimage. I have, however, found strength in discovering that, as a pastor, I accompany people who are seeking answers to the same questions. Many people in my community address these questions either by denying the faith 'given' to them by their parents, or by representing the God of their own faith as powerful and saving. The latter takes considerable courage and a strong faith because the suffering we face seems to suggest that God is not powerful and saving.

It is in this light that I believe people should judge the Kairos Document. It is an act of jealous faith by those who refuse to allow the God of their faith to be identified with the false God of South Africa's oppressive monstrosity. Albert Nolan's participation in this kind of theology has its origins in his experience of ministry to young people. Until 1984, he served as national chaplain to the Young Christian Students (YCS). This is a dynamic body of young Christians who are committed to serious reflection and transformative action in South Africa. As part-time chaplain to the Western Cape region of YCS since 1985, I have had the privilege of sharing in the kind of ministry that I am sure has contributed to Albert Nolan's analysis and theological reflections. Was it this ministry that gave him the conviction that in the apparent hopelessness of life under the boot of the most sophisticated repressive machine, there is hope?

This book is a powerful and systematic appeal to the reader to share in the recognition of grace and assumption of duty. These two things which are central to Christian living are summed up in Albert's clear understanding of *struggle*. I commend this book for intensive use by Christian reflection groups throughout the land. One may not agree with Albert's position on some of the issues raised, but no serious participant in the South African socio-theological debate can deny that this is a profound contribution to the debate.

As I have said, Albert's concept of struggle sums up the Christian message of hope and challenge. I cite the author's own words of tribute to the religious aura of the struggle for a human South Africa. It is 'a celebration of hope, the experience of communing, the self-sacrifice, the total commitment, the courage, the discipline and the willingness to live and to die for the struggle'.

Are these words not in the *spirit* of the classical Christian understanding of the way of the Cross? For those who live the daily life of struggle, these words are more than a recognition of their cause. They are refreshment which springs out of 'streams of living water' (Jn 7: 79). Indeed Albert Nolan is a son of the Church. When one looks back at the history of the Christian faith, one is amazed at the resourcefulness of the Church.

M. MALUSI MPUMLWANA
Guguletu, Cape Town
December 1987

Preface

What I have attempted in this book might be described as evangelisation rather than theology. It is an attempt to *preach* the gospel in South Africa rather than to *speculate* about its universal meaning. Despite the fact that I have made considerable use of theological research, this book is not an exercise in academic theology. Our situation is far too critical and serious for mere academic exercises of any kind, and yet for the same reason we cannot afford any kind of thinking that is not critical and rigorous. Perhaps one could describe what I have written as an attempt at doing theology in our context, and perhaps in the final analysis there is no great difference between doing theology and preaching the gospel. The book is addressed to South African Christians. The reader who is not a Christian, or not a South African Christian, will have to regard himself or herself as listening in to a conversation.

Some 77 per cent of South Africans would identify themselves as Christians. Hindus would account for 1,7 per cent, Muslims 1,1 per cent, Jews 0,4 per cent, while 1,8 per cent would describe themselves as adherents of the traditional religion of Africa. The remaining 18 per cent do not claim any religious affiliation. Among those who identify themselves as Christians, 88 per cent are black (de Gruchy, *JTSA* 51, June 1985). The fact that we Christians form the overwhelming majority in South Africa should serve as a warning to us of the danger of religious imperialism. That in itself would be a betrayal of the gospel (*JTSA* 56, Sept. 1986: 24ff). The special responsibility of Christians in South Africa lies not so much in our numbers as in the fact that there are Christians on both sides of the conflict.

My attempt to say something to *all* South African Christians, both black and white, has proved to be extraordinarily difficult. How do you speak simultaneously to people who, while they inhabit the same country, live in totally different worlds? Moreover, one may well doubt whether it is ever possible to say anything worthwhile to both the oppressor and the oppressed at the same time. In fact, in the course of writing this book I often wondered whether I would do better to write two books on the gospel in South Africa: one for those Christians who find themselves on the side of the oppressor and another for Christians involved in the struggle for liberation. In the end I decided to write one book, not only because Jesus himself preached to the oppressor and the oppressed at the same time and not only because the gospel of Jesus Christ is one and indivisible, but above all because the gospel is not, and can never be, neutral. Whether one writes one book or two, one cannot do so from a position of neutrality. In the first place, as I hope to show later, neutrality with regard to the conflict that is raging in South Africa today, is an illusion. And, in the second place, the gospel we preach will not be the gospel of Jesus Christ unless it takes sides with those who are being sinned against – the poor and the oppressed. It is from that point of view, as we shall see, that one must preach the gospel to both sides in South Africa today.

Another of the difficulties I had writing this book concerns individualism. Is it in any way possible for an individual author to say what the gospel means in our situation? And in any case who wants to hear the opinion of an individual Christian? It is precisely because I have come to believe that theology must be a community reflection rather than a private study, that I hesitated for a long time before writing this book. In South Africa today a new theology or new understanding of the gospel is being born out of the experience, practice and reflections of Christian groups and communities, and out of conferences in which Christians enter into dialogue with one another and with others who do not profess to be Christians. The results find written form in documents, statements, resolutions, articles and books that cannot be assigned to any one person as the sole author. Statements are made by bodies of Christians, documents (like the Kairos Document) have numerous signatories and books on theology tend to be collections of articles by several authors.

However, there comes a time when someone, as a service to the community, has to take the risk of tying up the loose ends, drawing out the implications of what is being said and believed, and presenting the Christian community with an articulate and systematic account of its faith. That is what I have been ambitious enough to attempt in this book. I write, therefore, not so much as an individual (although by force of circumstances much of the research had to be done alone), but as an attempt to represent and serve my fellow South African Christians, and in the form of a conversation with them.

This makes the usual acknowledgments that an author includes in a preface somewhat different in this case and considerably more extensive. I can name some of those who helped with the actual production of the book: Shaan Ellinghouse and Nan Oosthuizen who did such a good job in difficult circumstances with the typing, the Department of Religious Studies at the University of Cape Town which allowed me to make use of its facilities and resources, and Russell Martin, David Philip and Marie Philip who prepared the manuscript for publication. I hardly know how to thank them for being so helpful and cooperative in the production of this volume. But when it comes to the actual content of the book, it would be impossible to name individuals. There are many authors whose writings I have found useful and there are friends who read the manuscript or parts of it and made useful comments, but, by and large, the content of this book is the result of doing theology with people in thousands of meetings, discussions and arguments, and of the everyday experience of solidarity in the struggle. I have learnt more about what it means to be a Christian from the people of my country and especially from the youth in the townships, than I have ever learnt from books. I should like to think that all these people are, with me, the co-authors of this book or at least partners in the conversation that we shall be trying to conduct in this book.

List of Abbreviations

ABRECSA	Alliance of Black Reformed Churches of Southern Africa
ANC	African National Congress
AZAPO	Azanian People's Organisation
AZASM	Azanian Students' Movement
AZASO	Azanian Students' Organisation
AWB	*Afrikaner Weerstandsbeweging*
COSATU	Congress of South African Trade Unions
COSAS	Congress of South African Students
FEDSAW	Federation of South African Women
ICT	Institute for Contextual Theology
JB	Jerusalem Bible
JTSA	*Journal of Theology for Southern Africa*
NEB	New English Bible
NECC	National Education Crisis Committee
NEUM	New Unity Movement
NIV	New International Version
NUSAS	National Union of South African Students
PAC	Pan-Africanist Congress
par (parr)	parallel (parallels)
PFP	Progressive Federal Party
SACBC	South African Catholic Bishops' Conference
SACC	South African Council of Churches
SADF	South African Defence Force
SANSCO	South African National Students' Congress
SASO	South African Students' Organisation
SAYCO	South African Youth Congress
SPCC	Soweto Parents' Crisis Committee
SRC	Students' Representative Council
UCM	University Christian Movement
UDF	United Democratic Front

Introduction

The history of the preaching of the gospel in our country is closely bound up with our social, political and economic history. The preaching of the gospel in South Africa has never been politically neutral even when, in recent times, some Christians have imagined that they have transcended worldly matters like politics and economics.

The gospel that first came to our shores with Dutch and then British colonialism was a gospel that justified and legitimised colonialism, imperialism and European superiority. Despite their barbaric methods and attitudes, the colonisers firmly believed that what they were bringing to this part of the world was 'civilisation' and that the basis of this 'civilisation' was the message of Jesus Christ. The British never doubted that they were living and acting according to the gospel of Jesus Christ and that God had chosen them to 'civilise' and 'Christianise' vast areas of the world with their empire. Nor did the Boers who trekked further north from the Cape ever doubt that God was on their side and that their journey was like the journey of the Israelites to the promised land. In later times the so-called English Churches (Anglican, Methodist, Congregationalist, Presbyterian, Baptist and Catholic) would comment regularly and in the name of the gospel on the policies of successive white governments; while the white Dutch Reformed Churches were deeply involved from the start in the politics of the Afrikaner.

The original preachers of the gospel in South Africa were of two kinds: chaplains and missionaries. The chaplains were those who came to preach and minister to the colonial officials, soldiers and settlers. The missionaries were those who came to evangelise the indigenous and colonised people in this part of Africa. They came with all their divided traditions, denominations and mission societies, but the fundamental division they left us was the division between a white Church and a black Church, a settler Church and a missionary Church (de Gruchy 1979: 11ff). This was and still is a political division that cuts right through the different denominations and Church traditions. It has had a profound effect upon the development of theology, that is to say upon the way the gospel has come to be understood and preached.

It was out of the missionary Church that a prophetic gospel began to emerge. At one level it was embodied in certain prophetic figures: missionaries like Van der Kemp, John Philip, Bishop Colenso and Trevor Huddleston, and Church leaders like Beyers Naudé, Allan Boesak and Archbishop Desmond Tutu. At another level the voice of prophecy has been associated with bodies like the South African Catholic Bishops' Conference (SACBC), the Christian Institute, the South African Council of Churches (SACC) and the Institute for Contextual Theology (ICT). We could also mention the level of prophetic statements and declarations like the Catholic Bishops' statement (1957) that apartheid is intrinsically evil, the Message to the People of South Africa (1968) which rejected apartheid as a pseudo-gospel, the Belhar Confession (1982) which denounced apartheid as a sin, a heresy and a mockery of the gospel, the Kairos Document (1985) which challenged the Churches to side with the struggle for liberation, and Evangelical Witness in South Africa (1986) which called Evangelicals to repentance for not having preached a prophetic and radical gospel. (For these and other similar texts, see Villa–Vicencio 1986, de Gruchy 1983 and the Bibliography at the end of this book.)

However, at the most important and most basic level, the level that is sometimes called the grassroots, a simple, people's gospel has been preached, lived, celebrated and developed over a period of nearly a hundred years by the suffering people of South Africa. This is nowhere more evident than in that large group of people's Churches that have come to be called African Independent Churches. They now represent some 30 per cent of the black population and about 31 per cent of all Christians in South Africa, that is to say, between seven and eight million people in about four thousand different Churches. By any standards they are the biggest single phenomenon in the history of the preaching of the gospel in South Africa.

The gospel that is preached and practised in these Churches is not always or consistently prophetic. In fact they represent a bewildering complexity of interpretations and practices (ICT 1985: 14). Some are very traditional, in the sense that they have kept much of the teaching and practice of the missionary Churches. Others have much in common with charismatics or Pentecostals. Only a few could be described as preaching a 'social gospel' in the usual meaning of the term. What they have in common though, and what makes them different, is that they are totally *independent* of the missionary Churches and thoroughly *African*. Starting nearly a hundred years ago, African Christians began to break away from the missionary Churches partly because of white domination in those Churches and partly because African Christians were unwilling to exchange African customs for Western customs in order to be regarded as true Christians (ICT 1985: 21ff).

Independence meant religious freedom, the freedom to explore new ways of interpreting and living the gospel. In the event this meant not only shedding Western customs and trying to interpret the Bible in terms of African culture, but also trying to understand the gospel in terms of the black experience of suffering, insecurity and oppression. The results have varied enormously. There are many reasons for this. It would take us far beyond the scope of this brief introduction to elaborate upon these reasons. Suffice it to say that, whereas some very profound insights have been developed in these Churches, circumstances have not enabled them to produce an explicit and systematic theology as yet (ICT 1985: 25ff).

Black Theology did not arise out of these Churches. Black Theology is an explicit, articulate and scholarly reflection upon the Christian significance of black suffering and oppression in South Africa. It developed out of Christian student circles, in particular out of the 1971 black theological project of UCM

(University Christian Movement). It was an instant success and it proved to be the fundamental turning point in the history of explicit theology in South Africa. I say 'explicit theology' because much of what Black Theology articulated and systematised was already implicit in the preaching of the black Churches whether they were independent or not. Black Theology articulates a decidedly prophetic gospel.

Today Black Theology is faced with the dilemma of what is called the ideological split between Black Consciousness and the non-racialism that is associated with the Freedom Charter. Black Theology has been a theological reflection upon the meaning of Black Consciousness. If the majority of the people have now adopted the non-racialism of the Freedom Charter, what does this mean for Black Theology? It seems to me that what matters is not what name we give to our theology, but that it remains a genuine theological reflection upon what God is doing in our country today.

Nor should we be led to think that what we have said so far exhausts the history of the preaching of the gospel in South Africa. The Evangelical and Pentecostal movements have had an enormous impact upon the preaching of the gospel. But even here there is a clear distinction between those who support the present political system and those who reject it outright, as we see in the statement signed by 130 ministers in this tradition, Evangelical Witness in South Africa. And then there is the impact which the Latin American theology of liberation has had upon the preaching of the gospel in our country. We could also mention the influence of African theology and the developments in the Reformed tradition that centre around the BK (*Belydendekring*) and ABRECSA (Alliance of Black Reformed Churches of Southern Africa). Nor would one want to forget the developments in Christian student movements like YCS (Young Christian Students), CASA (Catholic Students Association) and SUCA (Students for Christian Action), to mention only a few of them. Unfortunately so many of the most profound insights into the meaning of the gospel for us today, insights that were expressed in sermons, Bible studies, prayers and discussions, have never been committed to writing. Once in a while, as with the Kairos Document, we get a glimpse of what is going on – the tip of the iceberg.

I have had the good fortune to have lived and worked in several parts of South Africa, to have travelled extensively and to have been involved with part of the huge variety of Churches and Christian organisations that we have in South Africa. My own conclusion is that Beyers Naudé was right when he said: 'Something new is groaning to emerge which will challenge the whole Church in South Africa to the depths of its being' (SACC 1986b: 123).

In South Africa today the preaching of the gospel is facing an unprecedented challenge. Our country has been experiencing a serious political crisis for some time and now the crisis has reached breaking-point. This alone presents those who believe in the gospel of Jesus Christ with a challenge. How does one preach the gospel in our present circumstances of conflict and crisis? But what makes the challenge really urgent and demanding is the simple fact that the gospel has been, and still is, associated with a political system that is now regarded by almost the whole world as a crime against humanity. Even more confusing and challenging is the way others use the gospel to avoid the issue by arguing that this crime against humanity has nothing to do with God and salvation in Jesus Christ, because it is a matter of politics and not religion. Meanwhile a growing number of concerned Christians in South Africa have come to associate the gospel with nothing more than mild, liberal attempts to modify or soften the prevailing system.

For years the suffering people of South Africa listened to all this and tried to make sense of it. But now the youth of the townships have lost patience with the Churches and with all the confused and contorted interpretations of the gospel. They are leaving the Church in their thousands. To them the gospel seems to be at best an irrelevant distraction and at worst an obstacle in the way of genuine liberation and peace.

It is out of the purifying fires of this challenge that a new understanding of the gospel is emerging – an understanding that is more faithful to Jesus Christ, more courageous and honest, and more rigorously and systematically thought out. It is not an attempt to save the gospel at all costs. The gospel does not need saving; it is we, the people of South Africa, who need to be saved. What hope of salvation does the gospel of Jesus Christ have to offer us in South Africa today?

1
What is the Gospel?

The Letter and the Spirit

If we were to take a cross section of South African Christians and ask them what they understood by the gospel of Jesus Christ, we would receive, I am sure, a surprising variety of answers. They would sum up the contents of the gospel message with a wide range of words or assertions including, perhaps, some of the following: love, forgiveness, salvation from sin, reconciliation, the rule or kingdom of God, the death and resurrection of Jesus, justice and peace, liberation from oppression or that Jesus is Lord, Saviour or Liberator. If we then went on to ask what exactly these words and assertions mean and what implications they have for the people of South Africa today, we would probably find that even those who use the same words to describe the gospel have quite different opinions about what it all means in practice, while others who use different formulations of the gospel might be discovered to be saying the same thing. To the outsider, and doubtless to some Christians too, this must be very confusing. The gospel *seems* to mean anything anyone wants it to mean.

And if we then turn to the Bible itself in an attempt to pin the gospel down, we will soon find that there is no fixed formula, no set of words that can be called the definitive message of the gospel. Sometimes it is summarised in one way and sometimes in another. Sometimes it takes the form of a prophetic proclamation like 'the rule (or kingdom) of God is near' or 'Jesus is the Messiah' and at other times it takes the form of a parable or a story or an account of something that happened. Matthew, Mark, Luke and John wrote whole books to communicate the gospel as they understood it.

I do not wish to suggest that there is no coherence in the Bible and that all these formulations are not compatible, but I do wish to point out that the gospel message is not like a telex message or a press statement. *It has no fixed verbal content.* The same gospel can be expressed in an endless variety of ways.

This becomes even more obvious when we study the variety of formulations that have been used in the preaching of the gospel down through the ages. What is clear is that different historical circumstances give rise to different formulations of what we call the gospel. In other words the gospel is, and has always been, *contextual*. The particular set of words or expressions that one may choose to use depends upon the language, culture, politics and needs of a particular time and place.

Where, then, is the continuity? What is it that remains the same down through the ages? What is it that makes all the different words and expressions one and the same gospel? An immediate answer that many Christians might give would be that it is not the *letter* that counts but the *spirit*. The gospel is not a new written law but a new spirit, a new attitude to life, a new way of thinking and acting (Rm 2: 29; 7: 6; II Cor 3: 6; Jer 31: 33; Ezek 36: 26). The letter or verbal content of the gospel might vary according to the circumstances but the spirit remains the same – unless of course it becomes a false gospel.

It is this distinction between the letter and the spirit that I want to take up and subject to a more rigorous analysis in this first chapter. It is crucial for any understanding of how we are to formulate the gospel in South Africa today. However, because words like 'letter' and 'spirit' are too vague, I want to take up this distinction in terms of the *content* and the *shape* of the gospel. I want to try to show that it is the content (letter) of the gospel that varies from time to time and place to place while the shape or characteristics or form or spirit of the gospel remains the same. There is a definite shape, certain definite characteristics, that any message would have to have in order to qualify as a true gospel, as the gospel of Jesus Christ for a particular people at a particular time.

The first and most general of these characteristics is that the message must be good news.

Good News

The word 'gospel' is derived from the old English word 'god-spel' which in turn is derived from the two words 'good' and 'spell'. And as everybody now knows this means 'good news'. The Greek word used in the New Testament makes this abundantly clear. *Euaggelion* means quite simply 'good news', and the verb *euaggelizontai* from which we derive our verb 'evangelise', means 'to bring good news'.

Behind the word 'gospel' then is the image of good news brought to a community, before the days of newspapers, by a runner or herald. It was Isaiah (or rather the author of the second part of the Book of Isaiah) who first used the expression to describe his prophecy of liberation from exile and slavery in Babylon (52: 7). It was indeed good news and the exiles welcomed it as good news. Jesus takes up the term from Isaiah to describe his prophetic message. He says that he has come 'to bring good news to the poor' (Lk 4: 18; 7: 22).

It has often been pointed out that the problem with what is preached in our churches today is that it no longer has the shape or character of good news. People may accept what is preached and believe it but they are unable to welcome it with joy and excitement, welcome it as real good news. It does not sound like news at all, let alone good news. Perhaps you have heard some of our present-day evangelists who use every modern gimmick to whip up some excitement about a message that very few can welcome as good news for us today. Other more sincere preachers try very hard to convince people that the gospel of Jesus Christ is good news for us today. There is something radically wrong if the message we preach cannot be welcomed spontaneously and immediately as good news. Of course it does happen. I have heard preachers in South Africa who do bring good news (see Bruwer in SACC 1986b: 68–70). We shall have to examine the conditions that make this possible.

When Jesus stood up and announced, 'The time has come; the rule of God is at hand', his audience welcomed the announcement as good news. They knew what he meant. The rule or kingdom of God embodied all their hopes and aspirations. To hear that the time had come for these hopes and aspirations to be fulfilled was real good news. When the disciples went out and proclaimed that Jesus was the Messiah, it was the news of the century. The excitement after years and years of waiting and praying would be difficult to contain. And when Paul brings the news that people can now be justified in the eyes of God by faith in Jesus Christ and that it is therefore no longer necessary to try to please God by observing all the details of the Mosaic law, the people must have breathed a great sigh of relief. What exciting news!

What Jesus and Paul and the others had to say remains true, but if I were to stand up in a church or on a street corner in South Africa today and repeat what they said using the same words, I would simply not get the same response. If I were to stand on a street corner and announce that the rule or kingdom of God is coming soon, I would be treated as some kind of religious freak. No journalist today would regard my statement that Jesus is the Messiah as newsworthy. Everybody knows that, or rather everybody knows that Christians have believed that for centuries. Nor would my announcement that we no longer need to observe the laws of ritual purity as laid down by Moses, engender much enthusiasm amongst the majority of the people of South Africa who have never had to observe those laws but are oppressed by apartheid laws.

If we simply repeat the formulas of the past, our words may have the character of doctrine and dogma but they will not have the character of good news. We may be preaching perfectly orthodox doctrine but it is not *the gospel for us today*. We must take the idea of good news seriously. If our message does not take the form of good news, it is simply not the Christian gospel.

We call something good news because of the effect that it has upon us. We are pleased to hear it. It makes us happy. And if it is really good news we would want to rejoice, to celebrate, to dance on the streets. Why? Because this news eliminates something that we feared, something dangerous, something we did not like, something bad or evil, and because it promises us in some way or another a better future. Good news is promising news. It makes us happy because it makes us *hopeful* about the future.

Another effect that good news has upon us is that it *energises* us (Brueggemann 1978: 13ff, 23, 62ff, 96ff). Good news can wake us up, shake us out of our lethargy and enable us to respond to the challenges of life. When we are feeling sad, depressed and hopeless, we do not have the energy to do things. Some good news can suddenly change our mood, pep us up, inspire and motivate us. We feel energised by it and ready to go out and face the world with all its challenges. Good news can give us courage and strength.

This was precisely the kind of effect that Jesus' preaching had upon the people of his time. And this is precisely what the preaching of the gospel in South Africa today, with rare exceptions, does not do for people or at least not authentically and spontaneously. One of the reasons for this is that we speak about hope and about motivation and about challenge and about what Jesus said in the past, but we have no news for the people, let alone good news. If the gospel is good news then it is not a message about hope and about challenge and about the past but it is the kind of news about our times that will create hope and energise people as Jesus did in his time. Good news is not a statement about hope, it is the kind of news that will generate hope (Soelle 1981: 77).

We are beginning to see the shape or form that our message would have to take if it is to be a gospel. It would have to take the form of news, the kind of news that generates hope and energy. Of course that is only the very broadest outline of the shape of the gospel. There is much more to it than that.

Jesus' message was designed to be good news for all the people of his time but only by being in the first place good news for the poor.

Good News for the Poor

We are all aware of the fact that what might be welcomed as good news by some people will be regarded as bad news by others. In situations of conflict and division as in South Africa today a newspaper headline that brings rejoicing and hope to some, brings sadness and despair to others. And even if it is news about something that will ultimately benefit everybody, in a situation of conflict and division not everybody will appreciate that. In such situations it is impossible to find any news that will be welcomed by everybody immediately and spontaneously as good news.

There can be no doubt that what Jesus said and did was good news for the poor and bad news for the rich and the powerful. The phrase that Jesus borrowed from Isaiah to describe what he was doing was not simply 'bringing good news' but 'bringing good news to or for the poor' (Lk 4: 18; 7: 22; Mt 11: 5). And even a cursory glance at what he said and did could leave no doubt that it would have been welcomed as good news by the poor but not by the rich. 'Blessed are you who are poor. . . . Woe to you who are rich' (Lk 6: 20, 24). The community of the future belongs to the poor ('*yours* is the kingdom', Lk 6: 20) and the rich will not be able to enter it, any more than a camel would be able to enter the eye of a needle (Mk 10: 25 parr).

There is no way of escaping this fact about the gospel of Jesus Christ. It is an extremely controversial and divisive issue today, but then it was an extremely controversial and divisive issue in the time of Jesus too. We are told that Jesus' own disciples were astounded (Mk 10: 24, 26) and that the Pharisees simply 'laughed at him' (Lk 16: 14). The rich and the powerful had no doubt that, however you looked at it, Jesus' message was bad news – such bad news that he had to be silenced forever and handed over to the Romans to be crucified.

Does that mean that the gospel is exclusively for the poor and that there is no good news for the rich? For Jesus the matter was extremely simple: there was no salvation for the rich while they remained rich, while they refused to share with the poor, while they continued to worship money instead of God (Lk 16: 19–31; Mt 6: 24). Jesus' advice or challenge to the rich is quite simple: sell your possessions and give up the worship of money (Mk 10: 17–22; Lk 12: 33–34; 14: 33). Jesus says this to the rich young man with love but without compromising. No compromise between God and money is possible (Mt 6: 24). In other words the news becomes good news for those who are rich only when they cease to be rich.

What that means for us today in practice is not immediately clear. We cannot simply transpose the advice that Jesus had for the rich of his time, to the rich of our time, and tell them to sell all their possessions. That may not be what the gospel is challenging them to do in our circumstances in South Africa today. It is not a matter of applying the gospel literally or to the letter. It is a matter of discovering the will of God for us today in the spirit of the message that Jesus delivered to the people of his time. There has been much research recently on the meaning of 'the poor' in the time of Jesus (Stegemann 1984: 13ff; Schottroff 1986: 6ff) and on the precise economic and social status of the first Christians (Gottwald 1983: 441ff). That is helpful and important, not because we are supposed to imitate or copy the lifestyle of the first Christians, but because it helps us to discover the shape or spirit of the gospel. Hopefully this will become clearer as we try to discover the contents of the good news in our circumstances in South Africa today. However, what we preach will not be the gospel of Jesus Christ, in fact it will be a false gospel, if it does not have this characteristic of being good news for everyone by being in the first place good news for the poor. That is part of the shape that any message must take if it is to be in truth the gospel.

The temptation, of course, is to water down the gospel, to soften the 'hard sayings', in order to preach something that everyone can immediately accept as good news. In fact the attempt to preach something that is not controversial and not divisive is self-defeating. We end up preaching abstract truths and vague generalities that are supposed to be equally applicable to everyone but, in fact, are good news for no one. If you try to please everyone, you end up pleasing no one. The Church that tries to avoid everything controversial will end up by becoming a very controversial Church. It will be criticised for sitting on the fence. It will be criticised for betraying the gospel. Any preaching of the gospel that tries to remain neutral with regard to issues that deeply affect the lives of people, like the issue of the rich and the poor, is in fact taking sides. It is taking sides with the status quo, even if that is not its intention, because its neutrality prevents change.

The only way that the gospel can be, in the final analysis, good news for all is by being, in the first instance, good news for the poor. The best thing that could happen to the rich would be for them to hear and be challenged by the good news for the poor.

But how can the gospel be news for anyone today, let alone good news for the poor?

A Prophetic Message for Our Times

The gospel has the shape and characteristics of a prophecy, a prophetic message for the times. The message that Jesus preached, even though its contents were different, had the same pattern or shape as the messages of all the prophets from Moses through the great classical prophets to John the Baptist and all other genuine prophets down to our own time. Jesus was immediately recognised as like the prophets of old and not like the scribes (Lk 7: 16–17; Mk 1: 22; 8: 27–28 parr).

The principal characteristic of a prophetic message is that it is not a timeless message (Von Rad 1968: 100–1). A prophet speaks to a particular time and about a particular time. The message is thoroughly timebound. The paradigm that shapes every prophetic message, no matter what its content may be, is simply this:

> the time has come,
> the day is near.

A prophetic message is always news because it is always about the significance of a particular time and a particular day. It is indeed a message about God but not about God in general, it is about what God is doing in these times.

Moses spoke to the people of his time about what God was doing in Egypt (the plagues) and about the liberation from slavery that God was going to bring about in the near future. To the next generation Joshua would have to speak about what God wanted then and about the entry into the promised land that was imminent. Amos, Jeremiah, Isaiah and the others who prophesied before the exile read the signs of their times, pronounced on the crisis of their times and prophesied a day of the Lord (Yahweh) when the leaders of Israel and their collaborators would be punished and taken into exile. The little-known prophets around the time of Jesus all announced that the time was ripe for some kind of action or change and that the day of liberation was imminent (Horsley 1985: 148, 152, 170ff).

Jesus' message was no exception to this rule. He too announced: 'The time has come; the rule of God is near.' The time was different and the imminent event was different but the shape of the message was the same. What Jesus had to say was news for his time and news about his time. If the gospel for us in South Africa today is to have the shape of a prophetic message, it must proclaim news for our time, news about what God is doing and about to do in our country.

What we are tempted to do, though, is to preach a timeless gospel of timeless truths that are equally applicable to all times and in all circumstances. Whatever value this might have, it is simply not the gospel; it does not even have the shape of news, let alone good news; it has the shape of doctrines, dogmas, principles, norms and eternal truths. No wonder nobody is able to welcome what we say as good news.

This temptation or tendency to preach a timeless gospel is the same as the tendency we saw earlier, the tendency to say something that is equally applicable to everybody – rich and poor, oppressor and oppressed. We shall come across this tendency again and again in the course of this book. I want to call it 'the universalising tendency'. Western theology seems to be based upon the assumption that nothing is true or valuable unless it applies to all people, at all times and in all circumstances. What one ends up with is an abstract God who deals with abstract 'man' in an abstract world.

The Bible provides us with a series of prophetic messages about what God was doing and saying in other times and places. This enables us to get some idea of what God is like – his character and personality you might say – and some idea of what God might be expected to do and say. In itself this is an abstraction. We have abstracted the characteristics and generalised attributes of God from what we are told about the wonderful works of God in the past. That is fine as long as we then use the abstraction to search for the same God in our times, to recognise the finger of God in our historical situation. For example, after reading the Bible we can draw the conclusion, as John does, that God is love. That in itself is an abstraction. We can then go on to look for the signs of genuine and effective love in our historical situation. When we find these, we find God alive and active in our midst. The gospel for us today is *shaped* by what the Bible says about God but its *content* is the latest news about the wonderful works of God in South Africa today.

A New Gospel?

The great distinguishing feature of the God of the Bible is newness. Yahweh is an historical God, which means a God who remains the same precisely by always doing new things in every new set of circumstances. It is the historical circumstances that change but a creative God can only remain a creative God by acting in new and unprecedented ways in each new situation. In the words of the Korean theologian, Moon Hee-Suk Cyris: 'History changes constantly and God's word is proclaimed in many different ways throughout history. But the fact that does not change is that God acts throughout history. He acts freely in history and his actions are not always repetitions of past actions. Often they are radically new.' (CTA-CCA 1981: 123) That insight is at the heart of all that Jesus and the prophets had to say (Von Rad 1968: 92–94; Brueggemann 1978: 100–101). It is interesting to notice how often the word 'new' is used in the Bible: a new song, a new heart, a new spirit, a new man (person), a new life, a new creation, a new covenant, a new age, new wine in new wineskins, a new heaven and a new earth, a new Jerusalem. 'Remember not the former things. . . . I am going to do a new thing' (Is 43: 18–19). 'Behold I make all things new' (Rev 21: 5).

Like all prophetic messages the gospel is not about 'the former things' but about 'the new thing' that God is doing today, about the God who is 'making all things new' in South Africa today. What we are searching for is not a new gospel but a gospel that is news. The gospel can only be the same as in the past if it continues to be about the new things that God is doing in our time.

This would seem to imply that we are no longer talking about the gospel as the message that was preached by Jesus Christ nearly two thousand years ago. We seem to have put all the prophetic messages of the past on a par with Jesus' message as we look for a new prophetic message for our times. Are we still talking about the gospel of Jesus Christ?

We have seen that the gospel message today must take the shape of good news for the poor; we have seen that it must take the shape of a prophetic message for our times; and we have said that it must be shaped by what has been said about God in the Bible in order to bring us the good news of what God is doing in South Africa today. But that is not all. To be the Christian gospel for today it must be rigorously shaped by the message that Jesus preached to his contemporaries. We had put Jesus' message on a par with other prophetic messages only in order to see the general characteristics of the gospel as a prophetic message. Now we must be more specific about the characteristics that would shape our message into the gospel of Jesus Christ for our times.

The Gospel of Jesus Christ

We find in Jesus the perfect human embodiment of all that we mean by God. His life, his death and his resurrection reveal something about God that transcends anything anyone else has ever said about God. Yet that in itself is not the Christian gospel. The good news that Jesus preached to his contemporaries was about what this God was doing in their world at that time, what this God was doing in and through Jesus. It has often been said that in Jesus the messenger becomes the message. That is true as long as one does not think that the gospel message has become doctrines about Jesus. Jesus is the message because of what he did or what God was doing in and through him at that time. Jesus is divine, but as Paul says, that in itself is not the good news. The good news is that 'God was reconciling himself to us in Jesus' (II Cor 5: 19). In other words the good news is about the practice of Jesus, the wonderful work of God that was manifested in the practice of Jesus.

And today? The good news about Jesus today is the good news about what Jesus as the risen Christ is doing in South Africa today or what God is now doing in and through the risen Christ. The importance of the resurrection is that we are able to treat Jesus as still alive, as our contemporary who is playing a role in our South African crisis and conflict. The good news about Jesus Christ for us today is the good news about the practice of Jesus in our country.

Our concern then is with the living God and the living Christ in our midst. And while we are on this topic our concern is also with the living Spirit of God, the Holy Spirit, who is moving and acting in the whole drama of events that we are experiencing in South Africa today.

The good news for South Africa will be shaped by what we read in the New Testament about God – about God who became flesh in Jesus and who moves people like a powerful Spirit. It will be shaped by what Jesus said about sin in his time and about salvation from sin and the rule of God – in his time. It will be shaped by the knowledge that Jesus came into conflict with the religious and political authorities of his time, that they arrested, imprisoned, interrogated, mocked, tried and sentenced him to death by crucifixion. It will be shaped by the belief that his death was nevertheless a victory and that he conquered death.

The gospel we preach today will refer to all these things and use them as its norms and guiding principles but they will not be the contents of the good news for us today. As Paul himself says, our concern now is not to 'know Christ according to the flesh' (II Cor 5: 16) but to 'have the mind of Christ' (I Cor 2: 16; Phil 2: 5).

Having the mind of Christ means more than just remembering what he did or copying his actions and quoting his words. Having the mind of Christ means tackling the problems of our times in the spirit in which he tackled the problems of his times. There may be some similarities between the problems of our times and of his times but there will also be considerable differences and the means available for solving our problems will also be very different. What matters is that we approach them with the mind of Christ, that is to say, in the same spirit. (See the 'correspondence of relationships' in C. Boff 1987: 146ff.)

Whenever this happens, whenever there is true discipleship or a true following of Christ, his practice becomes a present reality and he is in our midst. The good news of Jesus Christ today is the news about the presence of his mind, his spirit, his practice, his salvation in our historical situation. To preach another gospel (Gal 1: 8–9) is to preach a gospel that is not shaped by the paradigm of what Jesus said and did. The content of the good news that Paul is arguing about in Galatians concerns liberation from laws about circumcision and unclean foods (Gal 1: 11–2: 14). That is surely not the contents of the good news for us today. However for both Paul and ourselves the good news must conform to the mind of Christ, otherwise it is another gospel.

We must read the Bible and hear its stories in order to get the clues, but if we want to hear the latest news about God and Jesus Christ we must read the signs of our times.

The Signs of the Times

A prophetic message is one that is derived from a reading of the signs of the times. This is what all the prophets did, this is what Jesus did and this is what he told his contemporaries to do (Mt 16: 1–3; Lk 12: 54–57). Jesus describes the experience of reading the signs of the times as something that is as easy, as simple and as concrete as 'reading the face of the sky' in order to see what the weather will be like tomorrow. Just as in that part of the world 'a red evening sky' or 'a cloud looming up in the west' or 'a wind from the south' would indicate fine weather or a storm or a hot day, so do the signs of the times indicate what God is doing or planning to do in this place at this time. But as we would not be able to read the signs of the weather without some previous experience of what happens when the evening sky is red or when there are clouds in the west or a wind from the south, so we are not able to read the signs of our times without the information that the prophets and especially Jesus give us about what to expect from God.

The signs themselves are human events that we can see and experience. I suppose today we would call them public events – the kind of thing one might expect to read about in a newspaper. The process we call reading the signs of the times is the process of discovering the religious significance of public events, which means discerning, differentiating and interpreting them in relation to God. Nor is this done out of some kind of religious curiosity about where God fits into the picture but in order to understand what is really happening around us, where it is all leading to and what we are supposed to do about it.

This is the process of interpretation that we find going on throughout the Bible. For Moses the signs of the times must have included such public events as the oppression of the Hebrew slaves, Pharaoh's stubbornness (the hardening of his heart), the plagues and most of all the successful escape across the Sea of Reeds. Moses found God in these events and that is how he knew what he and the Hebrew slaves were expected to do. For the great classical prophets of the Old Testament the signs of the times must have included public events like wars and rumours of wars, power struggles amongst the great empires, the gathering storm clouds of Babylonian expansionism, shaky political alliances with Egypt, attempted reforms at home (King Josia), social injustice, greed and idolatry. They interpreted these and other similar events in the light of Exodus and the Moses tradition and drew their conclusions about what God was doing and planning and what the people ought to do now in those circumstances.

Jesus also read the signs of his times. He observed the menacing threat of Roman imperialism, the moral bankruptcy and hyprocrisy of the religious establishment, the increasing poverty, unemployment, sickness and misery of the poor together with their rising expectations of a Messiah and of a new age (Theissen 1978: 33ff; Stegemann 1984: 16ff; L. Schottroff 1986: 7ff) and the strong faith in God that showed itself in extraordinary healings (Nolan 1976: 30ff). Jesus had a very strong sense of the presence of God in these events and especially in his own activities. He could see that it was a very special moment, a *kairos*, and that God was active in a quite new way.

In the next generation we find Paul reading the signs of his time, which ranged from that most significant of all public events, the crucifixion of Jesus, to the surprising conversion of so many Gentiles. Paul interpreted these and similar events in the light of the Scriptures. Everything in the New Testament is an interpretation of current events in the light of the Old Testament or, as I should like to express it, their interpretation of current events was shaped by the Old Testament. The New Testament writers themselves describe the process as fulfilment. Everything in the Old Testament is being fulfilled in the events of their time. This means something more than just the fulfilment of the explicit prophecies of the past (though it includes that). It means that everything in the Old Testament can be seen as an archetype or symbol that is being completed, filled with content and made concrete by current events. Or to put it the other way, we can only understand the religious significance of current events by reference to what God has said and done in the past.

Much more study is needed of what the signs were in past times and how they were given a religious interpretation, but enough has been said to indicate what we ought to be doing today. There is much talk about the need to read the signs of our times but in practice it is very seldom done in a rigorous, conscious and systematic way. It is sometimes done by preachers in their sermons but it seldom appears in the writings and research of theologians. In fact the interpretation of the signs of the times is being pursued more vigorously today than ever before, but it is being done in a non-religious way by political analysts. On the whole God and the traditions about God are not being used to throw light upon the meaning of public events in our time and to determine what we ought to be doing about them. And even when this is done, it is so frequently done badly, unprophetically, timidly or in a manner that can only be described as superstitious.

At least one of the problems here is that we still treat the gospel of Jesus Christ as a message from the past and about events in the past that somehow must be 'applied' to our times. My contention is that the gospel for us today is the good news about what God is doing *in South Africa today* in the light of what God has done in the past.

Revelation and Experience

It might be thought that what we have said so far undermines the authority of the Bible and makes our human experience rather than Biblical revelation the normative criterion of gospel truth. This is *not* what I am saying. On the contrary the understanding of the gospel that I am suggesting enhances the authority of the Bible and the truth of what is revealed in the Bible. Although the authority of the Bible is understood in a variety of different ways in the Churches in South Africa, it remains an almost universal belief amongst South African Christians. That is not the problem. The problem is our understanding of revelation and its relation to experience.

In all modern theology and in all the most vital and energetic forms of Christianity in South Africa and more generally in the world today, from charismatics to liberation theologians, the emphasis is upon experience. We seem to be living in a world that is gradually rediscovering the value of experience. After many centuries of Western civilisation when ideas and principles dominated the lives of people (especially in religious matters) and when experience was felt to be hopelessly unreliable, we are now returning to the more natural and human attitude of trusting our own experience.

In South Africa the African Independent Churches broke away from the missionary Churches because the ideas, doctrines and practices of those Churches conflicted with African religious experience. They wanted a salvation that could be experienced in this life and did not have to be postponed until after death (ICT 1985). The Pentecostal and charismatic movement was also a kind of rebellion against a Church and a form of worship in which there was no religious experience but only doctrine and moral principles. Black Theology was based upon the value and importance of black experience over against dominant white ideas. The various forms of liberation theology describe what they are doing as critical reflection upon Christian praxis or practical experience, especially the practical experience of struggling for liberation. Monika Hellwig argues that 'the struggle of Christian theology in our times is to re-establish contact with the experience of contemporary Christians' (1983: 22). And in summing up what theology will be like tomorrow the French theologian Jossua says: 'No theology will be constructed without being founded on human experience, the experience of believers, or at least constantly tested against it' (*Concilium* 115: 108). For most people today and especially for the youth the person who argues from abstract ideas and principles and from book knowledge instead of speaking from experience and speaking to their experience is simply not credible.

This is no modern invention. We can trace it back to Luther and his rebellion against Rome, to Augustine and indeed to all people of all times who have not been dominated by imposed ideas. But most of all we can trace it back to the Bible and the revelations that we find recorded in the Bible.

There is no contradiction between revelation and experience (Schillebeeckx 1980: 45). The problem arises when we treat revelation as only a set of words and ideas that we inherit from the Bible. Revelation is also and more fundamentally an experience. The difference has been captured by the theological distinction between objective and subjective revelation.

Objective revelation is the ideas, doctrines, norms, principles and texts that we can abstract from the Bible (and tradition) and then contemplate like an object or body of 'knowledge' that has been revealed by God to people in the past. The Biblical teachings or the deposit of faith (as Catholics would call it) or the Biblical symbols (as some theologians would say) are indeed normative and authoritative. There is no need to deny that, even if we sometimes disagree about what these doctrines mean. In fact if we denied any authority to Biblical revelation we could not call ourselves Christians. But this is not the whole story. Revelation means more than that.

Subjective revelation is the subjective experience of faith. This happens when we have our eyes opened, when God reveals himself to us or, as some people would say, 'when we encounter the living God' or 'accept Christ as our personal saviour'. It is the discovery of God alive and active in our midst, it is the reading of the signs of the times. I am not concerned at the moment with the truth or falsehood of these experiences but only with the fact of religious experience.

A religious experience is not something abnormal. I am not speaking about the kind of thing one reads about in books on the occult or parapsychology. Nor am I referring to what some people would call 'mystical experiences' or 'private revelations'. A religious experience is a perfectly normal experience. It is simply an experience with a religious interpretation. There is no such thing as a pure experience. Every human experience is an *interpreted* experience (Schillebeeckx 1980: 31ff). If I am in the habit of viewing reality in personal terms, then an experience might be for me a personal experience. If I am in the habit of interpreting things politically, then the same experience would be for me a political experience. Similarly if I am in the habit of bringing God into the picture, then the same experience would be for me a religious experience: an experience of God speaking to me or calling me or challenging me or revealing something to me – in the signs of our times.

We shall have occasion to return to this point later in relation to our experience in South Africa today. Our concern here is to establish the reality of subjective revelation. It is the religious experience of God speaking to us now, God revealing something to us now. Perhaps it might help to call it a religious insight.

What then is the relationship between objective and subjective revelation?

In the first place the Bible itself is based upon the subjective experience of revelation. Moses, the prophets and all the other Biblical writers had their eyes opened by God to see what God was doing and saying in their time. They read the signs of their times. In this way a body of information about God and his ways was collected. For us this is objective revelation and it ends with the last book of the Bible in the sense that after Jesus no more new information about God and his ways is possible or needed. The revelation in Jesus is final and complete. It has a 'once and for all' character about it (Heb 9: 12). But that is not the end of subjective revelation. God still has to reveal himself and what he is doing in different times and places. And although this will not provide us with any new information about God in general, it will reveal God anew again and again in what God is now doing in the world.

To return to our argument about the gospel, then, the good news for us today is not simply objective revelation, the 'deposit of faith', the teaching of the Bible or of the Church, doctrines and dogmas, or even the revelations that were experienced by other people at other times. The gospel is the news about our time and our country that God is revealing to us today through the signs of our times, but this subjective experience of revelation is formed, guaranteed and normatively shaped by the message of Jesus to his contemporaries and by all that is revealed about God in the Bible. Objective revelation and Biblical norms are not the letter or *content* of the good news for us today but the spirit or *shape* that the gospel will have to take for us or for anyone else.

The Incarnate Gospel

The idea that the gospel needs to be contextualised is now generally accepted in South Africa as it is in most Third World countries. The gospel message that we have inherited in our different Churches was formulated in terms of European culture and colonial politics. As we have seen the African Independent Churches broke away from the missionary Churches in order to formulate and live the gospel in terms of their African cultural and political experience. Black Theology took up the same theme in a more academic manner, attempting to reformulate the gospel in terms of the black experience of oppression. The Kairos Document went a step further by starting from the present political crisis in an attempt to understand what the gospel means for us in our context of conflict and crisis.

The process is generally called contextualisation. But this can be understood in two ways. It can be understood as taking the *contents* of the gospel from the Bible (and tradition) and giving them a new *shape* in terms of our particular context. I have heard this described as receiving the contents of the gospel in a European colonial envelope and having to transfer the contents to a South African or black envelope. But the process can also be understood the other way round: taking the shape of the gospel from the Bible and tradition in order to discover the *contents* of the gospel in our contextual situation. This reversal of the usual understanding of the process of contextualisation is to my mind crucial for a proper understanding of the meaning of the gospel in South Africa today.

The debate about this process has generally centred around the meaning of Africanisation or indigenisation. Africanisation, it is being said today, does not mean adapting a Western gospel to African culture or thought patterns (Mosala 1986a: 112ff). According to the Cameroon theologian Ela, Africanisation means 'allowing the gospel to be reborn in Africa' (1986: 115). The inculturation of the gospel does not mean starting from the Western cultural expression of the gospel and extracting the 'pure contents of the gospel' which can then be formulated in new cultural terms. Apart from the fact that the original revelation was not given to us in terms of Western culture but in terms of Hebrew culture, the idea that one can hold the 'pure contents of the gospel' in one's head without any particular cultural language is simply an illusion (Villa-Vicencio 1985: 104, 106).

The misunderstandings about what we are doing when we try to contextualise the gospel can be seen most clearly when we describe it as the *incarnation* of the gospel. It is frequently said today that we must incarnate the gospel, make the word of God incarnate, in our situation. The idea is that you start with certain gospel values or gospel norms or gospel principles and then you introduce these into the situation from outside and 'apply' them to the issues and problems of our country. In that way you 'christianise' or 'evangelise' South Africa. But is that true? Is that what we are supposed to be trying to do?

In the first place this is an idealist way of thinking (Villa-Vicencio 1985: 105). We start with ideas and principles, and then 'apply' them to a situation. In this way of thinking experience and subjective revelation and the signs of the times are unnecessary and superfluous. But more important still, this process of incarnating the word of God is simply unbiblical. It is not we who must make the gospel incarnate in our situation, God does it and is already busy doing it. We discover the word of God, we discover what God is doing and saying today, in the signs of our times. Those who want to incarnate the gospel in our situation are thinking of the gospel as some kind of *moral ideal* that has to be lived or put into practice. But as we have seen, the gospel cannot be reduced to nothing more than a moral ideal. The gospel is good news for the poor, the gospel is a prophetic message for our time. You do not incarnate good news into a situation, good news arises out of a situation. The prophets did not 'apply' their prophetic message to their times, they had it revealed to them through the signs of their times.

The good news has definite moral implications. It is the kind of news that challenges us to act. But the good news is concerned with something more than morality or ethics. The good news is about the meaning of our times, about the significance of what is happening in our country, about what God is doing. It never ceases to amaze me that so many Christians, including so many 'progressive' Christians and so many reputable theologians, still speak about the gospel as if it were merely a moral ideal, a set of values – gospel values. I can only assume that that is why they still think of the gospel as something which has to be brought in from outside and contextualised or incarnated in our situation. But, as Boesak points out, we cannot begin to talk about ethics, morality and the will of God for us today *outside* of the context of what God is doing in our present situation (1977: 90–1).

Contextualisation, then, is the process of discovering 'what the Spirit is saying to the Churches' in our context today and this is done in the light of what the Spirit said to the Churches and the prophets and Jesus in the past. Incarnation means that God has already entered into our human situation, and now we must open our eyes in order to see where God is, what the risen Christ is doing and what the Spirit is calling us to do (SACC 1986b: 77–79). Or, to put it another way, contextualisation means naming our experience and our practice with religious words like sin, salvation, grace, temptation, the work of God, the powers of evil, the practice of Jesus, the power of the Spirit and so forth. As the theologian Gilkey says, theology 'presents an understanding of contemporary existence as that existence is interpreted through the symbols of the Christian tradition' (in Jennings 1985: 90). Because the good news is about the meaning and challenges of our present experience, the Spanish theologian Fierro can conclude that we must 'fashion a theology for here and now which makes no claims about holding true for other times and situations' (1977: 209).

Where Do We Start?

Do we start with the shape of the gospel as we find it in the Bible and then fill that shape with content from our experience and from the signs of the times? Or do we start with our experience in South Africa today and then form that experience into the shape of a Christian gospel? Do we start with the Bible or do we start with our context?

In one sense this is a false dilemma (Schillebeeckx 1980: 76–77). What we are dealing with here is not a one-way street from the Bible to the context or from the context to the Bible (Nicol in SACC 1986b: 79–80). What we are dealing with here is a circular movement that proceeds forward like a wheel. We move from Bible to context to Bible and back again, making progress all the time as we come to a better and better appreciation of both the shape and the content of the good news for us today. The theologians call this the hermeneutical circle (C. Boff 1987: 135ff). Hermeneutics is the study of how people interpret the Bible and the hermeneutical circle is the conclusion that our experience or context influences the way we interpret the Bible, and our interpretation of the Bible influences the way we live and experience the world. It is not a vicious circle because if we keep moving ahead we can correct our previous interpretations and change our way of living, which in turn improves our understanding of the Bible and so forth. It is a dynamic rather than a static way of coming to a better theory and a better practice, of coming to a deeper and deeper appreciation of the good news that God is revealing to us in South Africa today.

On the other hand you cannot write a book in a circular manner. You have to start somewhere and you have to end somewhere. In the course of writing you can try to move round in a circle deepening the argument as you go along. I have tried to do that, to some extent, in this chapter. One of the best examples of this kind of writing is the gospel of John. He moves round and round the same point while making progress through the life of Jesus. However it is impossible to maintain this circular movement all the time. You have to speak about one topic at a time and, as I have already said, you have to begin somewhere and end somewhere. Moreover you have to proceed from what is likely to be more familiar to the reader to what might be new or at least less familiar. Thus the question remains: where do we start?

I have chosen to start with the shape of the gospel. In this chapter I have already presented some of the broad outlines or outer contours of that shape. I have pointed out that it must have the shape of good news, of good news for the poor and of a prophetic message for our times. I have also emphasised that while its more specific shape will come from the Bible and especially from the New Testament, the contents of this good news must come from our experience and from our reading of the signs of our times.

In the next chapter I shall analyse the gospel category of sin. I shall then make use of that category to interpret our experience in our country today. But my analysis of sin in the Bible will already be influenced by our experience of sin and evil in South Africa. The circle is there. It is simply unavoidable. But you have to begin somewhere because you can only write in a straight line.

To avoid getting lost along the way the reader would do well to remember that when we ask about the gospel in South Africa today, we are asking about *the role of God (and therefore Christ and the Spirit) in our present situation of crisis and conflict.* This question is of vital importance for the future of our country as I hope to make clear in the course of this book.

The journalist Joseph Lelyveld gives the following account of a conversation between Steve Biko and Malusi Mpumlwana. It is based upon an interview the journalist had with Malusi.

Only two brief weeks intervened between Malusi's release and Steve Biko's arrest. There was time for only one long . . . conversation. Malusi tried to impart his sense of urgency about the need to consider the 'role of God in the situation'. . . . The conversation reached no conclusion, and then Biko left on the trip from which he never returned. It would be hard to exaggerate this irony: two close friends – one who had just been tortured, the other about to be tortured to death on behalf of what is supposed to be a Christian civilization in South Africa – and in the little time left to them, they talk about the 'role of God in this situation' (1986: 297).

2
Sin in the Bible

The gospel is about salvation from sin. That is one of the few statements that all Christians would agree about – in the abstract. However, once we begin to ask about the meaning or concrete contents of these two words 'salvation' and 'sin' all the differences begin to appear. And if we try to pin these words down to concrete events and activities in South Africa today, we will find that the differences of opinion become so great that what is sin for some is salvation for others and vice versa.

What we need then is a thorough investigation into the concrete meaning of sin in our situation in South Africa. Salvation makes sense and becomes real good news only when we are quite clear about, and feel very strongly about, what we need to be saved or liberated from. Christians have always called this sin.

The reader may find this and the next few chapters a bit gloomy and even depressing. But then sin is rather gloomy and depressing. The advantage of allowing ourselves to feel the full impact of sin and evil in South Africa today, however, is that it will eventually enable us to appreciate to the full the excitement and joy of the good news about salvation.

Sin is not a very popular word today. It conjures up visions of punishment and hell and produces neurotic feelings of guilt and seems to be chiefly a matter of sex. I wonder if there is any other word in the Christian vocabulary which has been so thoroughly misused and whose meaning has been so completely distorted. No wonder so many people are confused about it and prefer to avoid using it while others reject it outright. On the whole we have lost any real or genuine sense of sin and that in itself, as we shall see, deprives the gospel of much of its energising power.

Before we begin our investigation into the experience of sin in our country today, we shall have to ensure that we are using the word 'sin' in its true Biblical sense. We shall therefore devote this chapter to the main characteristics of sin as they have been understood and experienced in the traditions we inherit.

Sin and God

Sin is a religious word. When we look at some wrongdoing and call it a sin, we are bringing God into the picture. We are not simply saying that we think something is wrong, we are saying that God disapproves of it, that God condemns it, that it is an 'offence against God'. When we speak of something as a sin we are saying that in a religious sense the one who is being wronged or sinned against is God. Thus if we say that apartheid is a sin we are claiming that God condemns it and that God is offended and insulted by it (Oosthuizen 1973: 60–65).

There is another way in which God is brought into the picture by the use of the word 'sin': God is the one who punishes us for our sins. We could just say that 'crime does not pay' or that 'every dog has its day', but when we interpret this experience in terms of sin, we see the disastrous consequences for the sinner as divine punishment. This is what the prophets did. By reading the signs of their times the prophets were able to foresee the disastrous consequences of Israel's sinful activities and policies. It was this that they spoke about as God's punishment for sin.

Of course it does not always work out like this. All too often it is the innocent who suffer and continue to suffer while the wicked prosper and continue to prosper. The Bible recognises this as a major problem in our attempts to understand sin and God. We shall have occasion to return to this problem later.

Sin and Morality

Sin is also a moral word. When we call some wrongdoing a sin, we are claiming that it is not the result of chance or fate but that somebody is morally responsible for it, somebody is to be blamed for it. Sin implies guilt. We shall have to try to clarify the meaning of guilt in our South African situation later but here we need only note that when we say that something is a sin we are not only saying that God is involved, we are also saying that human beings are guilty or in some way responsible for it. What is being contradicted here is fatalism and determinism of any kind.

In the Bible and in early Christianity the concept of sin was developed in order to contradict, among other things, prevailing ideas about blind fate (Bloch 1970: 204–206). Both natural and social forces were experienced as so powerful, so unintelligible, so uncontrollable and so inevitable that they simply determined our fate. Human beings were helplessly in the hands of the gods and especially the god of fate (Moira) or their whole lives were determined by the stars (astrology). The tragedy of a life totally dominated by the inevitability of fate has been dramatically portrayed in the classical plays of ancient Greece.

The Bible roundly contradicts this fatalism. As the author Bloch says, 'the definitive contrast appears only in the Bible' (1970: 206). The concept of sin emphasises human responsibility, human guilt and the role of human decisions in determining the course of history. To see what is wrong as sinful is to see that it can be changed, that conversion and repentance are possible. And that is why the Church today still reacts to anything that is perceived as fatalistic or deterministic. Dogmatic forms of Marxism or Communism that are, or at least appear to be, deterministic are rejected. What is not often noticed, however, is the determinism and fatalism of so much Western thinking. One so often hears people saying: 'Human selfishness is inevitable.' 'There is nothing you can do about it.' 'You must accept reality as it is.' 'You cannot change the world.' This kind of fatalism denies the reality of sin and the possibility of hope.

However the concept of sin and human responsibility for evil should not be applied to events and situations blindly and indiscriminately. A careful study of the Bible will show that there are situations where it is impossible to impute guilt or where there is very little guilt or where guilt is not the most important factor in the situation. A study of the many Biblical words for sin, guilt, evil and wickedness and the way they are used in different contexts will make it clear that the Bible is not dogmatic about human responsibility for every possible form of evil in the world. To quote only examples that would interest us today, there are genuine accidents, mistakes and natural disasters like earthquakes. However what the Bible does do is compel us to look for the element of human responsibility for whatever is wrong in any given situation. And this is what we shall have to do in relation to South Africa today. Where and to what extent are we being sinful?

Sin and Suffering

The link between sin and suffering is maintained throughout the Bible but the nature of this link is not always clear. We have seen that the link can be understood as punishment but this only accounts for the suffering that frequently results for the sinner himself or herself. What about the terrible suffering that sin causes in other people? The great prophets grappled with the meaning of this kind of link between sin and suffering but it was only in Jesus that it was clearly and dramatically brought to light.

Jesus turned sin on its head. He reversed the whole meaning and concrete contents of the word 'sin'. Sin was not what the scribes and Pharisees thought it was, in fact it was the very opposite of what they thought it was. Jesus claimed that the religious (and political) leaders of his time were wrong about what displeased and offended God.

Jesus clashed not only with the Pharisees but with the whole Jewish establishment of that time: the scribes, the chief priests, the elders, the Pharisees, the Sadducees, the Herodians, the Essenes and the Zealots. They had some very serious differences amongst themselves but fundamentally they all belonged to and endorsed the same religious and political system. They had differences of opinion about whether the system needed to be reformed, or about how it needed to be reformed, or about how it was to be secured against pagan and especially Roman threats: by collaboration, by separation or by outright warfare. But they never questioned the system itself. Jesus did. And that was why he disagreed with them so radically about sin.

The system we are talking about is what scholars now call a

purity or holiness system. It was the current interpretation and daily application of the law of Moses. Jesus regarded it as a misinterpretation and a misapplication of God's law.

According to this system the whole of society and the whole of life must be ordered and classified in terms of greater or lesser degrees of purity or holiness. Thus, geographically speaking the centre of the world was the holy of holies in the Temple and then moving outwards in concentric circles towards diminishing degrees of holiness or purity were the sanctuary, the altar, the court of the priests, the court of the Israelites, the court of the women, the Temple mount, Jerusalem and the land of Israel. Beyond that there were no holy or clean places.

Then there was the classification of times like feastdays and fastdays with the Sabbath as the holiest of holy days. Things were also categorised as pure or impure, ranging from unclean foods to semen, urine, menstrual blood and dead bodies. And finally there was the classification of people, firstly according to their status with the chief priests as the holiest and all who were circumcised as holy and separated from the uncircumcised pagans who were therefore outside of the system. But people were further classified at any particular moment by their present degree of purity and this was determined by whether they had eaten unclean foods, been in contact with unclean things or ignored the boundaries of holy places and holy times or in any other way transgressed the law. In such cases ritual washings or sacrifices would be necessary to restore the proper order of things.

Nor was this a matter of private religious beliefs. Religion in those days was a public affair. The system of purity and holiness was the religious ideology that governed all economic, political and social relationships. The Temple was not only the heart and centre of all holiness and purity, it was also the financial centre, the national treasury and the basis of the whole economy (Jeremias 1969: 21ff, 73ff, 126ff; Belo 1981: 63, 80). Moreover it was also the seat of government and of the high court. Insofar as the Romans allowed the Jews to have some measure of self-government, the country was ruled by a religious council called the Sanhedrin (Jeremias 1969: 74). The seventy-one members of this council were appointed from amongst the wealthy families of the chief priests and the elders (lay nobility) and from the scribes (Jeremias 1969: 222ff, 236f). The high priest himself presided over the Sanhedrin and it met in the Temple. Thus all executive, legislative and judicial power was also centred on the Temple (Jeremias 1969: 72, 151, 236). The religious system of purity and holiness ensured that the centre of all economic and political power would be seen as a very holy and sacred place – God's own house or dwelling place.

Socially, people were identified, classified and separated according to their degree of purity and holiness and this included racial purity! The unparalleled research of Joachim Jeremias has shown that 'from a social point of view the whole community of Judaism at the time of Jesus was dominated by the fundamental idea of racial purity. The entire population . . . was classified according to purity of descent [because] the nation was considered God-given and its purity was God's will' (1969: 270).

The law in the time of Jesus, interpreted as a system of purity and holiness, sanctified the status quo, the structures of economic and political domination, effectively ensuring that those who had privileges would never lose them. It was a total system and not merely a religious system.

As for the question of sin, according to this system sin was any transgression of the law, any transgression of the boundaries laid down by the system. No clear distinction was made between what we would call moral laws and ritual laws. The law was the law whether it concerned stealing or unclean foods or holy places. To sin was to act against the system, to rebel against the system or simply to be outside of the system. Those who fell outside of the boundaries of holiness and purity were sinners – whether they knew it or not, whether they were born that way or not. Thus sinners included pagans, lepers, prostitutes, tax-collectors (who were classified as crooks), shepherds (who were classified as thieves), people of mixed race (because they were born of a sinful sexual union between a Jew and a pagan) and all the lower classes of people who were dirty and ignorant of the law. God was holy and he would have nothing to do with anybody or anything that was not pure, clean and holy.

Jesus rejected this system *in toto*. Not because he wanted to reject the Jewish faith. On the contrary he did it in the name of faith in the God of the Bible, the God of Moses and the prophets. This was not the meaning of the law and the prophets. This was not the intention of God. Jesus was quite sure about that and so he could confidently break Sabbath laws and laws of fasting or ritual washing, touch lepers, eat unclean food with unclean people, mix with prostitutes and other impure outcasts, declare all foods clean and prophesy that one day the Temple itself and all the holy places would be destroyed.

Jesus was relentless in his criticism and condemnation of all the upholders of the system. In no uncertain terms he pronounces woes upon the rich (Lk 6: 24–26) and upon the scribes and the Pharisees (Mt 23: 13–32). In fact he accuses *them* of sin. He accuses them of two great sins: the idolatrous worship of money (Mt 6: 24 par) and hypocrisy. As Jesus sees it, their prayers are hypocritical, and so are their fasting, their almsgiving and even their questions (Mt 6: 1–18; Mk 12: 15). He accuses them of being serpents, a brood of vipers, whited sepulchres, blind guides, deceivers of the people who make their converts twice as fit for hell as they are, who put heavy loads upon people and who rob widows. They are the sons of those who murdered the prophets (Mt 23: 1–39).

It is the upholders of the system, the holy and pure ones, those who have conformed most assiduously and meticulously to the dictates of the system, who must be regarded as the real sinners (Mt 12: 34). They are the ones who offend God (Lk 16: 14–15).

On the other hand the people who were officially classified as sinners were Jesus' friends: the poor, the sick, the unclean, 'the rabble who know nothing of the law' (Jn 7: 49). 'He is a friend of prostitutes and tax-collectors' (Mt 11: 19). He mixes with them, eats with them, encourages them, tells them not to feel guilty because God forgives them and will not hold their supposed or possibly real faults against them. They are the ones who will inherit the land (Mt 5: 4) and the rule (or kingdom) of God when it comes (Lk 6: 20–21). They are the salt of the earth and the light of the world (Mt 5: 13–16).

But why? Why this total rejection of the system and of almost everything it stood for? Why this total reversal of the meaning of sin? Because God wants mercy not sacrifice (Mt 9: 13; 12: 7). Because in the eyes of God people and their needs are more important than the Sabbath and the Sabbath only has meaning insofar as it serves the needs of people (Schottroff 1984: 126). Because what makes you sinful is not the unclean foods that go into your mouth or the unclean things that you touch, but what you do and say, what comes out of you (Mt 15: 10–11). Because in God's court of judgment what you will be asked about is not holiness and purity but whether you fed the hungry, clothed the naked and visited those who are in prison (Mt 25: 31–36). Because if you want to be like God you must be compassionate or sensitive to the suffering of people (Lk 6: 36).

Sin is an offence against God precisely because it is an offence against people: 'Whatever you do to even the least of these people, you do to me' (Mt 25: 40, 45). There is no such thing as a sin that does not do any harm to anyone. At the very least, sin harms the sinner (now and in the future); at the most it harms millions of other people (now and in the future). The starting point for Jesus is suffering. Sin is about suffering, about making people suffer, allowing them to suffer or ignoring their sufferings. In the last analysis sin is not a transgression of law but a transgression of love. In the eyes of Jesus the system of purity and holiness as a system of law was itself sinful because it was the loveless cause of a great deal of suffering in that society.

Sin becomes visible in suffering. The seriousness or gravity of a sin must be measured in terms of the amount of pain and suffering it causes. That is different from the measure of *guilt* involved. In the Catholic tradition there are three conditions for a serious sin: full knowledge, full consent and grave matter. The degree to which people know what they are doing and the degree to which they give consent to it will determine the degree of their guilt or responsibility for what happens. But the gravity or seriousness of what is actually done must be measured by the amount of pain and suffering that it inflicts upon people. This we call grave matter.

Sin and Blindness

Sin is blind. It is impossible to sin without some kind of self-deception or blindness. This again is most clearly revealed in Jesus' analysis of the sin of the scribes and the Pharisees.

To say that the scribes and the Pharisees were shocked by Jesus' attitude to sin would be an understatement (Mt 15: 12). How could they possibly accept that those who transgressed the law were not necessarily sinners and those who kept the law were the real sinners? It was true that the law was a heavy burden and that it sometimes caused hardship. But that was the will of God and in any case some of the scribes were trying to apply the laws less harshly and with more sensitivity. There was no reason to reject the whole system.

At first they listened to Jesus, giving him the benefit of the doubt. But as time went on they felt more and more threatened by him. This man was clearly a sinner himself (Jn 9: 24; Mk 4: 15). More than that, he was a blasphemer, he was dangerous, he was misleading the people. For the sake of the system, the nation and the holy places he had to be eliminated (Jn 11: 46–50).

From Jesus' point of view the scribes and the Pharisees were blind (Mt 15: 14). Their whole education and training in terms of the system of purity and holiness had made them blind. Unless they could be born again, unless they could start again right from the beginning, they would never be able to see the truth – the truth about the law and the prophets, the truth about themselves, the truth about Jesus and the truth about sin. But the 'sinners' could see it. Those who were 'mere children' as far as education and training in the intricacies of the law were concerned, *they* could see what Jesus meant. Those who did not benefit from the system of purity and holiness but suffered under it, *they* were not blind. That is why Jesus could thank God 'for hiding these things from the learned and the clever and revealing them to mere children' (Lk 10: 21).

The Biblical image of blindness is often spoken about today as false consciousness. Because of their position in society, some people are unable to see what is really happening. They are conscious of themselves and of the world around them but their consciousness or awareness is false. They look but they cannot see; they listen but they cannot hear (Is 6: 9–10; Mat 13: 14–15). The concept of false consciousness, however, does not take the element of guilt or human responsibility into account. Blindness can be innocent or guilty.

The blindness of the Pharisees was not innocent. They were not like people who genuinely want to see and try hard to understand but because of their education and social conditioning are simply unable to see. This kind of blindness can be cured with time as in the case of Nicodemus. But there is another kind of blindness. It is the blindness of those who do not want to see or, more precisely, the blindness of those who are blind to their own blindness and who are therefore convinced that they can see perfectly clearly. Most of the Pharisees, it seems, were like that. When Jesus points out that they are blind, they are astonished. 'We are not blind, surely?' Jesus replied: 'Blind? If you were, you would not be guilty; but since you say, We see, your guilt remains' (Jn 9: 40–41). Today we call it culpable ignorance.

Behind this kind of blindness is the fundamental accusation that Jesus levels against the Pharisees and the whole purity system: hypocrisy. For Jesus hypocrisy is not just one amongst many possible sins that a person can commit. Hypocrisy is a fundamental characteristic of all sin. It is the element of self-deception or blindness that is present in all sin.

Hypocrisy is a lie. It is the attempt to live a contradiction as if it were not a contradiction. Jesus continually pointed out the contradictions in the lives of the scribes and Pharisees and in the whole system of purity and holiness. There is a contradiction between appearance and reality, between what they say and what they do, between the whitewashed exterior and the corruption within, between the plank in their own eyes and the splinter they are trying to remove from another's eye.

The whole situation was fraught with lies and contradictions. Everything was upside down. Things were not what they appeared to be, but were the very opposite of what they appeared to be. For anyone who remained in the system personal hypocrisy and blindness were unavoidable. The system itself was blind and what it required of people in the name of God was blind obedience regardless of the cost in terms of human suffering. The leaders and propagators of the system were 'blind guides' and Jesus could picture the whole scene as the blind leading the blind towards the edge of a precipice (Mt 15: 14) while they protest loudly and confidently that they know what they are doing (Jn 9: 40–41).

Hypocritical blindness is a characteristic of all sin. We can only sin by fooling ourselves at that moment about what we are really doing. We try to deceive ourselves by making excuses for ourselves. We lie to ourselves. Christian theology has always recognised this characteristic of sin. In the words of one theologian 'sin deceives itself about its sin *and* about its self-deception' (Brown 1981: 74). Sin is doubly blind and that is what makes it so extraordinarily dangerous to human life and limb.

The Sin of Omission

One of the most serious and widespread ways in which we deceive ourselves about our sin is by saying to ourselves (or to others): 'But I didn't *do* anything.' Doing nothing when I should have done something is a sin. We call it a sin of omission.

Millions upon millions of people in the world today are suffering not merely because of what others are doing but also because of what far too many people are not doing. In fact when those who are suffering do nothing themselves to throw off the yoke of oppression, they too are guilty of the sin of omission. It is so easy for us to blame others who are actively involved in making the policies that cause so much suffering, while we excuse ourselves with the illusion that we are not responsible because we have done nothing.

Perhaps, as Harvey Cox has pointed out, the most serious sin in the world today is the sin of sloth or apathy (1969: 37ff; 1968: ixff). It is the sin of not caring, not deciding, not taking responsibility and of avoiding the issue by saying that it is not my business. Harvey Cox calls it the sin of being less than human (1969: 40ff). We allow ourselves to be passive objects and part of the crowd, instead of becoming subjects of our own history. 'The apathetic avoidance of politics is the sophisticated way in which we, like Cain, club our brothers (and sisters) to death' (Cox 1969: 46).

This was also true of the scribes and the Pharisees. Jesus does not only accuse them of placing heavy burdens upon the shoulders of people, but also of 'not lifting a finger' to remove those burdens (Mt 23: 4). By omission they 'have neglected the weightier matters of the law – justice, mercy, good faith' (Mt 23: 23). In the parable of the sheep and the goats, people are excluded from the rule (or kingdom) of God only because of their sins of omission. They did *not* feed the hungry, give drink to the thirsty, visit prisoners and so forth (Mt 25: 31–46).

How easy it is for us to deceive ourselves into thinking that doing nothing is not sinful.

The Powers of Evil

Sin in the Bible means something more than individual acts of wrongdoing. There is another dimension to the whole experience of sin. In very general terms we could say that it is the corporate or social dimension of sin (Durand 1978: 89). We have only to think of how the prophets condemned not merely the individual sins of individual people but also, and much more frequently, the sin of whole nations and empires including the sin of Israel itself as a nation. In fact the social dimension of sin is the major concern of all the Biblical writers. This is not immediately obvious to the reader today because of the way the Bible speaks about this dimension. It does not speak about it in terms of social, corporate or collective sins or in terms of structures or systems, but in terms of false gods, demons, devils, evil spirits, principalities, powers and the law.

It is not possible to give even a brief outline of the characteristics of sin in the Bible without saying something about Satan and other evil spirits, the powers of evil. Some of you will appreciate this, particularly, but not only, those who are still close to the traditional African understanding of evil spirits. Others whose thinking has been formed by Western science will find any reference to devils and spirits somewhat disconcerting. It sounds like superstition and, of course, often enough especially today it is merely superstition. But it need not be and in the Bible it is used to say something very important and very powerful about sin and evil. Without this dimension of sin and without some way of symbolising it, we shall not be able to appreciate to the full what we are up against in South Africa today.

There is considerable confusion amongst Christians about the role of sin in our country. Is sin to be found in the individual or in the structures, in the hearts of people or in the social system of apartheid? The accusation levelled against so-called 'social gospellers' or 'liberation theologians' is that they have located sin in the unjust structures rather than in individuals and that they therefore want to bring salvation by changing social structures instead of working for a change of heart in individual people. Some try to avoid this dilemma by saying that there are two kinds of sin, personal sin and social sin, and by arguing that we must convert individuals and change the structures at the same time.

The trouble with all of this is that it is not based upon a sufficiently coherent understanding of sin. For example, what do we mean by a social sin? Does it mean the collective guilt of a nation or society? But what does collective guilt mean? It cannot mean that a person becomes guilty merely by being born into a particular nation, society, class or race. That would make one's guilt involuntary and involuntary guilt is a contradiction in terms. We can only become guilty by actively or passively participating with others in the same sin. But does that mean social sin is simply the sum total of the individual sins or individual guilt of the members of that society? The Bible is talking about much more than that.

The Bible does not make a distinction between two kinds of sin, personal sin and social sin. Sin is to be found in the individual and in the nation or social structures but in quite different ways. The personal and the social are two dimensions that are present in every sin. All sin is both personal and social at the same time. All sin is personal in the sense that only individuals can commit sin, only individuals can be guilty, only individuals can be sinners. However all sins also have a social dimension because sins have social consequences (they affect other people), sins become institutionalised and systematised in the structures, laws and customs of a society, and sins are committed in a particular society that shapes and influences the sinner.

One way of expressing this is to say that personal sins are objectified or embodied in social structures through which our sins cause suffering in people and through which others are influenced to become sinners. In this sense apartheid can be called sin although it cannot be called a sinner. The distinction is between the subjective (personal) and objective (social) dimensions of sin (Brown 1981: 75–81).

Put like this, the distinction is very abstract and intellectual. The Bible has a more concrete and powerful way of expressing the social dimension of sin. It speaks of the powers of evil in the world.

The people of Israel experienced sin in two ways. They experienced themselves as sinners when they had not been faithful to Yahweh their God, and they experienced themselves as sinned against when the powerful empires of ancient times, like the Egyptians, Assyrians, Babylonians, Greeks and Romans, threatened them, attacked them, massacred them and enslaved them. These were the original evil powers that Israel feared. These were the nations whose sins were condemned by the prophets.

To understand how Israel and the first Christians experienced this threat we should remember that every nation was thought of as having its own god or angel or spirit. Thus when any of these nations became cruel and oppressive their national god was thought of as having become a demon, a devil or an evil spirit (Caird 1956: 5–10; Wink 1986: 87–99, 110–116). The wicked oppressor was therefore experienced as the embodiment of some evil power that threatened the lives of ordinary people in much the same way as a great lion or a monstrous beast or a dragon (see especially Dan 7 and Rev 12, 13 etc.).

In New Testament times Paul speaks about this social evil as the principalities and powers, the authorities, thrones, lordships or the rulers of this world (Col 1: 16; 2: 10, 15; I Cor 2: 6; 15: 24; Eph 2: 2; 6: 12). When all of these powers are seen together as one threat they are spoken of as the god of this world or Satan, the prince of devils (II Cor 4: 4; Mt 12: 24–27). The whole world is then experienced as being in the grip of Satan (Jn 12: 31; 14: 30; 16: 11). In the words of Walter Wink, 'Satan thus becomes the symbol of an entire universal experience of evil' (1986: 24, 25). So also the principalities and powers that we read about in the New Testament 'represent organised evil, evil embedded in the structure of society' (Caird 1956: 84). Today most people would refer to the same thing as social forces. But the term 'social forces' is too intellectual; it does not capture the experience of something that is terrifyingly threatening and blindly and mercilessly cruel.

Sin and Temptation

The powers of evil also have another side to them. They are not only oppressive, they are also tempting. The experience of sin always includes an experience of temptation. Temptation is a kind of pre-condition for personal sin. Nobody sins without first being tempted. We could even describe sin as the experience of giving in to temptation.

Evil in itself is not attractive. It cannot tempt us without deceiving us and presenting itself as something that is good and attractive. That is the seduction. We are blinded and allow ourselves to be blinded to the truth about what we are going to do or not do. This is very well depicted in that great Biblical story about sin, the story of Adam and Eve. The serpent is the tempter who deceives Eve and then Adam by disguising evil as good and making it look attractive.

The people of Israel were tempted again and again by the false gods, the gods of other nations. The way of life, the security and the benefits they offered to those who accepted them were a constant temptation. The powers of evil can put us to the test and try to co-opt us. The experience of being tempted by something evil is symbolised in the Bible as an encounter with Satan, the great tempter (see, for example, Mt 16: 23). 'Satan did not begin life as an idea, but as an experience' (Wink 1986: 10). This can be a very concrete experience of daily life as we shall see when we begin to analyse our experience of sin in South Africa today.

The powers of evil, then, as the organised sinfulness of

nations or social systems, have two functions: to oppress and to tempt, to cause suffering and to seduce people into participating in the sinfulness, to coerce and to co-opt.

Sin and Law

'It is remarkable how, in one passage after another in Paul's epistles, the law duplicates [the] functions . . . attributed to Satan' (Caird 1956: 41).

We have seen how Jesus turned sin on its head, how he saw the system of law in Israel, the purity or holiness system, as itself the cause of suffering and evil. It was not only the pagan nations and the Roman Empire in particular that oppressed people; the interpretation and application of God's law in Israel at that time was also oppressive. It had become an evil power. What is more the Pharisees and others had been totally blinded and deceived by it. The law had become a temptation to sin.

Paul takes up this theme with some remarkable assertions about the law. While he affirms that the law itself is not sin (Rm 7: 7), he recognises that it has been perverted and absolutised. It has become an instrument of sin and therefore a demonic force from which we need to be saved (I Cor 15: 56; Rm 6: 14; 7: 8–13; 8: 2; Col 2: 13–14).

Once again it is a social system that has become a demonic force or evil power.

'Original Sin'

The term 'original sin' does not come from the Bible. It was coined by the Western or Latin Church to refer to some of the things that the Bible does indeed say about sin. However, it was around this concept of original or inherited sin that the Western Church developed some of its wildest theological speculations, for example, that we all share the guilt of the sin committed by Adam and Eve and that this guilt is passed on to us biologically, in the act of sexual intercourse by which one is conceived. Although some of this still lingers on in popular Christian thought in the Western world, today all theologians, without exception, reject this way of formulating the doctrine of original sin. Rahner is emphatic about it: 'The notion that the sin of

Adam has been transmitted to us biologically, as it were, has absolutely nothing to do with the Christian dogma of original sin' (1978: 110).

But then what does original sin mean? As a very broad generalisation, the meaning theologians give to this term 'original sin' might be summarised as the general sinfulness of the world which goes back to our human origins, which we inherit by being born into a sinful world and which gives rise to our human weaknesses (Durand 1978: 115–131). But what does the Bible say about this particular dimension of sin?

The stories of the first eleven chapters of Genesis (creation, Adam and Eve, Cain and Abel, the flood and the tower of Babel) were, among other things, Israel's theology of sin in narrative form. The stories are meant to explain how the world became so corrupt (6: 11, 12), so full of violence (6: 11, 13), so divided (11: 7) and so full of hardship (3: 14–19). It was not God who made it that way. Human beings are responsible for it. The personal sins of Eve, Adam, Cain and many others changed the world and its social structures and this in turn influenced other people to be sinful.

But it was above all Paul in the New Testament who took up the theme, focusing on the sin of Adam and developing the social dimension of sin not only as the sin of a particular nation or society, but as the universal sin of the whole human world from its very beginning. This objectification of sin in social structures and relationships takes different forms at different times and in different places, but it is a universal phenomenon that has been there from the time of Adam.

In Romans 5: 12–8: 13, Paul speaks of sin (in the singular) as an objective reality that has dominated history since the time of Adam. It is like a power or a master that rules over us and enslaves us. Moreover, sin does this to us from outside of us and also from within us. As an external reality sin manifests itself *through* the principalities and powers and the law. As an internal reality it manifests itself as a force that dwells in us and divides us against ourselves, in other words, as the experience of human weakness or alienation.

What is being pointed out here is that the powers of evil, the oppressive structures and systems, the perversion of God's law and our human weakness are all the result of personal sins. It is human beings starting with Adam who have made the world to be like this. As Caird puts it, 'the powers [of evil] owe their hold over humanity to sin' (1956: 84). In later times this came to be known as 'original sin'. It might be more appropriate to call it 'the sin of the world' (Jn 1: 29).

This is all very abstract. We have been trying to 'abstract' certain characteristics of sin from the Bible and from the Christian tradition. This is necessary if we are to be accurate and rigorous in our search for the concrete reality of sin in our situation in South Africa today. However, it is only when we discover the concrete reality of sin that we can begin to appreciate the value of these abstract characteristics.

By way of conclusion, then, before we turn to the realities of our experience in South Africa, we can sum up the characteristics or shape of sin as follows.

Sin is a religious word that speaks of God as the one who is sinned against and the one who punishes sin.

Sin is a moral word that indicates human responsibility and guilt.

The criterion for sinfulness is not law but suffering. Sin always causes suffering.

Sin is blind, hypocritical and self-deceptive.

We sin not only by what we do but also by what we do not do, by omission.

All sin is both personal and social because although only individual persons can commit sin, their sins have social consequences and these can be objectified, embodied or institutionalised in structures such as nations, social systems and laws.

These embodiments of sin or sinful structures are the powers of evil in the world.

The social embodiments of sin are also the means by which sin causes suffering in the world and the means by which people are tempted to commit further sins.

Original sin or the sin of the world is a way of speaking about all the social embodiments of sin and the influence they have had upon all of us since the beginning of the human race.

3
A Crucified People

Suffering

Sin becomes visible in suffering.

The extraordinary increase of suffering in the modern world has become one of the central concerns of all modern theologians from European theologians such as Moltmann, Metz, Schillebeeckx and Rahner to the black theologians of the USA and South Africa and the liberation theologians of the Third World. Suffering has long been the central theme of black Christianity in South Africa, especially in the African Independent Churches (ICT 1985: 30). If one were to try to discern the new starting point for modern theology and spirituality in most of the Christian world today, one would have to say that it is suffering. The sufferings of so many millions of people on this planet are one of the most fundamental signs of our times.

Academic theologians, who do not necessarily suffer much themselves, are learning to approach the subject of suffering with more and more care and sensitivity. Suffering is not an abstract idea and the theologian who treats it as an abstract idea that has to be related to other abstract ideas like sin and God is being unforgivably insensitive. Suffering is a painfully concrete reality that can only be approached with fear and trembling. One dare not speak about suffering in general (Metz 1980: 114). One dare not lump together the discomfort of a headache or the inconvenience of losing a mere luxury with the pain of a mother who sees her children dying of starvation or a person who is at the mercy of cruel torturers day and night. They are simply not the same kind of thing and to put them together under the same general heading of suffering is to distort reality. Schillebeeckx tries to indicate something of this by distinguishing between everyday suffering and 'the barbarous excess of suffering' (1980: 725). This is what I would call real suffering. Once one has experienced or been exposed to real suffering, the pinpricks of discomfort and inconvenience pale into insignificance.

But can anyone who has not experienced an excess of suffering or real suffering say anything worthwhile about it? I think it is possible provided one approaches the matter with extreme sensitivity and bases oneself upon what the real sufferers themselves say about their suffering (de Gruchy 1987: 99). I am not given to being autobiographical but in this instance it is necessary for me to declare my qualifications, limited as they are, for saying anything about real suffering.

I grew up in a white working-class family in a racially mixed part of Cape Town. We were not really poor. My father was a skilled labourer and often out of work. There were times when we went to bed slightly hungry or when we couldn't go to school because we had no shoes or because my mother was in such debt that she couldn't even borrow fourpence for the trainfare to school. But that was not real poverty or real suffering and we never ever thought of ourselves as poor or as suffering. Perhaps this was because my mother made us painfully aware from a very early age of the real sufferers. When we complained of the cold, we were told that we were lucky to have a roof over our heads. When we made a fuss about a toothache, we were told that other people had to suffer much more than that. Out of respect for the real sufferers we should not cry over a mere toothache.

It was not until much later in life that I came into contact with the indescribable sufferings of the people of my own country. I knew about the starving millions in India but it was only later that I discovered the starving millions in South Africa. I remember being powerfully disturbed when hearing stories about the wounded soldiers abandoned in the trenches during the First World War or stories about Nazi concentration camps, about the cruelty of the Japanese army and about priests who were, I heard, tortured in prisons in China. It was only later that I discovered with horror that these things were happening under my very nose in South Africa. As a priest I was exposed not just to stories but to the daily horrors of real suffering in real people. Like anyone else I have had the usual hardships and tough times but I have never regarded that as suffering. Of real suffering I can only say that I have seen it, I have touched it and I have become marginally sensitive to it. Nothing more.

Others have written about suffering in South Africa far more eloquently and far more comprehensively than I am able to do. Others have written from personal experience of real suffering or on the basis of far more information and a more extensive exposure to it. But I must say something if I am to allow the reality of sin and therefore the gospel to become visible to the reader.

Humiliation

The most characteristic form of suffering in South Africa, though by no means the worst form, is the suffering of humiliation. Anyone who is not legally classified as white is treated as inferior not only by individual whites but by the whole system of laws with their 'whites only' restrictions. This legalised humiliation, this systematic attack upon the dignity of so many human beings, has shocked and scandalised the world. Everyone knows that throughout the world one comes across prejudice (racial prejudice, ethnic prejudice, national prejudice, political prejudice) but how a government can actually demand by law that the majority of its citizens be systematically humiliated is beyond the comprehension of anyone who has not been brought up as a white South African. What is also beyond the comprehension of the international community, however, is the depth of suffering involved in this daily humiliation. Only people who have suffered humiliation from every side, from day to day, can tell us what it means in terms of human suffering.

They say, 'We are treated like animals.' In fact they also point out that very often animals such as pets or cattle and sheep are given far more care and consideration than they are given. They speak of the humiliation of being treated like dirt, like something unclean and despicable, something that will contaminate a white person who gets too close. One becomes less than an animal, less than a precious object or possession, a nobody, a non-person. When whites speak about 'South Africans' or about 'people' they mean other whites. Blacks are simply not taken into account. It is as if they didn't even exist. Of course not all whites are the same. There are exceptions but that does not bring much relief to the daily diet of humiliation.

Jesus was keenly sensitive to such humiliation. He went out of his way to make contact with those who were humiliated and rejected by the system of purity and holiness – the outcasts of all kinds. He not only treated them as persons and challenged them to treat one another as persons, he also preached a gospel in which they were persons of very special value in the eyes of God.

In South Africa today, despite this onslaught upon human dignity, many people have recovered their pride and self-worth; indeed some have never lost it. In recent times it was the Black Consciousness movement that developed this self-assertiveness and recovery of dignity. Today people can laugh at the arrogance of white superiority and see it for the foolishness, the stupidity and childishness that it is. White arrogance can be seen as degrading to whites rather than to blacks. The new generation of militant youth and workers has taken this recovery of dignity even further, but that is our topic for another chapter. The suffering caused by legalised humiliation remains for very many people although it is completely outweighed by other forms of suffering.

Workers

Before we turn to the intolerable sufferings of the millions of people in South Africa who are unemployed and who have no regular income at all, we must briefly draw attention to the suffering of the worker. Those who have jobs are regarded as the lucky ones, despite the incredible hardship of having to wake up every weekday morning sometimes as early as 2 a.m. to travel for anything up to seven hours, to do a heavy day's work, arrive home very late, have a quick meal and a short sleep before starting out again. The apartheid system demands that some people have to live as much as two hundred kilometres from their place of work. Life becomes among other things a battle against tiredness. Others live closer to their work in single sex hostels or compounds far from their families. Who can imagine the pain of such a life? 'Work has become', in the words of Buti Tlhagale, 'a curse' (Villa-Vicencio 1985: 128).

Wages are generally meagre and sometimes unbelievably low. The workers themselves speak of 'starvation wages'. The trade unions have been able to secure some improvements but in real terms, taking the rate of inflation into account, the wages of many workers in South Africa have decreased over the years and now, because of the escalating unemployment, these pittances have to be shared amongst an ever increasing number of people. Accurate statistics are not necessary to enable us to appreciate that the people are suffering. When they see how the 'bosses' live, they can only conclude that they are being cheated and robbed. 'You cheated them,' says James in his Letter, 'listen to the wages that you kept back, calling out; realise that the cries of the reapers [workers] have reached the ears of the Lord of hosts' (5: 4). I wonder what more James would have said if he lived in South Africa today.

And then there are the conditions of work: deep down in the mines, working a pneumatic drill all day, the constant danger of accidents, the lack of protective clothing in factories and so forth and so forth. Black workers in South Africa are haunted by the fear that they may become too sick, too weak or too old to continue working. You will be paid off. And what then? But worse still is the insecurity of knowing that at any time you might be retrenched. If you once lose your precious job, you might never again find another and starvation will stare you and your family in the face. The pain of such insecurity cannot even be imagined by those who have never experienced it.

Workers are mere objects, labour units, like pieces of machinery (Villa-Vicencio 1985: 129). In fact workers are often made to feel that they are worth less than the machinery in the mine or the factory or the white home in which they work. Machines are expensive, tireless, accurate and they never answer back. Machines don't have human needs. If the 'bosses' could replace the worker with a machine they would happily do so. How must it feel to be of less value than a machine and more easily disposable? And yet these are the lucky ones.

Unemployed

Nobody knows how many millions of people in South Africa have no work, no land and no income. Only God knows how many people have never had a job and never will have. In South Africa it is impossible to count them or to compile reliable statistics. If present trends are allowed to continue, the future with regard to unemployment is not only incalculable, it is too horrible to contemplate.

For blacks in South Africa, with very few exceptions, unemployment means hunger, starvation and death. There is no dole as in European countries and to qualify for unemployment benefits is beset with difficulties. The great mystery is how so many manage to survive for so long. Of course many of them do not survive, especially children, who die of malnutrition and related diseases in their hundreds every day. But others do survive and as far as one can see this is because of the massive relief work of the Churches and of organisations such as Operation Hunger or because of the sharing of the meagre wages and tiny pensions that some receive or because it becomes necessary to beg, borrow, dig in rubbish dumps or steal. Is there any wonder that the crime rate is so extraordinarily high in South Africa? In whatever way they manage to do it, millions of people do survive.

To have no work, to have nothing at all to do in life makes one feel even more useless than a mechanical unit in an assembly line. What meaning can life possibly have? Earning even a very small amount of money makes one feel that at least one is worth something. Hence the drive to conduct some kind of business in the informal economy, buying and selling something no matter how small. Hence too the enormous lengths to which people will go in search of a job. Against all obstacles, braving dangers of arrest and imprisonment, travelling thousands of kilometres, sleeping in the open despite freezing temperatures and walking the streets of unknown cities, people hope against hope that they may one day find a job. No wonder they are sometimes willing to take any kind of job no matter how low the wages are or how many insults they have to endure. Anything is better than the spectre of starvation or watching your children die of malnutrition or spending all your life begging.

Life in these circumstances is particularly hard for women. If they do find a job (usually as a domestic servant or in a factory), they have to do what is called 'the double shift': at work and then at home, perhaps with considerable hours of travelling in between. And then what about the children? On the other hand if they do not have a job and their husband has gone elsewhere to find work and he does not send any money, and the other men are offering money for sex and you have had to get used to sexual abuse anyway and the children are starving. . . . There is no end to the problems, the worries, the sufferings.

Homeless

This is only the beginning. There are so many other forms of suffering in South Africa. On top of everything else people are deprived of a place to live, of space to be, of the security of a home. Houses are sometimes so overcrowded that there is scarcely enough room for everyone to stretch out huddled together on the floor. Those who manage to put up a shack or some kind of shelter on a vacant piece of land or in the bush are classified as squatters. Sooner or later the bulldozers will come, sometimes in the middle of the night, and everything will be lost.

Except for a few privileged blacks, it is extraordinarily difficult to find a place to live, well-nigh impossible to get a house near one's workplace, always difficult to pay the rent, and there is little feeling of permanence and security. Perhaps the most cruel form of social engineering in South Africa is the policy of what is euphemistically called 'resettlement'. More than three million people have been uprooted from their homes, sometimes from land that they have owned for generations, or from the sacred places where their ancestors were buried, and dumped in dry, dusty places where there are no jobs and no land to work. Frequently they find that they have ended up in what is technically another 'nation', a Bantustan. The lucky ones are those less than two hundred kilometres from the nearest job opportunity, the rest just starve. According to those re-drawing the map of South Africa, millions more will still have to be 'resettled'. How can they remain unmoved by the absolutely inhuman cruelty of it all, the pain, the anguish, the suffering?

What we have in South Africa, then, are millions upon millions of people struggling to survive. The will to live and to live a decent human life is strong. People risk everything and get out onto the roads on foot, in buses, trains and taxis in search of a living. They are caught in roadblocks and sent back. They find themselves in the 'wrong' place at the 'wrong' time and end up in prison. Much of life is spent waiting and waiting, waiting for the bus, waiting for a possible job, waiting for a relative who might help you – hour after hour, day after day, month after month. It is the soul-destroying game of travelling and waiting. Even slave labour with the Hebrews in Egypt would be better than this. If you are to be treated as a mere object then at least as a slave you would be owned by somebody who has to feed and clothe you. Here you are simply thrown away and left to rot like a useless piece of rubbish. The suffering is immeasurable; it goes beyond what our minds can even begin to comprehend.

Punishment

The will to survive is strong. Somewhere along the line, when you feel you have really had enough, you might stand up and protest; you might begin to scream and shout and even to throw stones and burn buildings to make sure that your protests are heard; you might begin to resist the evil that is crushing you and killing you by joining an organisation of one kind or another; you might even take up arms. Anyone who dares to resist and to 'cause trouble' will end up enduring the ultimate form of suffering in South Africa: punishment.

Those who step out of line and 'cause trouble' are beaten up, mercilessly kicked and whipped, teargassed, wounded, killed, stabbed or hacked to death, petrol bombed and even burnt. When the police and the army do not do this themselves, they get their 'puppets' to do it: vigilantes, *'kitskonstabels'*, *'witdoeke'*, homeland police and various other death squads. The authorities call it 'black on black violence'. If you are without a job and hungry and don't really understand what is happening, you can easily be co-opted into the squads that deal with 'troublemakers'. At least that way you can eat and survive.

The other form of punishment is imprisonment. It is not so easy for the average black person in South Africa to get through life without spending some time in prison for some offence or other. Apart from the extraordinary number of laws that you could transgress or be suspected of transgressing at any time, you are in constant danger of detention without trial for resisting or being suspected of resisting the system. Detention without trial is quite simply a form of punishment meted out to almost anyone (black or white, young or old) suspected of promoting the struggle for liberation. We know about the hundreds of small children who are kept in detention, sometimes for long periods of time, because they might throw stones at the representatives of the system.

Detention is calculated to destroy people, to destroy their will to resist. This is made worse by solitary confinement, regular beatings and systematic, sadistic torture. There is no way of denying the enormous amount of evidence that has been collected about the indescribable horrors of torture in South Africa (see for example Foster 1987). No old-fashioned preacher who excelled in vivid and literal descriptions of hell could outdo the reality of hell in our prisons.

Response to Suffering

As Schillebeeckx has said, 'human reason cannot cope with concentrated historical suffering and evil' (1980: 671). It is difficult to face suffering in all its naked reality, so we bypass it with excuses: not all blacks suffer like this; whites also suffer; there are poor people in other countries too; it is not done deliberately; people *are* trying to do something about it; it's not my fault. The point, however, is that unless we, both white and black, face the monstrous reality of evil and suffering in South Africa we shall not find God and we shall not hear his good news of salvation from sin.

Nor is *pity* an appropriate response to real suffering. To pity those who are suffering is to add insult to injury. Nobody wants to be pitied. It is unfortunate that some translations of the New Testament have described Jesus' attitude to those who suffer as 'pity'. I do not think that even the English word 'compassion' is an adequate translation of the Greek original (Nolan 1976: 28). In the face of such an excess of suffering one can only stand in stunned awe and absolute horror before moving on to an attempt to grasp its significance, to understand what has brought us to this and to strive for a way out of it for all of us.

It is quite impossible to exaggerate the significance of real suffering. It goes beyond all human words. Poetry can capture something of it that statistics and mere description will miss. But even poetic images are inadequate and perhaps that is why in the last resort one can only have recourse to religious language, to the words and symbols of the gospel, to images that point to something boundless and transcendent.

The Cross

The cross is *the* Christian symbol. A cross on a building, a book, or a picture or hanging around someone's neck signifies some connection with Christianity. We bless with the sign of the cross, meditate upon the crucifixion and preach salvation through the cross. Christianity has rightly been called 'the religion of the cross'. Unfortunately, though, the Christian Churches have tamed and domesticated the cross. It has become a symbol of love and self-sacrifice, a symbol of the value of tolerating the daily burdens of life, bearing one's cross – and not much more. The extreme contradiction involved in taking this symbol of the most violent, disgraceful, dishonourable, scandalous and shocking form of execution known to the ancient world and making it into a sacred symbol, escapes the ordinary Christian today (I Cor 1: 22–25).

The cross was not merely an instrument of execution and death, it was a gruesome instrument of torture and punishment. Crucifixion was calculated to inflict as much agonising pain and suffering as possible for as long as possible. Some of its victims are said to have hung upon their crosses in unimaginable pain for days. Crucifixion was also a display of power and a warning to those who might contemplate the same 'crimes'. Crucifixion was a public event. The crosses were erected on a hill overlooking the city or along the roads leading into the city for everyone to see. The cross spoke loud and clear about what would happen to you if you dared to do what these men had done. (As far as I know there is no record of women being tortured in this way.) But what had these men done?

This instrument of torture and punishment was reserved for slaves and colonials who were not Roman citizens. Although most Roman citizens were somewhat hardened to violence and bloodshed, the cross was a form of punishment that was so disgraceful and so degrading that it was regarded as most uncivilised and unmannerly to even mention in polite society. They knew that as Roman citizens they would never be subjected to such degradation, no matter what they did.

It is possible that slaves and colonials were punished in this manner for crimes like theft but the evidence we have seems to indicate that generally the cross was a punishment for the 'terrible crimes' of trying to escape from slavery and political rebellion. Such people had to be taught a real lesson and everyone else had to be effectively warned about what happens to those who commit such 'crimes'. One can almost hear the Romans saying, 'This is the only language these people understand.'

When oppressed people rise up or try to escape from their slavery, the oppressor always pushes them down again with a display of force and violence. This we call repression. In the Roman Empire the cross was the great and effective *instrument of repression.*

I remember a Mass in Sebokeng celebrated by about thirty Catholic bishops during the height of the repression in that township in January 1985. During the offertory procession the people presented to their bishops the instruments of their repression: rubber bullets, teargas canisters, rent bills and chains. I remember thinking that these were the modern crosses, the symbols of repression that were being transformed like the cross into sacred symbols of our hope for salvation and liberation.

The Crucified Christ

If the Roman cross was an instrument of repression and torture, what was Jesus Christ doing up there on a cross?

Volumes and volumes have been written in an attempt to answer this question or to avoid it. But some things are beginning to emerge as incontrovertible. It was no accident. Jesus was not crucified by mistake. In the eyes of God Jesus was innocent, totally innocent. But in terms of the system that punished, tortured and executed him, he was guilty. Jesus was a threat to the system (Nolan 1976: 126–132).

We have seen how Jesus rejected the system of purity and holiness, the theoretical and practical interpretation of God's law that governed the lives of people in Israel at that time. But then why was he punished in this cruel fashion by the *Romans*? Why did the Jewish authorities hand him over to the Romans? They could have just stoned him as they stoned Stephen (Acts 7: 57) and as they were about to stone the woman taken in adultery before Jesus intervened (Jn 8: 3–11). The Romans had their own imperial system. What had Jesus done to subvert *their* system and to make it necessary for them to use their great instrument of repression to put him in his place and to be a warning to others?

Many people today think that the Jewish system was a religious system and that the Roman system was political. That is an anachronism (the mistake of reading back a modern idea into the past). Neither the Jews nor the Romans made any such distinction between religion and politics. The system of purity and holiness was both religious and political at the same time. The imperial system of Rome was also both religious and political. This ought not to be so strange to us in South Africa. Apartheid is both a political and a religious system. That is why it can be called a heresy and why the Kairos Document can speak of a 'State Theology' (1986: 3–8).

The Jews and the Romans observed two distinct religions that were also two distinct political systems. The two were frequently in tension or even open conflict but by and large they collaborated with one another and accommodated one another – for the sake of peace. In fact the imperial system of Rome was known as the *pax Romana* – the Roman peace. The colonial policy of Rome was to be at peace with its colonies and to maintain peace in those colonies by allowing the political and religious system of the 'natives' to continue and even by supporting it, provided the colonials did not reject Roman rule or refuse to pay taxes.

Those who rebelled against Rome in the name of their own Jewish system of purity and holiness were troublemakers and disturbers of the peace and they were duly repressed by massacres and wholesale crucifixion. This was the lot of the Zealots and other similar groups. They were zealous for the law interpreted as a system of holiness and purity. But this was not Jesus' position. He rose up against the Jewish system of that time as itself a system of oppression which caused intolerable suffering. He wanted to replace it with something he called the rule of God. The Romans would not have understood this but what was clear to them was that here they had an even more radical troublemaker and political rebel. He wanted, it seemed to them, to overthrow the collaborating Jewish authorities and their whole system of law and order and to make himself the Messiah or King of the Jews. That would indeed undermine the whole system of Roman peace. It could not be tolerated.

Jesus suffered and died on a Roman cross because like Moses and the prophets of old and like the other prophets and prophetic leaders of his time (Horsley 1985: 135–187), Jesus was horrified by the sufferings of the people, shared in their sufferings and was determined to do something about their plight. Jesus was one of the oppressed struggling to free all who suffered under the yoke of repression. That is the meaning of the cross.

One of the great discoveries or revelations for the first Christians was that all of this took place 'according to the Scriptures'! 'You foolish people! So slow to believe the full message of the prophets! Was it not to be expected that the Messiah would suffer and so enter into his glory?' (Lk 24: 25–26)

According to the Scriptures

The frightening reality of suffering was a major theme of the Old Testament scriptures. Pain and suffering are described with extraordinary sensitivity and realism. We read about the great wailing and lamenting when the people have been destroyed and massacred. In the Psalms we hear the cries and appeals that were directed to God over the centuries by a suffering people. We are faced with the agonising questions that the prophets and other writers asked about the meaning of all this suffering. For the people of Israel suffering was an ever-present reality.

Unfortunately many translators and commentators, because they were acquainted only with personal hurt and private problems, interpreted all these references to suffering in a purely individualistic sense. It is true that on rare occasions reference is made to an individual who is persecuted (like some of the prophets) or who fall on hard times (like Job) or who is betrayed by a friend (like David); but, for the most part, passages about suffering in the Old Testament scriptures are depicting *the sufferings of an oppressed people.* It is only recently that scholars have begun to realise that the writers of the Old Testament (and the New) were fully aware of the fact that poverty and real suffering were caused by oppression (Hanks 1983: *passim*, Tamez 1982: *passim*; see also Nolan and Broderick 1987: 32–35; and Kairos 1986: 18–20). Only those who are blind to what is happening in the world and has been happening for many centuries, could imagine that the sufferings of the poor are the result of misfortune, chance, laziness or their own sins! It was Pharaoh who thought the Hebrew slaves were lazy (Ex 5: 8, 17).

Oppression is a fundamental Biblical category (Hanks 1983: 4). There are some sixteen different Hebrew root-words for oppression (Tamez 1982: 9; Hanks counts twenty root-words, 1983: 26, 40). Any people who had so many words for the same reality must have been very much preoccupied with the problem. As far as Israel is concerned that should not surprise us. For most of its history Israel was oppressed by the great empires and nations of ancient times: the Egyptians, Canaanites, Philistines, Assyrians, Babylonians, Persians, Greeks and Romans (Ps 129: 1–2). It was only for relatively short periods of time that they enjoyed the luxury of freedom and independence. However, much more painful was the experience of the poor of Israel who were oppressed by their own kings and rulers. Many of the descriptions of suffering are descriptions of internal or national oppression. In the words of the prophet Micah: 'They [the rulers of Israel] have devoured the flesh of my people and torn off their skin and crushed their bones and shredded them like meat' (3: 3).

In most of the Bible oppression is described from below. It is the experience of being pushed down, crushed and trampled upon (e.g. Ps 94: 5; Amos 2: 7; 5: 11; 8: 4; Lk 4: 18), the experience of being weighed down by an enormous burden or load (e.g. Ex 1: 11; 5: 6–18; Is 9: 3(4); Mt 11: 28). The poor of South Africa experience their oppression in the same way, and that is why they sing, *unzima lomthwalo* – the load is heavy.

The experience of oppression is fundamentally an experience of being impoverished, of becoming poorer and poorer. The Bible abounds in examples of this kind of suffering and it is described from the point of view of the poor: as the experience of being cheated and robbed by the rich (e.g. Neh 5: 1–15; Mi 2: 1–2, 8–10; Amos 8: 5–6; Ps 12: 5; Lv 19: 13; Jer 22: 13 and James 5: 4–6). The oppressed feel that they are the victims of lies and deceit (e.g. Jer 9: 1–8; Ps 56: 5). Worse still, they are the victims of cruel and murderous violence (e.g. Ps 94: 6; Jer 22: 17). They compare their fear and terror with the experience of being surrounded by lions, wolves, wild beasts or dogs, who are ready to tear them to pieces (e.g. Ps 10: 7–10; 17: 9–12; Ez 22: 25, 27; Is 56: 9–57: 4). Today in South Africa it would be the police, vigilantes and troops in the townships.

The words used to describe the oppressor in the Bible are the same as the words used anywhere by the oppressed themselves: the rich, the greedy, the arrogant and haughty, fat cows, exploiters, liars, idolaters, tyrants, sons (and daughters) of iniquity and violence, or quite simply and frequently the wicked, the enemy (e.g. Mi 2: 1–2; Amos 3: 10; 4: 1; Jer 50: 37–38; Zeph 3: 1, 3, 11; Ps 5: 9–10; 10: 3–4). It is not often noticed that the frequent references to 'the wicked' and 'the enemy' are references to the oppressor (e.g. Pss 58 and 59).

Oppression is humiliating and degrading, and often enough reduces a person to tears (e.g. Is 53: 3; Pss 6; 42: 3, 5, 9–11; 116: 6, 10) and produces cries and appeals for help. The message of the scriptures is that God does defend the cause of the poor, crush the oppressor and liberate the oppressed (e.g. Ps 7: 3). The author of Proverbs sums up the sinfulness of oppression with the simple statement: 'To oppress the poor is to insult their Creator' (14: 31). (For more texts and details about words for oppression, see Hanks 1983: 3ff and Tamez 1982: 8ff.)

Many Christians reading the Old Testament are led to believe that the people of Israel blamed themselves for their sufferings and that they saw their slavery and oppression as God's punishment for their own sins. That is simply not true, except in the case of those who were taken off into exile and slavery in Babylon; *and they were not the poor and oppressed of Israel.* It is clearly stated in the Second Book of Kings that those who were taken into exile were 'King Jehoiachin, his mother, his officers, his nobles and his eunuchs', in fact all the 'nobles and notables', 'the men of distinction' together with some 'blacksmiths', 'metal workers' and 'men capable of bearing arms'; but the 'humbler country people', 'the poorest people in the country were left behind' (24: 12, 14–16; 25: 11–12; compare Jer 29: 2; Dan 1: 1, 3). In other words the people who were punished for their sins were precisely the Israelite oppressors and their collaborators (Anderson 1979: 400; Clévenot 1985: 35). This was clearly God's exercise of judgment and justice.

But the problem of suffering remained. All too often the innocent continued to suffer. Who knows how many of the poor were massacred in the wars of oppression or left to starve in a devastated city and countryside (Book of Lamentations)? And all too often the wicked continued to prosper. Many of the prophets and writers of the Old Testament (especially Job) grappled with this problem.

Isaiah, or rather the author of the second part of the Book of Isaiah (40–55), came to the conclusion that the sufferings of Israel did have a meaning. In his famous servant songs he portrays the suffering people of Israel as a kind of collective prophet, a servant of God. In other words the oppressed nation of Israel (both those in exile and others) are called by God to play a prophetic role in the world (Gottwald 1964: 341–6; Von Rad 1968: 218–226). They are to become God's witness (43: 10–12),

God's tongue (50: 4), God's voice (50: 10) to bring true justice to the world (42: 1, 4, 6–7).

But the great new insight is that these people will be a prophetic witness to the world *through their suffering*. This is the meaning of the fourth servant song, the song of the suffering servant (52: 13–53: 12). The author presents us (all the kings, all the oppressors and the crowds in general) with the horrifying picture of a human being who suffers every imaginable kind of suffering: wracked with pain and sickness, disfigured by leprosy, rejected, despised, humiliated, oppressed and repressed, degraded and sentenced to death. The author was not attempting to speak of some individual who had suffered all of this (Von Rad 1968: 224). It is an inventory of the sufferings of an oppressed people.

And then as we stand there speechless, screening our faces (53: 3), appalled at the sight of something that no longer seems human (52: 14), suddenly we are told (in effect): 'Look, look carefully, because this is something that we have done.' It is our sins that have brought this about (53: 5, 6, 8, 11, 12). We thought the suffering people were being punished for their own sins (53: 4). In fact they are suffering the punishment or the consequences of our sins. Those sufferings and sorrows and sicknesses we see in the oppressed people are ours (53: 4), they are the punishment we deserve but they have to bear. Look at the suffering of the people (which may include some of us) in the face of this disfigured man and recognise that we are responsible for this suffering, all of us, some more than others and in a whole range of different ways. To bear witness to that is the prophetic role of a suffering people.

Sin becomes visible in suffering. Our sin becomes visible in the suffering faces of the poor and oppressed people of South Africa. God speaks to us through them as he speaks to us through his servants, the prophets. And he speaks to us first of all about sin, about our responsibility for the excess of suffering in South Africa today.

The Crucified God

We asked what Jesus was doing up there on a Roman instrument of torture and repression. We saw that his suffering was 'according to the Scriptures'. Christians from the beginning have understood this to mean that Jesus was the suffering servant spoken of in the Book of Isaiah. This symbolic figure who represents a suffering people becomes in Jesus an historical person. Jesus now represents all oppressed peoples, all who are humiliated, crushed, punished, beaten up, imprisoned, tortured and killed. Jesus also represents the suffering people of South Africa. And he does so by hanging on the cross – for our sins. When we look at his mangled body in agony on the cross we see what we have done to him and to the people he represents.

But there is one additional element here. Jesus also represents God. We say he is not only the servant of God, he is also the son of God. He is not only a prophet of God, he is the perfect image of the invisible God. And if that is so, then what we have hanging up there on a Roman cross is God – the crucified God! 'Christian faith stands and falls with the knowledge of the crucified Christ, or, to use Luther's even bolder phrase, with the knowledge of the "crucified God"' (Moltmann 1974: 65).

God has a special concern for the poor not because of their virtue but because of their suffering. God sides with the oppressed not because they are all so good and so religious but because they are the ones who are being *sinned against*. In religious terms the distinction between the oppressor and the oppressed is the distinction between the sinner and those who are sinned against. This applies in every sphere of life whether we choose to call it politics or not. There is oppression in the home, in the factory, in the convent and in the Church. And in every case God sides with those who are oppressed. To say this is to say nothing more than that sin is an offence against God.

Nowhere has this been revealed so dramatically, nowhere has the nature of sin been made so clear, as in the crucifixion of Jesus Christ. Sin crucifies God. That is just as true today as it ever was. Jesus was crucified some two thousand years ago but the gospel we preach today is not only about that past event. The gospel is about Christ being crucified today. It is about the crucifixion of the people of South Africa. This does not mean that we are simply *comparing* the suffering of our people with the crucifixion of Jesus Christ. The crucifixion of God in Jesus Christ *is*, for us, the crucifixion of the oppressed people in our country. Nor can we say that it is merely 'as if' God was being crucified today. God is being crucified in South Africa today. 'Whatsoever you do to even the least of my brothers and sisters you do to me' (Mt 25: 40, 45). There is no 'as if' about it.

Here, then, we have the beginnings of an answer to our question: where is God in South Africa today? God can be seen in the face of the starving black child. God can be heard in the crying of the children in detention. God speaks through the mouth of a person whose face has been disfigured by a policeman's boot. It is not their innocence, their holiness, their virtue, their religious perfection that make them look like God. It is their suffering, their oppression, the fact that they have been sinned against. Suffering makes God visible as the one who is sinned against. The suffering of the people of South Africa is one of the great signs of our times. It is a sign of God's presence as the crucified Christ. It is the sign of the cross.

That may be very revealing but it is small consolation to those who bear the burden of real suffering. What is the use of a God who is weak, powerless and oppressed? What is the use of a crucified God? It may be a consoling thought but how is it going to help us to be liberated or saved from suffering and from sin?

We shall attempt to answer these questions in later chapters but if we are to do this in a convincing manner, we shall first have to understand exactly how suffering is caused in South Africa, how the apartheid system works, who is responsible and where personal guilt fits into the picture. In fact we shall have to engage in a rigorous analysis of the dynamics of sin in our country. All of this will be necessary before the real good news can be heard.

4
Unmasking the System

What we experience first and foremost in South Africa is that somewhere between the sinner and the sufferer there is a comprehensive, all-pervasive and unjust system. On the one hand, what the suffering and oppressed people experience as the cause of all their sufferings is a social system. On the other hand, those who have come to acknowledge their responsibility for the excess of suffering in South Africa, recognise that this happens through the support they give, actively or passively, to the policy of apartheid. The system is experienced as the link between the sinner and those who are sinned against, the medium or channel through which sin causes suffering.

A Total System

We have seen how in the time and country of Jesus the whole of life was ordered and controlled by the purity or holiness system: the law. In South Africa the whole of life is ordered and controlled by another system: apartheid. When we call the particular interpretation and application of the Mosaic law in the time of Jesus a purity or holiness system, we are not saying that it dealt exclusively with matters of ritual purity, unclean foods and holy times and places. It was a comprehensive system that dealt with every aspect of life, private and public, religious and political. We call it the purity or holiness system because it was characterised by these practices; they were the dominant features in this particular interpretation of the law. Similarly when we speak of apartheid we are not referring only to those laws and policies that discriminate against people of colour; we are referring to the whole system with its security laws, press curbs and states of emergency and with its consumerism, money-making, labour laws and class conflicts. We call the whole system apartheid because its dominant characteristic is racial or ethnic discrimination. Some people now prefer to call it racial capitalism.

I am not particularly concerned about what we call it as long as we realise that it is a total system that orders and controls every aspect of life, including the way Christianity is to be interpreted and how religion is to be practised (Villa-Vicencio 1985: 112ff). Much has been written about the theological justifications for racism that have been so much part of the development of the apartheid system (e.g. Kinghorn 1986), and the Kairos Document provides us with an analysis of the 'State Theology' of today. To appreciate how much the system is also religious, we have only to observe the fanatical reaction by the establishment to Black Theology or liberation theology. And that is why it makes sense for the World Alliance of Reformed Churches to declare apartheid a heresy. It is just as heretical for us as Christians today as the system of the scribes and the Pharisees was for Jesus in his time. Apartheid is just as much a religio-political system as the purity or holiness system was. The only difference, in this regard, is that the characteristic features of their system were religious, whereas the characteristic feature of our system is racism.

Those who suffer under this system do sometimes refer to it as apartheid or as racism or as racial capitalism but more often than not they simply call it 'the system'. When the police come banging on the door at night the people inside will say: 'The system has come.' When the bulldozers come to flatten their houses it is because 'the system' has decreed that they must be removed. When the workers go on strike they are fighting 'the system' and when some people collaborate with the regime they are said to be 'working with the system'. The system is all-pervasive, controlling, ordering and dominating every aspect of everyone's life – both black and white, albeit in quite different ways. It is a total and totalitarian ideology (Villa-Vicencio in *Missionalia* 1980: 70ff).

Internal Colonialism

In the world of today the South African system is unique. There are similarities with other modern systems, for example, their consumerism, their exploitation of workers, their competitive individualism. We can even see how the South African system fits into the international network of exploitation and control. But the uniqueness of our history and material conditions has given rise to a system that is significantly different. One of the tools of analysis that we use to understand both the similarities and the differences is the concept of internal colonialism.

Internal colonialism (or colonialism of a special type, as it is sometimes called) is a way of saying that the system is similar to other forms of colonialism in the world (past and present) but that it differs from them because, whereas in other cases the colonisers and the colonised live far apart in separate countries, in South Africa the white colonisers and the black colonised live side by side in the same country. The colonialism is internal.

South Africa, like most of the world outside of Europe, was once part of European colonialism. The Cape was colonised first by the Dutch and then by the British. Natal was also colonised by the British; while the Transvaal and the Orange Free State were colonised by Dutch settlers (Boers) who for a while set up 'independent' republics. In the Anglo-Boer War, around the turn of the century, the British army defeated the Boers and thus brought the whole territory under the control of the British Empire. The European settlers in the four British dependencies came together, without any reference to the indigenous people of the country, to form what they called the Union of South Africa. In time this entity became independent of Britain.

The process was in many ways similar to the process of colonisation and decolonisation in other parts of the world. It was different in that it left behind in South Africa a system of internal colonialism or apartheid. Why did this happen?

In some parts of the world like the USA, Canada, Australia and New Zealand the indigenous people were so small in numbers or were so thoroughly decimated by the colonisers that eventually the European settlers emerged as the majority.

Thus when they became politically independent from Europe, they took their place among the white or European nations, as so-called 'developed' or 'First World' countries. In this 'new world' Europe had simply found a place for its rapidly expanding population.

In Africa and Asia, on the other hand, European settlers remained a small minority and therefore when these countries achieved political independence they emerged as 'underdeveloped', 'Third World' countries. In other words they passed from old-fashioned colonialism to what is called neo-colonialism. They gained some measure of political independence but they remained economically dependent.

South Africa fell between these two stools. On the one hand it was like North America in the nature of its European settlement and industrialisation; on the other hand it was like Africa and Asia with its majority of indigenous poor people. Whites therefore tend to perceive South Africa as partly a 'developed First World' country and partly an 'underdeveloped Third World' country; partly an extension of Europe or 'Western civilisation' and partly a world that has to remain colonised in one way or another. One hears white South Africans arguing that in the United States it was all very well to give blacks equal rights because there they are a minority that can be absorbed into the system. In South Africa blacks are in the majority.

However, the system of internal colonialism or separate development cannot be accounted for simply in terms of numbers. In Latin America the European settlers and the indigenous people merged and the exploitation continued in another form. Something similar happened in the early days at the Cape. It is true that a semi-feudal system based upon race was developed in the Boer republics but that was not very different from the racism of some South American countries or of the southern states of the USA. How and why was this racism transformed into the ideology of apartheid or internal colonialism?

What made all the difference in South Africa was the discovery of gold in 1886. Gold was also found in California and Australia, but what was discovered in South Africa was 'an endless treasure of gold' (de Kiewiet 1941: 5) and, what is even more significant for our inquiry, the gold was found in thin layers very deep underground. One hardly needs to emphasise how important gold is for the economy of the whole world. South Africa soon became and still is the largest supplier of gold in the world and there is enough gold here to carry on mining for hundreds of years to come. But it is low-grade ore and requires deep-level mining. Because of the very thin layers of gold, one ton of ore produces far less gold than in other places and most of these layers are about a kilometre underground. Consequently enormous profits could be made but only with vast numbers of cheap, really cheap, workers!

It was the initial need for cheap labour, for an exceptionally numerous labour force at an exceptionally cheap price, that made South Africa different. Without this need most of the indigenous people might have been eliminated like the native Americans or pushed into separate colonies outside of the 'golden areas'. What actually happened was that millions of black people were forced into a kind of 'slave' labour to dig the deepest holes and the largest network of tunnels on this planet. Pharaoh's little effort at putting up huge buildings and pyramids with forced labour was as nothing in comparison with this.

The system of internal colonialism is at its roots a system of forced labour. The system did not originate from the racism of the Boers or Afrikaner nationalism. It was developed by the white mine-owners and successive white governments for the purpose of profit-making. Racial differences were very conveniently exploited and when the National Party came to power in 1948 it simply perfected, streamlined and institutionalised the system and gave it the name 'apartheid'. Gold and racism was the winning combination. It turned South Africa into a capitalist's paradise. But why call the system internal colonialism?

Colonialism is a form of exploitation and oppression that has been exercised by imperialist nations for thousands of years. Throughout the Bible we read about the numerous imperial powers that colonised and oppressed Israel. But the greatest, the most extensive, the most long-lasting and the most ruthless form of colonialism in the history of humankind was and still is European colonialism (centred now in the USA).

Put quite simply, the purpose of all colonialism is money. In the old days the colonisers exacted a tribute or tax, in kind or in cash, from the colonised. European colonialism, however, was a way of acquiring more land, new markets, raw materials or cheap labour – depending upon which of these were available in the colonies. These were the commodities that were needed by the economy of Europe, by its particular way of producing or manufacturing goods (the capitalist mode of production). The European economy and its very successful way of producing goods were based upon the arrangement that some people would own the land, the factories, the mines and the machinery, while others would work for a wage. This divided the society into two basic classes: the owners and the workers. What motivated the owners to produce goods was the profits they could make and what was supposed to motivate the workers was their wages. In other words the incentive was money. But there is an inevitable conflict built into this system because higher profits require lower wages and higher wages result in lower profits.

Colonialism comes into the picture once the owners or their governments need more land, new markets for their surplus products, raw material not available in Europe or labour that is cheaper than the labour in the metropolitan country. Once the workers in a 'developed' country attain equal political rights they will succeed in obtaining higher and higher wages. The owners will then have to make greater use of migrant labour or move their factories to a poorer country. If any of this requires that other countries be colonised, that is to say, deprived of political independence, that will be done. But these days it is generally only necessary to exercise economic control over one's dependencies – neo-colonialism or economic imperialism.

In South Africa the white colonisers had already taken the land and the raw materials, especially the gold, but what they needed to colonise was the cheap labour. The only way to colonise the cheap labour within the same country was to devise a system of identity and separation. South Africa's 'First World' had to be set apart from its 'Third World' especially where political rights were concerned. There would have to be a way of creating separate identities for those who enjoyed the benefits of a colonising nation and those who were to remain colonised. It was not necessary to search for a criterion of identity, as racism was present already; it only needed to be systematised and controlled. Segregation and later apartheid involved the artificial and systematic creation of a white national identity (and within that an Afrikaner *'volksidentiteit')* in order to reap the benefits of South Africa's wealth and to exclude the colonised workers of African, Indian and mixed descent. The vast numbers of colonised people would have to be further divided in accordance with the principle of 'divide and rule' and located in separate 'colonies' or homelands, or at least in separate 'group areas'. It was the only way that the rich could remain rich and continue to make large profits. A certain number of workers (the white workers) could be included and given privileges and political rights but the rest of the people would have to remain colonised labour units (Stadler 1987: 103ff, 120ff).

Apartheid is a system of imposed separation and imposed identity. In this it has remarkable similarities with the system of purity and holiness. The Pharisees were 'the separated ones'. That was the very meaning of their name. The Essenes even went into the desert to ensure separation and to maintain their pure identity. The purity or holiness of places, times, food and people was calculated to set some people apart and to create a definite identity. A system of separation and identity is clearly a system of control.

A System of Control

Because the colonisers and the colonised existed side by side in the same country an elaborate and comprehensive system of control had to be devised. There are two ways of controlling people: by coercion or force and by co-option or persuasion. As has often been pointed out South Africa has used both methods to the maximum down through the years. I want to call the first social engineering and the second social conditioning.

To separate the races and to keep them apart required what must surely be the greatest exercise in social engineering in the history of humankind. People who worked together had to reside in separate group areas, to be prevented from mixing in the same restaurants, hotels, cinemas, or toilets, and forbidden to marry one another or have sex across the colour line. How else could they maintain their separate identities? How else could the whites maintain their feeling of superiority?

This was known as petty apartheid *(klein apartheid)* and some of it is no longer felt to be necessary. But the real job of social engineering was grand apartheid *(groot apartheid)*. This involved the creation of homelands or Bantustans with a programme of resettlement and forced removals to develop the fiction that some 80 per cent of the people had political rights in tiny, fragmented 'national states' in 13 per cent of the land outside the metropolitan areas. The system was trying to create its own small 'Third World' countries, its own colonies for the colonised labour force. They are nothing more than labour reserves and now that fewer unskilled workers are needed by the economy the homelands have become overcrowded dumping grounds for surplus people.

To get human beings (black and white) to accept this kind of social engineering required a tremendous amount of social conditioning. Today most of us know that we are socially conditioned by the society, culture or class in which we grow up. We are not socially determined because we remain theoretically free to transcend our social background. Very few people ever do and even then we never become entirely independent of the formative influences of our social environment.

Apartheid includes an elaborate system of social conditioning to legitimate itself. There are laws that make it all 'legal'; there is a bizarre ideology with myths about race or ethnicity and 'civilised' behaviour; there is an educational system that socialises children into a particular 'racial identity'; there is an elaborate system of propaganda, censorship and press curbs to control the minds and hearts of people; and finally there are forms of religious justification that appeal to one's conscience and 'fear of the Lord'. The onslaught upon the individual is total.

Security and Reform

Needless to say apartheid, even with its system of total control, has not succeeded and never will succeed. It is too full of contradictions and lies. Almost everything the system does turns out to be counterproductive in terms of its own goals. It sets out to create order and actually produces chaos. It sets out to generate wealth but produces more and more poverty for more and more people. Separation was supposed to avoid friction between the races, instead it created conflict. According to the great plan blacks were to be labour units who would be satisfied with their low wages but they turned out to be people who wanted to live like human beings.

Such an artificial, unnatural and contradictory system will inevitably lurch from one crisis to another. Each crisis calls for a measure of adaptation. Now, faced with its greatest crisis ever, the system has embarked upon a two-pronged programme of reconstruction that is known as 'security and reform'.

Security is simply a further extension of social engineering or coercion, only now it requires more force and more violence, comprehensive and lengthy states of emergency and total militarisation, including a policy of destabilising neighbouring countries. It is a last desperate attempt to force people to comply – at gunpoint. South Africa is being governed more and more by a State Security Council that reaches out to every corner of the country through its Security Forces and Joint Management Committees. They are responsible for ensuring, at all costs, that those who benefit from the system remain secure while everyone else lives in almost complete insecurity. What the system calls security is in fact ruthless military repression.

Reform is the other side of the coin. It is the new way of gaining some measure of legitimacy for the same old system and of conditioning people to accept the new security measures. It is a further extension of the old policy of co-option. Some of the laws regarding petty apartheid have been scrapped, although grand apartheid, the homelands policy, remains intact. Some Indians and so-called coloureds have been co-opted into the system by means of a tricameral parliament that gives them their own chambers to discuss their 'own affairs', with a proportion of votes on 'general affairs' that ensures they can never outvote the whites. An effort is being made to co-opt some urban blacks as community councillors and as possible future members of a National Statutory Council. On the whole the people boycott these toothless puppet structures.

More and more efforts will be made to win the minds and hearts of the people and to restructure the system. In the near future we might find ourselves with a carefully chosen 'multiracial' regime that tries to maintain the same system of exploitation and oppression in another form. But such reforms cannot work because they always come from the top, are designed to benefit the ruling class and will never allow the people as a whole to participate fully. That would endanger the whole system. The system cannot change itself to become something quite different. The system can only adapt itself in order to remain fundamentally the same. All its reforms are simply ways of self-adaptation that can only lead to more contradictions, more crises, more conflict and more chaos. The architects of the system and its reforms cannot see this because they are the blind leading the blind.

The Blind Leading the Blind

We have seen that one of the mechanisms of control is social conditioning. This might also be described as making people blind or blindfolding them in order to lead and control them. We have also seen how the system of the scribes and the Pharisees did this in the time of Jesus and that hypocritical blindness is a factor in all sin. In the next chapter we shall have to assess to what extent blindness in South Africa is hypocritical and therefore a matter of personal guilt. But first we must analyse more carefully the role of the system in this phenomenon that Jesus called 'the blind leading the blind'.

The principal means used by the system to deceive the white community and as many others as possible are separation, propaganda and education.

Internal colonialism has created two separate worlds within the same country and this has led to two quite different ways of perceiving the same situation. Visitors from outside often say that it is difficult to believe that people from the two worlds are actually talking about the same country. Those who move from one world to the other on a regular basis can see and hear the difference and, of course, most blacks do move into the white world every day when they go to work. On the other hand, whites hardly ever move into the other world. Most whites have never seen the inside of a black township or a black home. They know more about the geography of Europe than the geography of Soweto. They sometimes know more about the eating habits and igloos of Eskimos in Greenland than they know about the lives and the thoughts of their domestic servants and employees.

Moreover those blacks who work closely all day with whites dare not say what they think – for political and economic reasons. 'I could never tell the boss what I think about the struggle or the stayaway. I just say it was dangerous for me to come to work because of the intimidation.' Or in the words used by a male domestic to the journalist Lelyveld: 'If you go around showing what you're feeling inside, you'll be out of a job' (1986: 112). Few whites could appreciate Can Themba's plea for 'a little respite, brother, just a little respite from the huge responsibility of being a nice kaffir' (quoted by Lelyveld 1986: 262).

The closed white world creates the kind of blindness that we usually call the 'laager mentality'. One of the ironies or contradictions of the system of separation is that it isolates whites rather than blacks; it cuts whites off from reality but allows blacks to see both worlds. So that it is whites who need exposure to the other world, exposure to blacks as human beings, exposure to real suffering, exposure to reality.

However, in terms of blindness separation can only be effective when it is accompanied by consistent and carefully planned propaganda. The apartheid system controls all the mass media. Television and radio are state-owned, newspapers are controlled by press curbs and books are censored. People are only allowed to hear what the system wants them to hear. Television has become the perfect medium for manipulating people, for controlling their thoughts, their feelings and their access to information. This is done very effectively by remaining silent about much that is actually going on, by carefully selecting news items and arranging them in a particular sequence, by distorting what opponents of the system have said and then refusing to allow them to speak for themselves, and by propagating blatant lies. Again and again one has the experience of witnessing an event or speaking to eyewitnesses and then on the television listening to shameless and deliberate lies about what happened.

What is still worse, though, is the manipulation of the listener's emotions. Television and radio are used to instil fear into people. Most whites are now suffering from a near-paranoic fear of blacks, 'terrorists', radicals, the ANC and communists. In the 1987 whites-only election the National Party, despite its political confusion, despite the resignation of almost all its intelligentsia, was able to secure a landslide victory by simply playing on the fears of white people and then offering them security. Nothing blinds people more effectively than fear. Fear overcomes all doubts and all appeals to conscience. But unfounded fears are irrational and therefore very, very dangerous.

Education is the last of the forms of social conditioning that I would like to mention. Education in our country has become a way of preventing children from ever thinking for themselves and conditioning them from an early age to accept what they are told. A concerted effort is made to socialise young people into a system that is and must be, in every way, authoritarian. As we shall see, this no longer works for most black children but the majority of white children come out of school blinded by their highly educated ignorance and their inability to think for themselves. They have been socialised into a false consciousness.

The South African system is a typical case of what Jesus called 'the blind leading the blind'. To the blind the reality of South Africa is invisible: the suffering, the sin, the signs of the times, the good news of salvation and the reality of the living God.

We have been trying to understand the system: how it came about, how it works and what it does to people. We had already looked at the intolerable suffering that it causes for millions of people and we have just seen something of the dangerous blindness that it produces in other people. But there is something else that this system does to people, to everyone who does not stand up and resist it strongly. It is something that eats into the hearts of people, deprives them of their humanity and turns them into monsters. What we are referring to is the phenomenon that we call alienation. Apartheid must surely be one of the most effective systems in the world for generating alienation.

Alienation

People are alienated or estranged from one another when they treat one another as mere things rather than as persons, as objects rather than as subjects. People are alienated from themselves and from their own humanity when they begin to treat themselves as mere things or objects. Alienation destroys *ubuntu*. *Ubuntu* is the Nguni word for the traditional African experience of humanness. It refers to that sensitivity for other human beings and that experience of oneness with all human beings that enable one to become human oneself. The idea is captured in a saying that is known in all African countries south of the Sahara. In Sotho it reads: *motho ke motho ka batho;* a human being is a human being with, by and for human beings. It is this *ubuntu* that is destroyed by the system in South Africa.

We have seen how ruthlessly and systematically black people have been treated as mere labour units, as things that are needed in the process of producing goods and making money. Black workers have been stripped of everything that could make life even marginally human. In order to be used as profitable labour units they were cut off from their families, their culture, their history and their land (Mofokeng 1983: 21ff). Their low wages put even the goods they produced and the buildings they constructed beyond their reach. What was left to prevent them from thinking of themselves as mere objects and from treating one another as things instead of persons? The result would have been complete alienation and sometimes it has been. However, as we shall see later, many of the people have successfully resisted this onslaught and re-asserted their humanity against all the odds.

Most whites and other privileged people have not been so successful. The system produces alienation in them too – in another way. When you treat other human beings as mere units of labour and when you treat your money, your property, your privileges and your standard of living as more important than human beings, you begin to lose touch with your own humanity. And when you can only contact other people on the basis of their skin colour, their status within the system or their possessions, you have begun to treat them as objects, no matter who they are or how valuable they may be to you as objects. There is no human contact.

Whites (and all those who are co-opted onto their side) are blinded, numbed, isolated and cut off from reality. In the end they are alienated not only from black workers but also from themselves. As Boesak has pointed out, apartheid does not only prevent whites from understanding blacks, it also prevents them from understanding themselves as human beings (1977: 116, 147). You begin to value yourself not as a human being but as a white, as a privileged being, as a professional or even as a sex object. The results are disastrous.

The Symptoms of Alienation

I do not know much about the effects that other social systems have upon people, but in our country we are experiencing an appalling breakdown in mental health, physical health, social relationships and family life. In South Africa this breakdown seems to be worse than almost anywhere else in the world. It is the clinical psychologists, the social workers and the journalists who are beginning to sound the alarm bells. In a recent interview, Hendrik Kotze, director of the Unit for Clinical Psychology at the University of Stellenbosch, does not hesitate to assert that 'South Africa has one of the most psychologically ill societies in the world'. 'The problem had reached alarming proportions and was manifesting itself in frightening statistics' (*Star* 26.10.87). Kotze goes on to identify the root causes as 'the socio-political climate, . . . a materialistic lifestyle among whites striving for a high standard of living, . . . pressure to excel, conditions of poverty and often social disorder' (*Star* 26.10.87 and see *Sunday Star* 1.11.87). At its annual conference the Institute for Clinical Psychology 'adopted a major policy statement on the political situation, calling on the government to take note of the "irrevocable consequences" of its measures, including "the institutionalisation of racial discrimination", violence, indefinite detention without trial and solitary confinement, detention of children, media restrictions and the state of emergency' (*Argus* 9.9.87).

The stress and the strain of life in South Africa today take their toll on the body too. Statistics are difficult to obtain, but some believe that we have the highest death rate from heart disease and an alarming increase in cancer cases (*Sunday Times* 14.6.87, *Star* 26.10.87, *Sunday Star* 1.11.87). But it is above all in social behaviour that the symptoms of alienation can be clearly observed.

In the first place those who cannot cope with the situation, and there are many of them both white and black, resort to drink. Our alcohol consumption figures are amongst the highest in the world. Anyone who moves around amongst the different groups and classes in our country knows that an alarmingly high proportion of the population, both white and black, is under the influence of liquor a good deal of the time.

Liquor is part of our sad history. It was used on the mines as a form of control. The mine-owners started a profitable liquor industry to produce a very cheap brew to keep the workers 'happy'; more recently the township Administration Boards operated the beerhalls to defray their expenses; and the government forbade the private brewing of the wholesome traditional beer. In the Western Cape farm-labourers are still rewarded for their work with a 'tot' of wine. No wonder that during the uprising in Soweto in 1976, the youth burnt the beerhalls that had kept many of their parents and grandparents in a semi-permanent stupor.

But drink is not the only form of escape. Some escape into drugs or smoke dagga. Others find some relief in the consolations of religion or the distractions of sport. But it is to human relationships that we must turn to see how destructive our alienation has become.

Our divorce rate is the third highest in the world. Only the United States and the Soviet Union beat us to the divorce courts but perhaps that is because most family breakups in South Africa do not go through the divorce courts. In the white community there is a frightening number of battered babies and battered wives, not to mention family murders. And there is a growing incidence among white South Africans of family suicides. The husband who cannot cope any more shoots his wife, his children and then himself. Among white South Africans under 20, suicide is the third highest cause of death (*Sunday Times* 14.6.87)!

We have become a thoroughly violent society. This can be seen not only in the number of assaults, murders and armed robberies but also in the enormous number of road accidents. We seem to take out our frustrations behind the wheel.

However, the place where violence has really become a way of life, where violence has been systematically cultivated as a virtue that one can boast about, is in the Security Forces (white and black policemen, the army, homeland police, '*kitskonstabels*', homeland armies, etc.). Here, most of all, the security system makes young human beings into monsters. Some develop a Rambo identity as 'macho men' or 'tough boys' who want to be 'where the action is', provoking, assaulting, maiming and killing people who get in their way in the townships. This has to be seen to be believed (a frank account of this experience by a national serviceman can be found in the record of a court case in the *Weekly Mail* 22.5.87). It is the real ugly face of the system, not only in the intolerable suffering inflicted upon the people of the townships but also in the complete alienation of young men who have ceased to be human. No wonder they begin to take drugs and develop psychological problems. No wonder the highest suicide rate is amongst military conscripts (*Sunday Times* 14.6.87). No wonder some of the black youth are now responding with petrol-bombs, car bombs, hand grenades and necklacing. And now vigilantes and other similar groups are proving to be even more savagely violent than the Security Forces.

Our society is not falling apart, it has already fallen apart. It is no longer a human society of human beings with human relationships. Apartheid has brought us nothing but alienation, inhumanity, suffering, violence and death. The wages of the system is death. 'Sin lives by killing the human being . . ., by sucking the life out of those it kills. The law [the system] . . . reproduces and reinforces sin and therefore also leads to death.' This, at least, is Hinkelammert's interpretation of Paul's teaching about sin, law and death in his study of the ideological weapons of death today (1986: 133ff). Apartheid as a system can only lead to death and destruction. Moreover, those who are alienated from one another and from their own humanity are also alienated from God. They may talk about God, profess their belief in God and go to church on Sundays, but alienated people who have lost contact with all that is human have also lost contact with God. That at least is what the system does to anyone who does not resist its influence.

Idolatry

We have done some social analysis. We have tried to understand how the system works, how it arose and what it produces. But social analysis alone, valuable and vitally important as it is, cannot capture the totality of the experience of evil in South Africa today. To appreciate the full impact of the system, to bring the wrongness of the system to full consciousness, we shall have to make use of symbols – the traditional religious symbols of evil.

More and more today one hears the people in the townships speaking about the powers of evil that threaten them and the forces of darkness that have descended upon them. Again and again, and sometimes for long periods, the people have expected some respite, some concessions, some reasonableness from their oppressors, only to find any such expectations dashed to the ground by a new wave of repression. From about the middle of 1984 until the middle of 1986 there was considerable optimism. Surely this government will now fall and be replaced by something more reasonable. But what we all had to learn, in the words of Paul, is that 'our struggle is not against flesh and blood but against the rulers, against the authorities, against the powers of this dark world and against the spiritual forces of evil in the heavenly realms' (Eph 6: 12 NIV).

What we are up against are not human beings of flesh and blood, what we are up against is a monster. The system has a spirit of its own – an evil spirit. It is possessed by a demon. The agents and officials of the system cannot be reasonable and human because it is not they who are acting but the demon of the system that has blinded them, enslaved them and robbed them of their humanity. And if this demon must be given a name, then we must say that its name is Mammon.

Idolatry is not an outdated sin. It is not a sin that can only be committed by so-called 'primitive' and 'superstitious' people. It is the great sin of our country. We worship money – only we call it our standard of living. Jesus called it Mammon. It is an idol, a false god, a demon. The prophets of the Old Testament condemned the worship of the Baals, the fertility gods. But in the time of Jesus there was only one form of idolatry, only one false god, only one alternative to the worship of the true God – and that was Mammon. The choice was between God and Mammon. And one must choose. 'You cannot serve two masters.' There is no compromise (Mt 6: 24). 'Greed for money', says Paul, 'is the same thing as worshipping a false god' (Col 3: 5). In the first letter to Timothy we read: 'People who long to be rich are a prey to temptation; they get trapped into all sorts of foolishness and dangerous ambitions which eventually plunge them into ruin and destruction. The love of money is the root of all evil' (6: 9–10). That is even more true today.

The system in South Africa has a momentum of its own, a driving force that keeps it going. It is the incentive of money or profit. Money has become an object of devotion that bewitches people and casts a spell upon them. Money has become the measure of all value. Reality is then turned upside down so that things, products, commodities, and possessions have value, while people as people have no value. Money, a mere thing, is divinised, while people are treated as mere things or objects. We can do without people but we cannot do without money. Everything, in our system, depends upon money. It is our god and the pursuit of money is our religion (Hinkelammert 1986: *passim*).

According to Marx money has become a fetish. Webster's dictionary defines a fetish as 'a material object that is the abode of a supernatural spirit or power and that gains its potency from the indwelling of that spirit'. The spirit of money is the spirit of the system of apartheid. It is idolatry.

It would be impossible to exaggerate the evil of the system in South Africa. It has wrought havoc in the lives of people, caused a barbarous excess of violence and suffering, deprived people of their humanity, produced blindness, alienation and violent conflict. All that it can promise us is that the poor will become poorer and the blind blinder, that there will be more conflict, more bloodshed and total chaos – a veritable hell on earth. The system as a social force has gained a momentum or spirit of its own that drives it forward towards death and destruction. Our struggle is not against flesh and blood but against the evil spirit that is embodied in this system. It is 'the god of this world that blinds the minds' of its worshippers (II Cor 4: 4) and deceives them into believing that it is they who are fighting evil.

The final deception, the deception that makes the system truly diabolical, is its projection of its own evil onto others outside of itself. Projection is a well-known psychological phenomenon. A person who cannot face his or her faults projects them onto other people and then accuses them of the very things that he or she is doing. I remember giving a lecture on the evils of the South African system to a group of whites. After the lecture a woman got up and said that if what I spoke about was true then we were already a communist country. Communism for her was not a particular economic system, it was a word that meant oppression, suffering, people treated as objects, imprisonment and torture. She had just discovered that in our own country we do the very things we accuse communists of doing. She had just discovered that we have a beam in our own eye while we are looking at the speck in someone else's eye.

Listening to the almost hysterical campaign of propaganda against the ANC these days, one begins to wonder whether this too is not a projection of the evils of the system onto others.

Evil in its naked form cannot last long. It would soon be seen for what it is. To survive, evil must always be clothed or dressed up to look good. We say that when the devil comes to tempt us he has to come disguised as Christ. 'Many will come using my name,' Jesus says according to Mark. 'And they will deceive many' (Mk 13: 6). The evil in South Africa is dressed up to look like Christianity and makes use of the name of Christ. When the opposite of Christ comes disguised as Christ we call it the Antichrist. The system has become for us the Antichrist and many are deceived.

But those who suffer daily under the evils of the system are not deceived. When you are oppressed, when you are sinned against, when evil shows itself in all its nakedness and attacks you on every side, you will be able to see it for what it is. Those who have never experienced the cruelty and inhumanity of naked evil can still be deceived, but in the townships of South Africa we have seen it and felt it and we can no longer be deceived. It was 'the rulers of this world' who crucified the true Christ (I Cor 2: 8) and they continue to do so in our townships and prisons today.

Those who say that apartheid is a heresy or that apartheid is a sin are indulging in understatements. The Catholic bishops came closer to the mark some years ago when they declared apartheid to be 'intrinsically evil' (1957 Statement, see Prior 1982: 171). And in a more recent pastoral letter on hope they say: 'The government's policy has created hate and madness. It has done its Satanic work well' (Pastoral Letter, SACBC 1986). According to the Kairos Document, 'the god of the South African State . . . is the devil disguised as Almighty God – the Antichrist' (8). There can no longer be any doubt about it, the system in South Africa has become diabolical. That is a sign from God that we ignore at our own peril.

The system of purity or holiness that Jesus had to contend with was an enormous burden or yoke around the necks of the people. It weighed heavily upon them and caused much suffering, but can it really be compared with the merciless cruelty of our system? The upholders of the purity system were capable of handing over people like Jesus to the Romans for crucifixion, but would they have burnt the homes and all the belongings of thousands of people as in Crossroads or tortured people as in our prisons? I don't know, but I do wonder what kind of woes Jesus would have pronounced against the upholders of our system, the modern-day worshippers of Mammon.

The apartheid system is, without doubt, another of the great signs of our times in South Africa today. Through this sign God is saying something to us about the reality of evil, about the Antichrist, about the reign of Mammon and about what we all need to be saved from.

5
Sin and Guilt in South Africa

Human Responsibility

Social systems do not come into existence by themselves. They do not drop out of the sky. Nor are they simply a result of some kind of blind fate or social determinism. As we have seen, there were indeed certain material conditions and social forces that gave rise to the system of apartheid: colonial conquest, the colonisers' discovery of gold, the need for cheap labour and so forth. But they were not the only factors in the creation of this system. The process was not wholly determined and fated from the start. Even if it is difficult to see how it could have gone in any other direction, we cannot exclude the responsibility of human beings for the monster that has been created.

The system was created by numerous human beings in numerous ways. There were those who made the policy decisions along the way; there were those who supported and worked for the system; there were those whose greed, arrogance and hypocrisy made them fanatical architects of the system; and there were those who committed the great sins of omission by remaining silent and doing nothing to change the course of events. We can even point to those among the oppressed who did not join in the resistance but became passive accomplices in their own oppression. We can look back and see generations of sinners behind this system stretching back beyond South Africa and beyond colonialism into the distant past.

It is impossible for us today to assess the sinfulness and the guilt that created this intrinsically evil system. Some were obviously much more directly responsible for it than others. Some would have been more guilty because they knew very well what they were doing, while others would have been quite blind to the consequences of their actions or their apathy. Some may even have acted in what we call 'good faith'. Whatever the case may be, there is no way of denying that this monument to racism and greed was constructed by the sinfulness of human beings faced with certain material conditions and social forces.

It is equally clear that millions of people along the way were in no way responsible for the system that was so carefully constructed. They were the people who in one way or another resisted the onslaught of colonialism, racism and greed. They would include the indigenous people who fought the anti-colonial wars, the leaders, heroes, martyrs and countless other people who petitioned, protested, defied, mobilised, organised, struggled and died for justice and freedom down through the years. We shall have occasion to say more about them in Chapter 8.

But what about us today? Who is guilty and who is not? And how do people become guilty today?

Original Sin

With even a superficial awareness of what is happening to us in South Africa, we can experience ourselves as people who have inherited a system. Whether we benefit from it or suffer under it, the system is a given, something that was there before we were born; in fact the system is the social climate into which we are born. We cannot escape from it. We can fall for its temptations and go along with it or we can resist it unto death, but we can never simply avoid it. The system begins to affect us from the day we are born. As we grow up, it forms or at least tries to form our whole consciousness of reality. We are socialised into its false values of racism, individualism, selfishness, competition, possessiveness, and money as the measure of all value. From the beginning the system tries to cut us off from other human beings and to divide us against ourselves. We are socially conditioned into alienation. This is what the Christian tradition calls original sin.

Original sin is the sin we inherit. It is a given. It is something we are born into. In South Africa it is apartheid as a total system.

Perhaps more accurately, original sin is mediated to us in South Africa by the system of apartheid. And that is not a mere theoretical speculation, it is our experience. From a religious point of view, the system can be experienced as original sin.

People are taught to believe that the human weakness or alienation they experience is an inherent characteristic of human nature – 'our fallen nature'. One hears Christians saying, 'We are selfish by nature; there is nothing we can do about it; we are all sinners.' Nothing serves the interests of an evil system so effectively as this kind of false belief that what is evil is our human nature. This then becomes part of our general blindness, our false consciousness. It does not take much awareness and critical reflection for us to discover that our weakness and our alienation are products of the system of sin we inherit. Original sin is a reality, but it is a reality into which we have been socially conditioned.

How much we are affected from birth by the false, worldly values of the system will depend upon which sector of the society we are born into. In a working-class family or in a rural African family the perversities of individualism and competition are far less prominent. The natural instinct of co-operation and sharing is needed in order to survive. But even for such people the world of work in South Africa will soon begin to introduce its alienating demands for competition, possessiveness, money-value and cheap labour units. Unless they resist it, people begin to see one another as objects – black and white objects.

Those who grow up in a white family or any up-and-coming middle-class family are socialised from a very early age into selfishness, possessiveness and superiority. It is like the very air we breathe. It gets into our lungs, divides us against ourselves and perverts our very humanity. This is most obvious in the case of racial prejudice. Many white South Africans are now beginning to discover how they were socialised by the system into the unnatural attitude of racial prejudice. The same is true of the other inhuman and alienated attitudes that we find in ourselves. Our humanity is certainly twisted and distorted but this is not the result of a biologically inherited nature, it is the result of a socially inherited system. The cumulative effect of the sins of the past has been objectified or institutionalised in a sinful system that now influences all of us, albeit in different ways, from birth. That is our experience of original sin.

But it is not yet personal guilt. What we have described so far is simply our alienation, our weakness, our vulnerability. There is another experience before we come to guilt: the experience of being tempted by the system.

Temptation

The great temptation is 'to conform to this world' (Rm 12: 2), to fall for its seductions and lies. In our case this means the temptation to go along with the system of apartheid – actively or passively, part of the way if not the whole way. It is a matter of daily experience that the system tempts us with its offer of rewards, benefits and privileges for those who conform and with its threat of punishment in various forms for those who do not conform.

The offer of rewards and benefits is not in itself evil. What is evil is that the rewards and benefits are for some and not for others and are offered to some at the expense of others. That is the injustice that cries to heaven for vengeance. It is obvious that only those who qualify to benefit from the system will be tempted by it. Those who suffer under the system and are deprived of its rewards and benefits will not find it in any way attractive or tempting. And yet even they can be tempted to think that it would be more beneficial or at least less painful to go along with the system than to reject it and struggle against it. The system can punish you so severely for resisting it. You are tempted to do nothing.

We must look more closely at the experience of being tempted. What is so attractive about the system of internal colonialism, especially for whites, is that it offers wealth, possessions, luxuries and the imagined pleasures that money can buy, in short, a high standard of living. I remember once trying to stop a group of young whites armed with bicycle chains from beating up school children from Soweto who had come into a white suburb. When I asked the white youth why they were threatening to do this, they replied, 'To maintain our standard of living.'

Advertisements ensure that people believe in the value of these 'standards' and the system guarantees that these 'standards' will be maintained and improved for the privileged ones and even for some others if they agree to collaborate and conform. We need to begin to experience advertisements as real temptations. They tempt us to buy things we really do not need and to believe in the valuableness of things that have no real value in comparison with the value of people as people. Otherwise we will fall all the more easily for the propaganda of the system that tempts us with its unjust and oppressive ways of rewarding us with a high standard of living.

Those who are not white can also be tempted. The system tries to co-opt people by 'buying' them. An offer of thirty pieces of silver can tempt someone to become a Judas, an informer. To what extent have those who opted to participate in the tricameral parliament, homeland governments and community councils been tempted by the high standard of living that is offered them? There were no doubt other factors, other things that also made the offer tempting, for example, security, status and the illusion that one can do something to improve the system from within. Whatever form it takes, temptation must be recognised for what it is. This is especially difficult when you are unemployed and the system offers you a job in the police force, as a vigilante, in a homeland army or in the civil service. Some temptations are almost irresistible; nevertheless, we need to see them for what they are. The attempt to 'buy' people will be stepped up as the system tries to solve its problems by means of increasing co-option.

Another of the benefits offered to whites is a perverted sense of dignity or self-respect. When alienation has deprived you of your humanity and everyone has become a mere thing or object, you begin to experience a desperate need for some kind of dignity or self-respect, for something that will give you value and worth in your own eyes and in the eyes of others. The system then offers you the privilege of superiority on the basis of your 'whiteness'. You are better than people of other races, you are worth something, you are more 'civilised', you are superior, you are not like these 'kaffirs' and 'hotnots', you belong, you are acceptable. For people with a low self-esteem it is very easy to be tempted by this. Even for those who are not white it is tempting to accept 'honorary white status' in business or in the tricameral parliament or in homeland governments.

Some of the other benefits and rewards would include security for those who feel insecure, fearful and anxious; armed protection for those who feel vulnerable; unwavering certainty for those who are beginning to doubt and who cannot face the responsibility of making their own political decisions. The system lets you off the hook; you can sit back and do nothing.

The other side of the coin is the threats and punishments meted out by the system. Whites on the whole are terrified of stepping out of line lest there be that visit from the security police, and, who knows, maybe detention, maybe interrogation, maybe the loss of one's precious job? The threat to the oppressed is much greater. It becomes tempting, at the very least, to keep out of trouble, to sin by omission.

One of the remarkable things about South Africa is the fact that so many millions of people can no longer be tempted by anything the system has to offer or frightened by any of its threats, even the threat of torture and death. People reject the small benefits or concessions as mere 'sops', and any attempt to buy off a few individuals with huge benefits and privileges is rejected precisely because it is offered to some and not to all.

In the cycle of sin that we have been analysing, temptation is the weak link. Temptation can be resisted. It is at this point that the cycle of sin can be stopped and reversed. As we have seen, sin (in the circumstances of certain material conditions and social forces) causes the system to come into existence, but the system in its turn does not cause us to sin; it *tempts* us. The system conditions us in that direction, it influences our decisions, it applies pressure but it does not determine or force us into sin. We remain free to resist it – difficult as that may sometimes be. The cycle of sin is not a vicious circle of cause and effect. There is the weak link of temptation that places the responsibility for the continuation of the cycle of sin squarely upon our shoulders.

However, if we do succumb to temptation, if we do choose to 'conform to this world', if we are seduced into the sin of actively or passively supporting the system and worshipping Mammon, we become guilty of sinning against God.

Guilt

But can blind, ignorant and alienated people be guilty? Serious guilt requires full knowledge and full consent. To what extent do whites and their collaborators *know* what they are doing? To what extent is the suffering they cause unintentional?

Jesus had to face the Pharisees with their guilt in no uncertain terms. They were blind, but their blindness was no excuse because they were unwilling to have their eyes opened, they were unwilling to concede that they might possibly be wrong, they were insisting that they were not blind and that they could see perfectly well. That, precisely that, Jesus says, is their guilt: culpable ignorance (Jn 9: 40–41).

We have seen that the only way we can commit a sin is by deceiving ourselves, blinding ourselves to the truth about what we are doing. We have all had the experience of suppressing the voice of conscience or putting certain disturbing thoughts out of our heads in order to succumb to temptation. Nobody who is on the side of the system can claim that they do not experience even a twinge of conscience when they hear the accusations of the oppressed and of the whole international community. Those who *know* that they are suppressing doubts are guilty. Those who feel that they cannot allow such doubts to come to full consciousness lest those doubts turn their world upside down, are guilty. They harden their hearts as Pharaoh did. They look without seeing and listen without hearing (Is 6: 9–10; Mt 13: 14–15) because any alternative appears to be too disturbing to contemplate.

It is impossible to measure such guilt and quite unnecessary to do so. The degree of guilt involved makes no difference to the consequences of the sin, to the amount of suffering it may cause. Someone who is only vaguely aware of what he or she is doing or not doing and someone who knows full well what he or she is doing or not doing can support the same system with the same devastating results for other people. The seriousness or gravity of the sin is not dependent upon the degree of guilt involved.

We saw earlier that there is a distinction between full knowledge and consent on the one hand and grave matter on the other hand. Unfortunately most Christians tend to believe that the seriousness of a sin must be measured in terms of the degree of knowledge and consent involved, the degree of guilt, regardless of the gravity or seriousness of the matter. Thus trivial sins which cause very little harm to anyone at all are treated as serious sins when they are committed with full knowledge and full consent; while sins that cause an enormous amount of suffering are not taken seriously because the sinners were only vaguely aware of what they were doing and did not really intend to cause so much suffering.

But once we begin to understand how Jesus turned sin on its head, how he saw sin in terms of the suffering it caused to human beings rather than in terms of whether some law or other, no matter how trivial, was being transgressed, then we gain a new perspective on sin and guilt. Our primary concern becomes the suffering of people, and guilt is relevant only because those who are responsible for this suffering must be made fully aware of what they are doing. Must we then make people feel guilty? Must we try to increase feelings of guilt in people who do not feel much guilt? Did Jesus set out to make the scribes and the Pharisees feel more guilty?

There are those who think that if we felt more guilty about the system and if we could make others feel more guilty, we would all repent and change the system. But guilt is not like that. In itself and by itself guilt is not productive. In fact it tends to become a psychological complex that is destructive rather than constructive. It makes us hate ourselves, it makes us defensive, it drives us to fanatical forms of self-punishment to compensate for our feelings of unworthiness. Whites who get involved in the struggle for liberation out of a sense of guilt prove to be more of a hindrance than a help.

Jesus did not preach guilt, he preached forgiveness. Guilt must be acknowledged only in order to be forgiven and forgotten. Jesus brought the guilt of the scribes and the Pharisees and the other upholders of the system to the surface because once they acknowledged it, it could immediately be forgiven and forgotten. Past guilt must not be allowed to linger on, it must be transformed immediately into responsibility, with others, for the future. What is important then is that we become aware of what is actually happening, why it is happening, and our responsibility for it. In this way we can put guilt into perspective. For example, one is not guilty because one is white but because one supports the system and succumbs to its temptations. Thus, once one stops supporting the system, actively or passively, one's guilt ceases, it has been forgiven and forgotten.

Guilt must first be faced and acknowledged. One of the things that enable the system to continue is the suppression of guilt: making excuses for ourselves and putting the blame on others. It is easy to find scapegoats. We can blame the Afrikaner, the National Party or the white Dutch Reformed Church. Or we can simply blame all whites. But such 'scapegoating' does not help us to change the system. What is emerging so clearly in South Africa today is that our struggle is against a system that, while it was invented by whites and perfected by Afrikaner nationalists, is perpetuated by anyone who supports it, collaborates with it, becomes its puppet or refuses to join in the struggle against it. If this makes us feel guilty, then let us face it and deal with it.

For a Christian, dealing with guilt means believing that God forgives those who repent. We have already seen that in sinning against people we sin against God and that God is the one who is being crucified in the suffering of the oppressed people of our country. One of the advantages of this religious perspective is that if God represents those who are sinned against, then God can forgive us our guilt on behalf of those who are sinned against. However, God does this only when we acknowledge our guilt, repent of our sins and make some real changes in our lives.

The Cycle of Sin

Before we move on to the more complicated issue of misplaced guilt, I should like to crystallise and clarify the cycle of sin or dynamics of sin that we have been analysing in this and in the previous two chapters.

In the beginning of Chapter 4 we referred to our experience of the system as something that comes between the sinner and the sufferer. Thus the first line of development that we need to recognise is this: sinner → system → sufferer. In this chapter we have pinpointed the experience of how the system affects the sinner – original sin, alienation, temptation. There is therefore a line back from the system to the sinner. This can best be depicted as a circle or cycle of sin. Perhaps the diagram below will help.

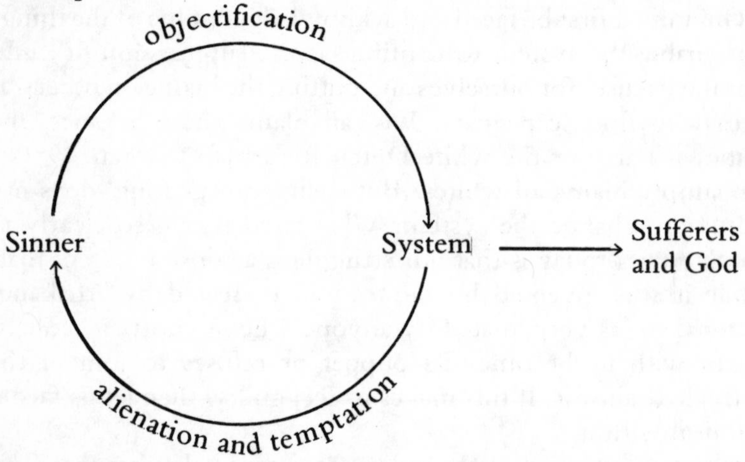

Here we can see that those who are sinned against are outside of the cycle of sin. God too, as the one who is offended by sin, is outside of the circle. We can also see that the relationship between the sinner and the system, the personal and the social, is dialectical or circular. There is an interaction between the two. And then finally, as we have already pointed out, the weak link is temptation. We can resist temptation, remove ourselves from the cycle of sin and join God who is on the side of the oppressed.

But is this not the cycle of racial and political sins, the sins of what is called 'social injustice'? What about all our other sins? What about the sins of those who are oppressed? Are there not some sins that escape this cycle?

Sins are not isolated, individual deeds. The sins of individual people in a society are interrelated and interwoven into a complex network of sinfulness. One sin influences another and each sin is socially bound up with every other sin in the same society. All sin, as we have said before, has a social dimension and the cycle of sin is perpetuated through the social system with its laws, customs, traditions, conflicts, contradictions, propaganda and temptations. There are no private sins because we are all affected by original sin and original sin is part of the cycle of sin we have been describing.

Thus many of the sins that may appear to be outside of this cycle are in fact side-effects of the cycle. We have seen how the alienation that is produced by the system leads to drink, drugs, sexual abuse, suicide and murder. Crime is clearly a result of the social circumstances in which people find themselves. The system, indirectly and unintentionally, tempts some people to become criminals. It is the supreme value given to money, and perhaps the fact of extreme poverty, that tempt people to steal from one another in more or less sophisticated ways. Sexual sins can surely be reduced to forms of selfish gratification that treat others as mere sex objects. That too is a result of our alienation – treating one another as objects. It is the whole social system that teaches us to do this.

But what about other forms of oppression? We have spoken about the oppression of colonised blacks and the oppression of workers and of the poor in general, but what about the oppression of women, of children, and the aged and the forms of oppression we find in homes, parishes, convents and schools? One could try to depict these as different cycles of sin with different people as the oppressed. But that would be deceptive. We do not live under several social systems. The system is one. It incorporates forms of oppression that can also be found elsewhere and in non-capitalist societies, for example, the oppression of women. All the forms of oppression and therefore all the forms of alienation and sin are interrelated. It is true that a person can be oppressed in one respect and an oppressor in any other respect – such as a black worker who oppresses his wife. But the system is one. In South Africa today when the youth of the townships make their demands they call for a democratic, unitary, non-racial and non-sexist society.

Are we all sinners then? In a sense we are, and that can be a sobering thought for many of us. But there are sins and sins! Some sins are simply trivial and others have immeasurable consequences. To put the sin of supporting a system that crushes, starves and kills vast numbers of people under the same general heading as the misdemeanour of telling a small lie is to distort reality. We saw this earlier in relation to suffering. It is the 'universalising tendency' again. We may all be sinners but we do not all commit the same outrageous crimes against humanity.

And this brings us finally to the sins that are not sins at all – what I call misplaced guilt.

Misplaced Guilt

The Christian conscience of a considerable number of our people in South Africa has been seriously deformed by the system, aided and abetted by many of the Churches. Thus guilt is deflected from our real sins onto activities that are in themselves trivial or innocent or even virtuous. We have seen how Jesus had to face the same problem with the scribes and the Pharisees. The system of purity or holiness made people feel guilty about the wrong things. Jesus had to turn sin on its head, to re-direct the misplaced guilt of so many of the people of his time – oppressor and oppressed.

It is not necessary for us to attempt an assessment of all the things that various people feel guilty about today. That would take us too far afield, especially if we were to try to enter into all the debates about the nature of sexual sins. But there are certain 'sins' that are used by the system as a form of control. One of the most effective ways of ensuring that people will censure themselves is to make them feel guilty about *any form* of disobedience, pride, doubt, criticism, suspicion or anger. Here, more than anywhere else, the Churches (sometimes unwittingly but with few exceptions) have collaborated with the system in South Africa.

We need to look briefly at each of these 'sins', at this network of misplaced guilt or false morality. In general its subterfuge is to take something that would be wrong in some circumstances and make it sinful in all circumstances. The effect is to make people thoroughly passive and submissive. We must deal briefly with disobedience and pride and then with doubt, criticism and suspicion, and finally with anger.

Disobedience is the so-called sin of not being submissive to every established authority and every law, no matter what it might demand of us. Once someone is in power, no matter how illegitimate that may be, once something is declared a law, no matter how unjust and evil it may be, we are made to feel guilty about disobeying. And people do feel guilty even when their disobedience is the only moral response in the circumstances. We have been conditioned to feel that we are holier, more spiritual and closer to God when we are submissive.

The Kairos Document has pointed out how 'State Theology' uses Paul's statement about obeying the government (Rm 13: 1ff) to make people feel guilty about any kind of disobedience (1986: 3–5) and how the concept of 'law and order' is used to make people who resist 'feel that they are lawless and disorderly . . . guilty of sin' (1986: 5). Anyone who does feel guilty on account of this has a misplaced sense of guilt. We are *not* sinning, because, in the final analysis, 'we must obey God rather than man [human beings]' (Acts 5: 29).

Pride is an ambiguous word. It could mean arrogance, like the arrogance of white superiority, or it could mean that sense of dignity and worth that we all ought to have as human beings created in the image and likeness of God. Too many Christians have been made to feel guilty about anything that expresses their human dignity and worth. Humility does not mean that we must treat ourselves as worthless objects, as doormats to be trampled on by everybody. To tell people whom the system treats as mere labour units, that they must humbly accept their lot otherwise they will be guilty of the sin of pride, is to add insult to injury and to outdo the system in wickedness.

A black youth once told me that he was unable to pray those words in the Mass: 'Lord, I am not worthy to receive you.' He said the system in South Africa told him every day that he was not worthy. He was not about to stand up and *admit* that he was not worthy. He still had some human pride left, he said. Of course the words of that prayer were written for people who are inclined towards arrogance, towards an overestimation of their own worth. In this prayer God does not want us to deny our human dignity and worth. What kind of a God would that be who treats us like objects in the same way as the system does?

On the whole black Christians in South Africa are now very well aware of this. Black Consciousness and Black Theology have successfully eliminated this form of misplaced guilt among black Christians. But there are still some Church circles where the poor and the oppressed are taught a false humility that plays into the hands of Satan.

When we are taught that it is unchristian to doubt, to be critical and suspicious, regardless of the circumstances, we are being made to feel guilty about criticising the system, about doubting the truth of its statements and suspecting its motives. We are taught that this is unfair and uncharitable and that we should give them, no matter who they are, the benefit of the doubt. As a generalised statement applicable in all circumstances, this is not true. It is unchristian and irresponsible. Doubt, criticism and suspicion can be destructive of good community relationships, but in circumstances of oppression and injustice they must be cultivated as virtues. As responsible human beings and as followers of Jesus Christ we must criticise the world, we must become suspicious of the false values of the system and of the people who peddle them, we must be ever doubtful, questioning and vigilant with regard to those who in their blindness are doing the work of Satan. Anything else would not only be naive, it would be allowing ourselves to be deceived. The system would welcome anything that makes people feel guilty about ever doubting, criticising or suspecting its motives. In the words of Harvey Cox: 'Why has our theological tradition concerned itself so obsessively with insubordination as the chief expression of sin? Part of the answer can be given in the single word, *politics*' (1969: 42).

Finally, there is the 'sin' of anger. That needs to be treated separately and more extensively.

Anger

Anger is not always a sin. There are times when it can be a virtue, a moral strength. In the Bible anger, and even wrath, are frequently attributed to God. Jesus was angry at times too. His anger was manifested not only by his act of driving the traders and money-changers out of the Temple courtyard with a whip (Jn 2: 13–22 parr), but also by his pronouncement of woes upon the rich and the hypocrites and by his reference to Herod as 'that fox' (Lk 13: 32). Jesus, like all the prophets, became really angry when he saw the injustice, the self-righteousness, the blindness and the callousness of those who made other people suffer. The anger of God is the anger of those who are sinned against, the anger of the oppressed and of all those who live in real solidarity with the oppressed. It is the experience of indignation at the sight of human cruelty. This anger is part and parcel of any genuine and strong love for people.

Anger can also be a sin, but that is the anger of selfishness. It is irrational and destructive. Alistair Campbell in his book, *The Gospel of Anger*, points out that 'anger can be used constructively or destructively'. 'The destructive use', as he says, 'is well-known.' The constructive value of anger, on the other hand, is that it 'provides a basis for communication' (1986: 64). What anger communicates very effectively is that the situation about which one is angry is very, very serious – in fact it is intolerable. Anger is the natural and human way of speaking the truth and there is simply no unemotional or intellectual substitute for it. This is said very clearly in Ephesians: 'Therefore, putting away falsehood, let everyone speak the *truth* with his or her neighbour, for we are members of one another. *Be angry* but do not sin; do not let the sun go down on your anger' (4: 25–26 RSV).

Anger can lead to sin but *only* when you let the sun go down on it, that is to say, when you nurse it, bottle it up, harbour it in the form of resentment or bitterness, or when you plan revenge. The sin is not the anger but the nursing of it. The New English Bible translates the sentence about not letting the sun go down on your anger as 'do not let sunset find you still nursing it' (Eph 4: 26 NEB). In the Sermon on the Mount when Jesus speaks of anger as the equivalent of murder, the NEB rightly translates the verse: 'Anyone who nurses anger against his brother [or sister]' (Mt 6: 22).

Anger about being sinned against must not be nursed. It must be expressed and communicated because there is no other way of saying what must be said. However, anger is more than just a way of communicating the truth. Anger is a very powerful driving force. Those who cannot get angry are weak and ineffective. Love without anger is not only pale and apathetic, it is not love at all. The forms of politeness and 'niceness' that are cultivated in some Christian circles no matter how serious and sinful the situation becomes, are a travesty of what is meant in the Bible by the word 'love'. In fact those who remain 'gentle' and 'nice' in all circumstances are timid and fearful cowards. A love that is vigorous, determined and effective is an angry love. Anger must not be nursed, it must be transformed into drive, energy, determination, creativity and courage. That is what is happening in South Africa today.

Those who cannot get angry about what is happening in South Africa have no real love for people. If the demand or challenge of the gospel is that 'you must be compassionate as your Father is compassionate' (Lk 6: 36), then we must also learn to share God's anger. Moreover, if we have no experience of anger about what is being done to people, we also have no experience of God.

Those who tell the oppressed that it is sinful to be angry are playing into the hands of Satan. The system has a vested interest in anything that makes people feel guilty about their anger at what is being done to them. The system is terrified by the prospect of black anger.

Those who are angry with the system but feel guilty about their anger, have a misplaced guilt. The Churches will have much to answer for in this regard. In her article on 'The Power of Anger in the Work of Love', Beverley Harrison sums up her concern about the lack of anger in church life with a sentence that says it all: 'We Christians have come very close to killing love precisely because anger has been understood as a deadly sin' (Supplement to *Union Seminary Quarterly Review* 1981: 50).

Most of the oppressed Christians of our country have seen

through the attempts to make them feel guilty about their anger, just as they have seen through the attempts to make them feel guilty about their human pride and dignity and about their doubts, criticisms, suspicions and disobedience towards the system. They are not going to allow themselves to become passive and submissive. The gospel that is emerging here is assertive, determined and powerful. Many white Christians feel personally threatened by this kind of Christianity, not only because of its anger and rebelliousness but also because of the possibility of violence. We shall tackle the question of violence in Chapter 8; what concerns us here is the fear and guilt about anything that is strongly emotional.

One of the frequent criticisms of the Kairos Document, mostly made by white Christians, is that it was too emotional. How could a Christian document express so much anger and indignation? One can only wonder what such critics make of the anger and indignation of the prophets and of Jesus himself. In fact what do they make of the Bible's frequent references to the wrath of God?

God is angry, God is absolutely furious, about what is being done to people in South Africa today. I say that without any hesitation. There is simply no other way of communicating or expressing the barbarous excess of suffering, the magnitude of the evil and the seriousness of our human responsibility for what is happening in our country. What we have seen so far in our search for where God is to be found in our situation today, is that God is the one who is being sinned against, God is the one who (in Christ) is being crucified by the system, God is the one to whom we are answerable for our share of the guilt. Now, all that remains at the end of these chapters on sin in South Africa, is that we take seriously the anger of God. God is present in our situation in a mood of anger and indignation. This is no mere religious speculation. The anger of God has become visible for all to see in the anger of the people.

6
Salvation in the Bible

The Christian answer to sin and evil is salvation. But what does salvation mean? Before we begin our search for the reality of salvation in our circumstances in South Africa today, we shall have to be clear about the meaning of salvation in the Bible. Here again we must remember that the characteristics of salvation we outline in this chapter are only the shape or skeleton of salvation. We shall try to put flesh on that skeleton in subsequent chapters.

God's Responsibility and Ours

Salvation is a religious word. Whatever the origins of the word may be, today when we talk about salvation we are understood to be talking about something religious, something to do with God. It is God who saves people. It is God who saves the world. And it is God who will save South Africa. It may not be immediately clear what that means in practice but it would make no sense to speak of a salvation that did not come from God. The Bible is quite clear about that. Salvation is God's responsibility, God's work.

On the other hand the Bible is equally clear about the fact that salvation is our responsibility as human beings. Human beings have to repent, to change and to take action otherwise there will be no salvation. In the story of Exodus there would have been no salvation or liberation from slavery for the Hebrews if they had not stood up and marched across the Sea of Reeds at low tide. For the prophets there was no hope of salvation for Israel unless the people repented and made some radical changes. For Jesus it was not enough to believe and to say, 'Lord, Lord'; one had to do the will of the Father (Mt 7: 21–27). And Paul says, 'You must work out your own salvation in fear and trembling' (Phil 2: 12 NEB). It is also a human project, the work of human hands. The Bible describes this as a covenant or contract between God and human beings.

There is no fatalism or determinism about salvation, any more than there is with regard to sin and evil. Salvation is not a form of magic. The religion of the Bible is precisely the rejection of all magical solutions to problems. God does not manipulate people like toys or robots. God is not the great tyrant or oppressor who treats people as mere objects. In fact God's salvation appears precisely at the moment when people start becoming subjects of their own history, when they begin to take responsibility for their own future.

This paradox or apparent contradiction between God's responsibility and human responsibility has taxed the minds of Christian theologians down the centuries. It has given rise to interminable debates about divine grace and human freedom, about predestination and free will, about God's action and human action. We have a real problem here. To say that salvation is both God's responsibility and ours does not mean that salvation comes partly from God and partly from us. It is not a matter of co-operation or a 'joint effort' between God and human beings. As Thomas Aquinas says, salvation comes totally from God and totally from human beings. Not that we are being asked to believe in some kind of mysterious contradiction. Clearly words like 'responsibility' and 'work' are being used here in two quite different senses. God's responsibility and work are simply not the same as human responsibility and human work. What then do we mean by God's responsibility or God's work or the wonderful works of God? What do we mean when we speak of God at all?

We shall have to return to these questions in Chapter 9. What needs to be stated emphatically at this stage, however, is that any idea that we as human beings can sit back and wait for God to save us, or just pray and then hope that God will intervene, is simply heretical. It has nothing whatsoever to do with the salvation we read about in the Bible.

Salvation from Sin

Salvation in the Bible is salvation from sin *in all its dimensions*. The danger always is that we might be tempted to relate salvation to only one dimension of sin or to only one element in the whole cycle of sin. We need to have our guilt removed but we also need to overcome the consequences of original sin: weakness and alienation. We need to be saved from our own sins but we also need to be saved from the sins of those who oppress us. The Hebrew slaves had to be saved from the sins of Pharaoh and it was within that process, in the desert, that they came to terms with their own sins, their own alienation, their own worship of the golden calf. The plea in the Psalms is for salvation from one's enemies despite one's own guilt. Salvation in the Bible is the victory over the powers of evil that oppress us, alienate us and tempt us – over the whole cycle of sin and evil. The bottom line is that we need to be saved from suffering and from everything that causes people to suffer.

In practice the content that is given to the word 'salvation' by different people depends upon their circumstances and their perceptions. It depends upon what they experience as their need for salvation and what they perceive to be wrong or sinful in their situation. Thus some will feel only the need for forgiveness to deal with their feelings of guilt, others will feel the need for justice to put right what is wrong in society, others will think that all we need is reconciliation to overcome the conflict, and still others will want liberation from oppression. Each of these projects will then become the content of the word 'salvation'. Clearly everything depends upon one's perception of what is really needed. Without a correct and comprehensive understanding of the dynamics of sin and evil in our situation, salvation will be given a limited or false content.

Salvation includes the forgiveness of sin (liberation from guilt) but it cannot be reduced to that alone (Schillebeeckx 1980: 832–3). The most serious heresy of European Christianity, especially in the last few centuries, has been the reduction of the gospel to little more than the salvation of souls. I make bold to call it a heresy. Technically I suppose I would have to say that it was a material heresy rather than a formal heresy because it was not deliberate. European Christians, as far as one knows, did not choose to go into heresy, they simply drifted into it. Perhaps some of them could be accused of culpable ignorance. I don't know and at this stage it doesn't really matter.

What seems to have happened is that the only need for salvation that was experienced by European Christians who benefited from capitalism and colonialism was the need to have their feelings of guilt removed. They felt no need, and could not imagine how anyone could feel any need, to be saved from oppression, from an excess of suffering, from the powers of evil, from the system. All such matters were conveniently excluded from the arena of religion and salvation by the device of calling them material and worldly problems. The gospel is only concerned with 'spiritual' matters like the struggle with guilt and forgiveness that take place deep in the individual soul. All that God is concerned about is guilt and punishment for guilt. God is too pure and 'spiritual' to get involved in such mundane matters as money, colonialism or 'the dirty business of politics'. Religion is a private matter between God and the individual soul because guilt is a private affair. The individual Christian who is 'saved' from guilt by Jesus will be rewarded after death in that other world where there are no material problems like suffering and poverty.

This kind of 'Christianity' is not Biblical. It takes one aspect of salvation, the need to be saved from individual guilt, and then re-interprets the whole Bible in terms of that need so that everything else in the Bible, everything that is concrete, material, political and down to earth, is 'spiritualised'. Thus, for example, the story of Exodus and the journey to the promised land becomes the story of the individual soul on its journey to heaven. The poor and the oppressed become 'those who know their need for God', which means those who know that they are guilty and need to be forgiven by God.

In the end even the one aspect of salvation that these people have tried to preserve becomes distorted. Guilt is taken out of its context in the whole cycle of sin and therefore misplaced so that it becomes neurotic (a guilt complex). Moreover, forgiveness divorced from the totality of salvation does nothing more than ameliorate some of the symptoms of guilt to make one feel a little better about it. In fact the whole thing becomes self-contradictory. On the one hand one professes to believe in *selfless* love and on the other hand one is caught up in the extremely *selfish* pursuit of one's own salvation, one's private rewards in heaven. This kind of religion does not even begin to tackle the problem of sin. By leaving the system intact it does not even solve the problem of guilt. The cycle of sin continues unabated. It was the 'spiritualisation' and privatisation of religion that enabled the system of exploitation and colonialism to be justified, enabled it to expand through the world and to cause the most barbaric excess of suffering in the history of humankind. This kind of religion is, without doubt, the opium of the people.

It is no coincidence that this form of religion is being revived today and vigorously promoted all over the world with the help of massive television programmes and worldwide campaigns. Nor should it come as a surprise to find that it is being strongly promoted in South Africa to prop up a crumbling system. What may surprise us is the discovery that the privatisation of religion is a recent phenomenon in South Africa and that it is linked to the recent process of secularisation amongst whites. Traditionally the Afrikaner had no problems with a social and political understanding of Christian faith. The Great Trek was the new Exodus. The *'volk'* was the people of God, the new Israel. We can disagree with that, but we cannot call it a 'privatised' or 'spiritualised' form of religion. In the process of secularisation, as God was excluded increasingly from public life, from politics, economics and social formations, religion was understood more and more to be solely a matter for the individual soul (Villa-Vicencio 1985: 112ff).

This may fool those who benefit from the system because the only need for salvation they now feel is the need to be absolved from guilt. But it does not fool those who suffer under the oppression. That is why 132 Evangelical Christians (mostly ministers) from the townships could take a prophetic stand against this kind of right-wing evangelicalism in their document, Evangelical Witness in South Africa (1986).

Let me not be misunderstood, though. Guilt is a part of the dynamics of sin, and liberation from guilt or the forgiveness of sin is an important aspect of salvation in the Bible. Those political activists who ignore the problem of white guilt and any other guilt in our situation in South Africa are overlooking an important factor in the struggle for liberation and salvation. The gospel or good news of salvation can help to redress this imbalance provided it brings us a message of total and effective salvation from suffering and from all that causes people to suffer.

Salvation and Power

The language of salvation in the Bible is the language of power. The extensive studies of Walter Wink have made us aware of how 'the language of power pervades the whole New Testament' (1984: 7ff, 99). The same can be said about the Old Testament. The question of sin and salvation is fundamentally a question of power.

God is power – almighty power! This does not only mean that God's power is greater than the powers of evil in the world, it also means that all power has its source and origin in God. That is why Jesus could say to Pilate: 'You would have no power over me if it had not been given to you from above' (Jn 19: 11). That is why in the controversial Chapter 13 of Romans Paul can say that 'all government [literally "power"] comes from God' (13: 1). But what we see in the powers of evil, in the awesome power wielded by oppressive systems in the world today, their military, political and technological power, their power over the minds, hearts and bodies of people, is a colossal *abuse* of power. The power in such systems comes from God. The abuse comes from sin.

Salvation is a question of power and the use of power. The process of salvation is an almighty struggle for power and its aim is victory over all the powers of evil.

It is amazing how frightened most Christians become when you begin to talk about real power, about a conflict of power or about the struggle for power. The writer Charles Elliot believes that 'the traditional Christian coyness about power' has become 'pathological' (1987: 83). Nothing has so emasculated the gospel, nothing has rendered its message of salvation so weak and powerless, as our inability to face the issue of power. Lord Acton's much quoted statement that 'all power corrupts and absolute power corrupts absolutely' is simply not true. If it were, God would be the epitome of absolute corruption. It is the abuse of power that corrupts. That may be what Lord Acton meant but it is not what he said and it is not what Christians mean when they use his statement to avoid the issue of power.

The distinction between the right and wrong use of power or authority is made by Jesus when he says: 'You know that among the pagans their rulers lord it over them and make their authority felt. This is not to happen among you. No; anyone who wants to be great among you must be your servant and anyone who wants to be first among you must be your slave, just as the Son of Man came not to be served but to serve . . . ' (Mt 20: 26–28).

Service is the key. Power should be used to serve people, to protect them, save them and give them freedom. When power is misused to dominate, control and oppress people, it corrupts. Power is abused when it is exercised for the benefit of some at the expense of others. Power is a service when it is exercised for the benefit of everyone. The power that serves is a power that is shared by all. The power that dominates cannot be shared. Boesak calls this the difference between 'power over others' and 'power with others' (1977: 47). In South Africa today we call it people's power: power that is shared by all, for the benefit of all and as a service to all. The Bible calls it God's power.

From the point of view of the worldly abuse of power, God's power of service and freedom appears to be weakness (I Cor 1: 18–28). From the point of view of God's power, the oppressive abuse of power can be seen to be in fact weakness because it is contradictory, false, blind, sinful and doomed to failure. At present the powers of evil might still have the upper hand but victory is certain. Salvation means victory (Schillebeeckx 1980: 508ff).

In the Old Testament this is clear enough. It was the power of God that triumphed over Pharaoh's riders and chariots to save the Hebrew slaves. It was the power of God that triumphed over the Canaanite kings and the Philistines. It was the power of God that enabled David to triumph over Goliath. All the stories are the same. What appears to be weakness turns out to be strength usually because the enemy is outwitted by a more subtle power.

In the New Testament Jesus emerges as a man of tremendous power and authority (Mk 1: 22, 27; Mt 28: 18; Nolan 1976: 121–124). His life is portrayed as a great drama of conflict with demonic powers (Mk 1: 23–34; 5: 1–20), with Satan, the prince of this world (Mt 4: 1–11; Jn 12: 31) and, as we have seen, with the system. When the power of Jesus and the power that he was able to generate in the poor became a real threat to the abusers of power, they hit back, crushing him to the ground and displaying his broken body on their instrument of repression. The crucifixion of Jesus appeared to be a victory for the powers of evil. But they were wrong. The powers of evil had been outwitted and Jesus' death on the cross turned out to be *his* victory over *them* (Jn 12: 31–32). As Paul describes it: 'He disarmed the principalities and powers and made a public example of them, triumphing over them on the cross' (Col 2: 15 RSV; see Wink 1984: 55ff).

The abusers of power thought that by killing Jesus and by displaying his body on a cross as a warning to others, they would destroy the power that was in him. They used all the might of *their* power against him but what they did not realise was that you can kill the body but you cannot kill the spirit (Mt 10: 28), especially when that spirit is the power of God, the Holy Spirit. All they succeeded in doing was to 'draw all men [people] to him' (Jn 12: 32) and to enable his power to be transferred to the people. That is the meaning of the outpouring of his Spirit at Pentecost (Acts 2: 1–13).

There are two things that we must be very clear about if we are to appreciate the paradox of the cross. Firstly, the death of Jesus was, in one sense, a *failure*. 'In a straight historical sense Jesus failed in his life's project' (Schillebeeckx 1979: 640). He set out to destroy the power of the system of purity and holiness and to replace it with the power or rule of God. The time was ripe. The opportunity was there. The rule of God was near. All that was missing was repentance. 'The time has come and the kingdom of God is close at hand. Repent, and believe the good news' (Mk 1: 15). What Jesus needed was the co-operation of the people, especially those who were oppressed by the system. They had to be converted and filled with the power of God. And that is precisely what did not happen, at least, not on a large scale. In that way the project was a failure and Jesus' death was a victory for the system.

Secondly, what we need to appreciate is that the cross was a success, a victory for Jesus, *because* it led to the outpouring of the power of the Spirit and the creation of a new people of God, the Church (Schillebeeckx 1979: 646). It turned out to be a tremendous act of creative power because, as in the story of Exodus, God created a new people, a new Israel. It was after his death and because of his death that Jesus began to succeed where he had previously failed: in the spreading of God's power amongst the people (Lk 24: 49). The powers of evil tried to destroy him but he rose up again – not as some kind of ghost to haunt them, but in a new body, a risen body, which is the people of God. Paul leaves us in no doubt about that: 'Now you together are Christ's body' (I Cor 12: 27). 'The Church is Christ's body' (Eph 1: 23; 5: 29–30; Col 1: 24), the embodiment of his power and his Spirit (I Cor 15: 43, 44; compare also Rm 12: 4; I Cor 12: 12–30; Phil 1: 20).

The death and resurrection of Jesus Christ was a powerful saving work because it gave the almighty power of God, the power of the Spirit, to the people. It was a victory over the powers of evil because it outwitted them and 'disarmed' them. But the final victory was yet to come: when Christ will 'put all his enemies under his feet' (I Cor 15: 24–28), when 'they will be defeated by his followers, the called, the chosen, the faithful' (Rev 17: 14).

Whatever happened to this victory? Whatever happened to the tremendous power of God that was given to the people? We may well ask. I suppose you could say that somewhere along the way the almighty power of God was 'spiritualised' and domesticated. There have been some notable exceptions in the long history of the Church, but all too often the power of God became mere ecclesiastical authority! In recent times there has been a renewed interest in the power of the Spirit. But all too often this has become a private possession of those who have been 'baptised in the Spirit'. I do not wish to decry the very real power of the Spirit that does exist in the Church today, but it seems to become rather shy and timid when it enters into the public arena. Many Christians today opt out of the power struggles that are going on in the world by saying that they must identify with the powerlessness of God who is suffering with the poor and the weak. But that is only one side of the cross and although it is important, as we saw in the chapter on our crucified people, there is another side to the cross: its power and its victory. Wallowing in our weakness is of absolutely no value to anyone. While some people continue to do this in the Church, the struggle between the powers of evil and the almighty power of God continues to be waged outside of the Church.

Personal and Social Power

The fundamental problem seems to be, once again, an emphasis upon the personal dimension of God's saving power and a neglect of its social dimension. In South Africa we first became aware of this, at least as far as power and salvation were concerned, through the writings and sermons of the black theologians. They had to face the issue of black power. Was it or was it not the power of Christ? (See, for example, Boesak 1977: 46–71.) Today what we have to face is the reality of people's power.

The personal dimension of God's saving power is clear enough. It is the inner strength that replaces our human weakness. It is the power of courage, commitment, love and an unshakeable hope that overcomes our alienation and makes us powerful subjects of our own history. But this does not happen without new structures, structures of power. God's saving power, somewhat like sin, is objectified or embodied in new structures: Church communities, but also political organisations. Structures of true power are structures that embody the right use of power: the power of service, the power of sharing, the power of solidarity and love, the power of faith and commitment, the power of hope. In the name of justice and freedom it is these embodiments of God's saving power that will confront the systems of sin and evil. Victory is certain.

Parallel to the cycle of sin and evil, then, is the cycle of saving and creative power. It is a cycle because while the power of the Spirit that is in us is objectified in structures of true power, these structures in turn have an influence upon us. They strengthen and support us, they encourage us and make us whole. The social embodiments of sin, as we have seen, have the opposite effect. They produce alienation, weakness and the temptation to sin. Both cycles are very real and very concrete. However, until we come down to earth and give this idea of God's power in the world some real content in terms of our experience in South Africa today, it remains little more than an interesting idea.

The Promise of Salvation

The one indisputable result of all theological research during this century and of the massive scholarship that has been brought to bear upon the Bible (by scholars of all persuasions including atheists) and the result also of so much Christian reflection upon the Bible especially in recent times, is simply this: *the Bible is a book about hope.* Hope is not only the central theme of the stories that have been handed down to us as the Word of God; hope is also what gives the Bible its abiding fascination, its power to inspire and motivate, its undying relevance. Hope was introduced into the world by the Bible or, more correctly, God was revealed to the people of the Bible as the God of hope. God is the author of the Bible because God is the author of hope.

The basis or grounds for hope that is offered to us in the Bible are the *promises* of an all-powerful God. The Bible is not a book about a salvation that has been achieved and finalised in the past; the Bible is about the promise of salvation in the future. There are stories about powerful saving events, about victories over the powers of evil, but they are not final, at least for us they are not final. We still stand in need of salvation, and the victories of the past are for us signs, symbols or promises of a salvation that is yet to come. Even Jesus' victory on the cross was not final as a victory. It was the definitive revelation, the definite promise of a final victory over the powers of evil. The Bible is the story of the promise. The Word of God is fundamentally always a word of promise. There have been fulfilments of the promise along the way but these fulfilments then function, at least for us, as promises for the future.

In the words of Paul to the Romans: 'Everything that was written long ago in the Scriptures was meant to teach us something about hope from examples Scripture gives of how people who did not give up were helped by God (15: 4; compare Heb 11: 1–40).

In each age what we hope for is salvation from sin. What this means in practice in any particular age will depend upon the form that sin takes in that time and place. The object of our hope, then, is that the sins of our time, the sins that beset us, oppress us and tempt us *today,* will be overcome. That is what God guarantees and promises.

The crucial question, however, is when? When will God's promises be fulfilled for us? When will salvation come for us? Must we wait until the next life? Must we wait until the last day?

The Day of Salvation

In the Bible the day of salvation is referred to in a variety of ways: the day of Yahweh, the day of the Lord, the day of judgment, the day, that day, the days to come, the latter days, the coming of the reign of God. However it may be designated, the consistent message about this day throughout the Bible is that *it is near.* What the prophets stood up to proclaim was not simply that there would be a day of reckoning but that it was near (e.g. Is 13: 6, 9; Jer 46: 10; Ez 7: 7, 12; 30: 3; Joel 1: 15; 4: 14; Zeph 1: 7, 14; Zech 14: 1). What Jesus stood up to proclaim was not that one day some time the reign of God would come (everybody knew that) but that 'the time has come and the reign of God is now near' (Mk 1: 15; Mt 4: 17; Lk 10: 9, 11; Rm 13: 11–12). That was the good news (Mt 4: 23; 9: 35; Lk 5: 43; 8: 1).

What is being referred to throughout the Bible is the same

kind of time, the same *kind of day*: a day of victory for God that is close at hand. What is clearly not being referred to is the same calendar day. A word is necessary here about the meaning of time in the Bible.

There is a fundamental and crucial difference between the concept of time that is typically Western and the concept of time that is typical of the Bible – and indeed of other non-Western peoples. Time in our Western way of thinking is a measurement. It is thought of in terms of numbered dates and hours that can be recorded and measured with clocks and calendars. The image of time here is the image of one long continuous line that can be measured with numbers or dates: these are like empty spaces which can then be filled with events of greater or lesser importance. This typically Western way of thinking about time is called chronological or quantitative time. It is very useful and practical especially for modern efficiency but it is not what the Bible means by time.

'Today one of the few things of which we can be quite sure', says Gerhard von Rad, 'is that this concept of absolute time, independent of events, and, like blanks on a questionnaire, only needing to be filled up with data . . . was unknown to Israel' (1968: 77). For Israel, for Hebrew thinking, to know the time was not to know the date but to know what kind of time it was. There is 'a time for giving birth and a time for dying; a time for planting and a time for sowing; a time for destroying and a time for building; a time for tears and a time for laughter . . . a time for war and a time for peace' (Eccl 3: 1–8). Everything has its time and what matters is to discern what *kind of time* it is – by reading the signs of the times. Is it a time for waiting or for acting? Is it a time for going to war or for making peace? In the liberation struggle in South Africa we know about the need to discern what kind of time it is. Is it a time for speaking out or keeping silent? Is it a time for protest and mass mobilisation or a time for consolidation and organisation?

I am not suggesting that in Western thinking there is no concept of the *kind of time* we might be living in. We do refer to good times and bad times and hard times and war-time and so forth. Nor am I suggesting that the Bible knows nothing about chronological time. There are constant references to something that happened 'in the eighteenth year of King Jeroboam' or whatever. But in the Bible the emphasis is upon the kind of time, and we should be careful not to interpret this as a date on the calendar.

The day of salvation, then, is a particular kind of time. It might entail a victory for Israel in a particular battle or the downfall of one of the great empires that oppressed them (Von Rad 1968: 95–99) or the day the rulers of Israel are punished with exile or the day the lion lies down with the lamb (Is 11: 6–9; 65: 25) and swords are melted into ploughshares (Is 2: 2–5; Mic 4: 1–5), when there will be no more evil to fear (Zeph 3: 15) and all tears will be wiped away (Is 25: 8), when the 'leaders' in the 'tyrannical city', the 'proud boasters' have been 'removed from your midst' (Zeph 3: 1–5, 11–18), when peace and justice reign supreme (Is 32: 16–17) because the law has been written in the hearts of the people (Jer 31: 33) and the Spirit of God is in them (Ez 36: 26).

Jesus also spoke about a time of salvation that was near. He described it as the coming kingdom or reign of God. Here again Jesus was in fundamental disagreement with most of his contemporaries, especially the scribes and the Pharisees. Just as he reversed the current meaning of the concept of sin and returned to something more akin to what the prophets had been saying, so also he changed the meaning of salvation that was current in those days and returned to something more akin to what Moses and the prophets had been saying. Just as many of his fellow Jews at that time thought of sin as a transgression of the law (the system of purity and holiness), so also many of them thought of the day of salvation as the last day.

The idea that one day this world will come to an end in a great cosmic upheaval and that salvation will come in the next world, belongs to a set of ideas that we call *apocalyptic*. I do not wish to deny that there will be a last day of some kind or that there is any after-life. That would be foolish and presumptuous. But if we are going to avoid any misunderstanding about the basic meaning of salvation in the Bible, we must put apocalyptic beliefs into proper perspective (Koch 1972: 11f; 130f). They are not central to the Biblical meaning of salvation.

The Apocalyptic Last Day

Apocalypse means revelation. But we use the word 'apocalypse' or 'apocalyptic' to refer to those special revelations that were introduced into Judaism in the second century before Christ under the influence of the Persian (Iranian) philosophy of Zoroastrianism (Russell 1964: 18ff; Belo 1981: 72ff). It seems that for nearly three hundred years some of the scribes or sages indulged in elaborate speculations about the end of the world and produced a whole library of books on the subject (Charles 1963: 167ff). These books, with the exception of the Book of Daniel, were never included in the Old Testament. In the time of Jesus and the early Christians, apocalyptic ideas were still current and they had a decided influence upon the understanding of salvation that developed after Jesus. Strangely enough, after the destruction of the Temple in A.D. 70, the Jewish scribes or rabbis abandoned this way of thinking about salvation, while Christians perpetuated it in an adapted form. This is most obvious in the last book of the New Testament, which is actually called the Apocalypse. But the influence of apocalyptic ideas can also be seen in other parts of the New Testament (Charles 1963: 362ff).

What are these apocalyptic ideas? What were the historical circumstances that gave rise to them? What was Jesus' attitude to apocalyptic thinking and what influence do they have even today upon the Christian understanding of salvation?

The following would be some of the most important ideas introduced for the first time by the apocalyptic writers:

The history of the human race develops according to a fixed and predetermined divine plan. It is part of God's plan that the powers of evil will cause more and more suffering and oppression until eventually on the last day of history God will destroy this world and establish the kingdom of God. All that human beings can do is prepare themselves as individuals for the last judgment by keeping the law. On the last day there will be great signs from heaven and the Messiah or Son of Man will come down from heaven, while the dead will rise from their graves. Those who are saved will enter heaven (paradise) while those who are condemned will be cast into the fires of hell (Gehenna).

The apocalyptic writers believed that the last day was near and that with enough wisdom and learning one could calculate when it would come. They were fascinated by calculations based upon the stars and upon symbolic numbers in the scriptures. (For more details about apocalyptic ideas see Russell 1964: 205ff or Koch 1972: 28ff; Charles 1963: 167ff.)

The claim of the apocalyptic writers was that this divine plan had been revealed to them (or to others before them) in dreams and visions. Hence the rather weird and exotic imagery that is associated with the apocalyptic: dragons, beasts, heavenly beings in conflict, stars that fall from the sky, symbolic numbers and so forth.

This is a far cry from the simple and direct messages of the prophets (Von Rad 1968: 271ff; Koch 1972: 36ff). The prophets interpreted the signs of the times; the apocalyptists interpreted dreams, visions, numbers and the signs of the stars. The prophets foresaw the future consequences of present trends. Their prophecies were therefore *conditional*. They warned about what would happen if people did not change and promised a day of salvation if people did change, because 'God relents when humans repent' (Jer 26: 13, 16–23; Amos 7: 3, 6; Jonah 3: 10; 4: 2; Ex 32: 14). In other words what humans do or do not do today makes a difference to what will happen in the future. Human beings can be the subjects of history, the agents who make history. For the apocalyptic writers this was impossible. Everything was determined beforehand by the divine plan. Human beings remained free to keep the law or not, but the course of history was decided by God alone. This was an unbiblical return to a form of determinism.

The prophets spoke about a day of judgment or a day of salvation that would take place in this world. The apocalyptists spoke about a day of judgment and salvation that would take place in a world beyond time and history. For the prophets there was indeed a qualitative difference between the present time of suffering and a future day of salvation, but this was not the same as the other-worldly supernaturalism of the apocalyptic visionaries (Von Rad 1968: 91ff).

The prophets had a message for a particular people at a particular time in a particular place. The apocalyptic writers produced a comprehensive history of all times and epochs with a message that was presented as universally and eternally valid. Apocalyptic universalises the promises of God and the day of salvation (Russell 1964: 94; Sobrino 1987: 85). In so doing apocalyptic in fact divorces salvation from any particular time and place and people, and from the signs of any particular times. The irony of this is that the universal hopes of apocalyptic were a response to particular historical problems and experiences in Israel during the second century before Christ. Apocalyptic ideas could only have been introduced into Judaism because they gave some kind of meaning to what people were experiencing at that time. Moreover, they could only be perpetuated or revived in similar historical circumstances. What were these historical circumstances?

Israel's Darkest Hour

In the second century before Christ there was a strong feeling of hopelessness and helplessness in the Jewish community, especially amongst the learned or educated people. With the Hellenistic King Antiochus IV, the oppression and persecution of the Jews became more acute and more destructive than ever before. Antiochus was determined to wipe out the Jewish religion once and for all. Jews were not allowed to keep the Sabbath, to circumcise their children, or to abstain from eating pork. They were ordered to burn every copy of the Hebrew Bible and to worship the pagan god Zeus, and indeed to worship Antiochus himself as a god. Worse still, the Temple itself had been desecrated by the 'abomination of desolation', an altar to Zeus (I Macc 1: 41–64).

Anyone who disobeyed these orders or resisted was killed by Antiochus' patrolling soldiers. The upper classes of Jews had already adopted Hellenistic culture and religion, the high priests were totally corrupt collaborators and now many more Jews were opting for obedience to the pagan oppressor rather than death. The magnificent hopes of restoring the nation after the exile had been dashed to the ground. It was Israel's darkest hour and there was no prophet in the land (I Macc 4: 46; 9: 27; 14: 41) to interpret these evil times and to find some signs of hope for the future.

The response of the Maccabees was to flee into the hills, form a guerilla army and fight back. Thus began the protracted Maccabean revolution. But the 'learned' seemed to have believed that this would be of 'little help' (Dan 11: 33–34; Von Rad 1968: 281). After so many years of oppression and persecution, and with everything getting worse and worse by the day, the educated people developed a deep pessimism about the world, about politics and about any human effort to change the course of history. There are many educated people in South Africa today who could identify very easily with this feeling of pessimism.

It was in these historical circumstances that the apocalyptic writers came to the conclusion, in dreams and visions, that the only way to continue to believe in God's justice and God's promises was to believe that despite appearances, God was in control, God had a plan and that everything was happening according to that plan. People could make some sense of their sufferings and their powerlessness by believing that one day God would intervene *from outside of this world and regardless of what human beings might or might not do*. This gave people some measure of security, but it also made them passive observers or spectators. God was going to do everything for them.

How did Jesus respond to such ideas?

Jesus and Apocalyptic

Jesus was not an apocalyptic dreamer. He was a prophet with a prophetic message for the people of his time. It was immediately obvious to the people that he did not speak like the learned scribes of his time (Mk 1: 22 par; Jn 7: 15) but like the prophets of old, like 'Elijah or Jeremiah or one of the other prophets' (Mt 16: 13). He spoke about things that God had '*not revealed to the learned and the wise* but to mere children' (Lk 10: 21 par). Jesus related simple stories or parables about everyday life; he did not give visionary accounts of a heavenly world like the apocalypses of the learned and the wise. He refused to speak about signs from heaven and drew attention to the signs on earth, the signs of the times (Mk 8: 11–13; Mt 16: 1–4; Lk 11: 16; 12: 54–56). In fact he calls those who ask for signs from heaven 'an evil and unfaithful generation' (Mt 16: 4; Lk 11: 29). And when it comes to calculations about the day or the hour when God's reign might begin, he emphatically denies that anyone could make any such calculations (Mk 13: 32 par; Acts 1: 7; for the scholarly discussion of this question see Koch 1972: 57ff).

However, Jesus was a son of his time. He thought and spoke in the religious categories and the religious language of his time. What he had to say was astonishingly new, but for the most part this had to be communicated in the religious language that people were accustomed to. Jesus seems to have been acutely aware of the fact that this was like putting new wine into old wineskins (Mt 9: 17 parr). Sometimes he found it necessary to discard the old wineskins altogether, like the religious practices of fasting (Mt 9: 14 parr) and ritual washings (Mt 15: 2 par) and religious words like 'clean' and 'unclean'. He also developed new religious practices like breaking bread together, and new religious words like Abba, Father. But for the most part he had to give new content to the religious symbols of his time. And at least some of the religious categories that were current at that time were derived from apocalyptic writings.

We all know, and I have already drawn attention to the fact, that religious words can change their meaning from one historical context to another; but we are indebted to John Riches for a detailed analysis of how this happens and how Jesus reworked the religious language of his time (1980: *passim*). John Riches distinguishes between the core-meaning of a word and its numerous associations (1980: 22ff). Thus, while a word keeps its core-meaning, 'it may receive new associations and be stripped of old ones' (1980: 23). That is precisely what Jesus did.

Everyone knows, for example, that Jesus thoroughly reworked the meaning of the word 'Messiah'. He stripped it of associations that were royal, military and nationalistic, and associated it with service, humility and the poor. He did much the same with the concept of God (Riches 1980: 145ff). We have seen how radically he altered the contents of religious words like 'sin' and 'the law'. It seems to me that he did the same with apocalyptic categories like 'the last judgment', 'resurrection', 'heaven', 'hell', 'the age to come', 'the coming of the Son of Man' and 'the kingdom of God'. However it is extremely difficult, if not impossible, for us today to determine how Jesus reworked these religious categories. In most cases we simply do not have enough evidence to work on, and in any case the gospels are overlaid with the associations which the early Christians had developed around these words, and their associations were decidedly influenced by apocalyptic thinking. We have only to remember how the early Christians waited eagerly for the return of Christ as the heavenly Son of Man descending on the clouds. This is far more like an apocalyptic vision than the down-to-earth hopes for the poor and the oppressed that Jesus spoke about.

Fortunately it is not necessary for us to know how Jesus reworked all the religious language of his time. Our task is to rework the religious language of our time in the spirit of Jesus. But there is one religious term that Jesus used very frequently, which is somewhat easier to analyse and which is indispensable for any understanding of Christian salvation. It is the term 'kingdom of God'.

The Kingdom of God

The kind of theology that many of us have been promoting in South Africa and elsewhere has sometimes been called 'kingdom theology'. In trying to understand what it means to be a Christian in a situation of oppression and struggle we spoke about our belief in the coming of God's kingdom, our commitment to kingdom values and our task of working for the kingdom. But what is now beginning to emerge is that as a religious symbol for our times and for our experience, the kingdom of God is *inadequate*. It has become like an old wineskin that is wearing thin, bursting at the seams and allowing the new wine to spill out. The word 'kingdom' has too many unfortunate associations that cannot be easily discarded. It is associated with royalty, monarchy and absolutist rule. What we want today is not a kingdom but a republic, a democracy.

Moreover the English word 'kingdom' is sexist. The original Hebrew and Greek words (*malkuth* and *basileia*) were not sexist. They refer to a monarch who could be either male or female.

Still more serious is the association of the word 'kingdom' with a place or a territory, like the Kingdom of Lesotho or the United Kingdom of Great Britain. What is the territory that will be covered by the Kingdom of God? The whole world? Does that mean that all other nations and governments will disappear? Apart from anything else, this appears to be far-fetched and hopelessly remote from our present struggles. Here again the Hebrew and Greek words do not refer to a territory. They refer rather to the dominant *power* at a particular time, as in the English expression 'during the *reign* of Queen Elizabeth' or 'in Elizabethan *times*'. Thus more and more Christians today prefer to speak about the reign of God or the rule of God rather than the kingdom of God.

But this does not solve all our problems. The kingdom or reign or rule of God is still associated with the idea of a perfect society, a utopia, an ideal world which can only be partially realised at any particular time and place. This way of thinking is abstract and idealist. The reign of God becomes like one of Plato's perfect ideas that can never be experienced fully in this life. It belongs to another world, a world of ideas or heavenly realities. But is this what Jesus was talking about? Is this what salvation means?

The reign of God was a well-known religious symbol in the time of Jesus. It had a definite core-meaning and a whole range of different associations. Its core-meaning might be described as the power that had been displayed in the wonderful works of God from Exodus to the victories of David (Riches 1980: 92). This was the way that God had *reigned* or displayed his sovereign power in the past, and in the time of Jesus everyone knew that. But by then people had come to associate the reign of God with various other matters. We can isolate at least four of these.

Many of Jesus' contemporaries, especially the scribes and the Pharisees, associated the reign of God with keeping the law. They believed that they were saved or justified by their meticulous observance of every rule in the system of purity and holiness. And they spoke about this as taking upon themselves 'the yoke of the kingdom' (Riches 1980: 95). In other words God reigned now only in the minds and hearts of those who kept God's laws about purity and holiness.

In the time of Jesus many people also associated the reign of God with the last day. This was the apocalyptic association. The reign of God would finally be established on earth once this wicked world had been destroyed on the last day. God would then rule and judge the world through a Messiah or Son of Man who would come down from heaven on a cloud.

Thirdly, in the minds of a considerable number of people the reign of God was associated with national independence. However, this was not understood in the same way as we would understand it today. The Jews who wanted their nation to be independent from Rome did not believe that every nation had the right to be independent, but that Israel should not be ruled by Caesar or any other pagan king because God alone was their king. Thus, for them the reign of God meant replacing the reign of Caesar in Israel with a Jewish government that worshipped the true God. This, of course, was the position of the Zealots and other similar groups, and it should be remembered that what they were zealous for was the law, the system of purity and holiness.

Finally, there was yet another aspiration that was vaguely associated with the reign of God. It was not well thought out and was never clearly documented, although recent research is bringing it to light more and more (as we shall see in the next chapter). It was an aspiration which the poor associated with the reign of God, namely, liberation from their sufferings. The poor were becoming poorer and the burden of suffering was becoming intolerable. They do not seem to have understood why or how this was happening. Nor do they appear to have had any clear idea about how they would ever be liberated from their sufferings. But they did put their trust in God. Thus, without any clarity about what it would entail, the poor and uneducated people, like Simeon, Anna, Zachariah and their circle of friends, 'looked forward to the consolation of Israel' (Lk 1: 25) or 'the liberation of Jerusalem' (Lk 1: 38). According to Luke, Mary looked forward to the time when God would reign on earth as God had done in the past by 'pulling down the mighty from their thrones and exalting the lowly' and 'by feeding the hungry and sending the rich away empty'. This was 'the promise made to our ancestors' (Lk 1: 46–55). Zachariah believes in the prophetic promises that 'God will save us from our enemies and from all who hate us' (Lk 1: 71), grant us freedom from fear (74) and 'guide our feet into the way of peace' (79).

This is what the reign of God meant to such people. It was what one might call the faith of the poor. In the next chapter we shall have occasion to return to this 'simple' faith in its various forms.

It is clear that the ideas associated with the reign of God are not always mutually exclusive. The Pharisees would have believed in the reign of God as the observance of the law *and* as the salvation that will come on the last day. The Zealots would have believed in the observance of the law as well as national independence without necessarily excluding the other associated ideas. The poor might well have had some vague belief in the other ideas that were associated with the reign of God. For many it was probably just a matter of emphasis.

Jesus and the Reign of God

In the circumstances, Jesus decided to focus attention upon this religious concept, to discard some of the ideas and practices associated with it, to develop others and to build up a powerful image of what it would mean *for God to reign on earth*. A careful study of Jesus' own practice and of all that he is reported to have said about the reign of God in parables and metaphors, leads to the conclusion that in his experience the reign of God is associated with four ideas.

The first is clearly the association with the poor and their yearning for liberation from suffering. Hence his work of healing the sick and feeding the hungry, and his insistence that what pleases God is to feed the hungry, give drink to the thirsty, clothe the naked and visit the sick and those in prison (Mt 25: 31–46). His own agenda is to set the downtrodden free, open the eyes of the blind and open the doors of the prisons while giving hope or good news to the poor (Lk 4: 18–19). It is the poor, the hungry and the miserable who are blessed because the reign of God belongs to them (Lk 6: 20–21). The liberation of the poor from sickness and guilt is the work of God, an act of salvation and a sign that *God is beginning to reign* (Lk 11: 20; Mt 11: 2–5; Mk 5: 34; 10: 52; Lk 17: 19; 18: 42; in the Greek of the New Testament 'to heal' and 'to save' is the same word).

Secondly, there is a set of agricultural parables that make it clear that Jesus associated the reign of God with a project for which both God and human beings would be responsible. The agricultural images of ploughing, sowing, planting, growing and harvesting are used in several parables and sayings as images of the reign of God (Mt 13: 4–9, 24–30, 31–32; Mk 4: 26–29; Lk 9: 62). In the first place what this shows is that Jesus did not think of the reign of God as something that comes only on the last day. It is a *process* that begins now with the work of ploughing, sowing and planting, and reaches completion with the work of harvesting. Nor is there any reason for assigning the time of harvesting to another world at the end of time. The project, including the harvesting, is not portrayed as the work of God alone. Jesus made use of the image of an agricultural project precisely because it illustrates so well the relationship between the work of human beings and the work of God. Ploughing, sowing, planting and harvesting is the work of the farmer. But the actual growth of the plants or trees is the quiet and invisible work of God. This is made very clear in Mk 4: 26–29:

> This is what the kingdom of God is like. A man throws seed on the land. Night and day, while he sleeps, when he is awake, the seed is sprouting and growing; how, he does not know. Of its own accord the land produces first the shoot, then the ear, then the full grain in the ear. And when the crop is ready, he loses no time: he starts to reap because the harvest has come.

The invisible but very powerful work of God is also represented as the phenomenal growth of a tiny mustard seed (Mt 13: 31–32 parr) and as the secret action of the yeast or leaven that makes the whole batch of dough rise in the oven (Mt 13: 33 par). In the reign of God, then, we can discern both the finger of God and the work of human hands. For Jesus, unlike the apocalyptic writers, the reign of God or salvation includes a human initiative whereby people become the subjects or agents in an historical project.

Jesus himself is our great example of this human work. He took the initiative by his words and his deeds and he taught the poor who followed him to do the same. Today we call this work with its aims and strategies *the practice of Jesus* (Belo 1981: 244ff; Echegaray 1984: 74ff). What was Jesus' practice?

Jesus set out to change not only the government or rulers of his time, but the whole social, political, economic and religious system (Lk 4: 18–19). And he set out to do this not only with words but also with actions. His actions, like his words, were appropriate to those times and circumstances and are not necessarily appropriate to our times and circumstances. Jesus' practice was based upon his reading of the signs of *his* time, as we shall see in the next chapter.

The gospels give us a glimpse of this new practice. We are introduced to a man who began the process of liberating the poor from their sufferings by healing the sick, dispelling the fear of demons, encouraging the weak and powerless, teaching people to share what they had and doing so himself. Moreover he confronted the system, ignored its purity regulations, argued with the upholders of the system, led a demonstration by riding into Jerusalem on a donkey, staged a sit-in in the Temple courtyard and drove out the traders and money-changers with a whip, was confronted by the authorities, went into hiding, was betrayed by an informer called Judas, was arrested, interrogated, beaten, mocked, put on trial, sentenced to death and finally tortured to death on a Roman instrument of repression.

Jesus had warned his disciples about this. They would have to follow in his footsteps – unto death (Mt 10: 11–31; 16: 24–26). The reign of God was a process or project, a way to salvation that would be no easy road.

This brings us to another of the ideas that Jesus associated with the reign of God: total commitment. A number of sayings and smaller parables make this abundantly clear. The reign of God and its justice must be our first priority (Mt 6: 33). We should treat the reign of God as a precious pearl or a treasure in a field for which we are willing to give up everything else (Mt 13: 44–46). Once we put our shoulders to the plough we must not look back lest we deviate from the straight line we are trying to plough (Lk 9: 62). The human work involved in the coming of God's kingdom does not admit of compromise or hesitation. It is a matter of life and death.

The fourth and last association that we can detect in the parables and sayings of Jesus concerns the reign of God as a community of people. The work or project of salvation is depicted as the gathering together of people in a household or a city, or around a festive meal (Nolan 1976: 44). That is what begins to happen now in small communities and finds its fulfilment in a new society of people. We today would speak about this as mobilising people and building new structures in order to work towards a new society or nation.

However, what transforms these communities or societies into the reign of God and the work of salvation is the way people in them relate to one another and to others. They are joyful, happy and celebrating communities of brothers and sisters who love one another, help one another, serve one another, forgive one another, share with one another and are even willing to die for one another. In other words they live together in *solidarity*, and yet they remain open to others and are without any thought of taking revenge upon their enemies (e.g. Lk 14: 7–24; Mt 12: 36–50; Lk 6: 27–38; Mt 5: 38–48; Acts 2: 42–47; 4: 32–35). They are communities with a purpose, with a goal, communities that are part of the divine project that Jesus called the reign of God.

Salvation Today

The salvation preached and lived by Jesus was clearly not apocalyptic. However, it was not long before some of his followers began to interpret his simple stories in apocalyptic terms. A very clear example of this would be the way in which Matthew, after giving us the simple parable of the wheat and the weeds (13: 24–30), then supplies an interpretation of it in terms of the Son of Man, the devil, the angels, the end of the world and the fires of hell (13: 36–40). Throughout the New Testament we find Jesus' very direct and powerful message overlaid with elements of apocalyptic thinking.

What we have seen, though, is that the fundamental problem with apocalyptic is not its language and its highly symbolic imagery, but its supernaturalism which excludes the work of human hands and its closely related tendency to universalise the day of salvation, thereby divorcing it from this time and place. The highly symbolic imagery can be powerful and effective as in the New Testament Book of the Revelation (Schüssler–Fiorenza 1981: 16ff). But the supernaturalism is disastrous for any understanding of the concrete meaning of salvation in the Bible, and indeed for any understanding of the concrete meaning of salvation in South Africa today. Modern eschatology (the theological study of the last day) does try to strip the last day of its supernaturalism. But the *eschaton* or last day is still thought of as the end of *all* history for *all* people for *all* time. The result of this universalising tendency is that it still removes the day of salvation from particular historical struggles and postpones it until the end of time, far out of the reach of particular peoples who are struggling with particular manifestations of sin and evil in particular places at particular times. In short, it makes the day of salvation or the reign of God irrelevant.

This is not what Jesus did. He spoke about a concrete practice at a particular time and in a particular place as the coming reign of God. The day of salvation which he looked forward to and which did not come in his time, was a day that would have been final and definitive for a particular people at a particular time. Whatever Jesus may have *thought* about a last day for all people and for all time, what he *spoke* about, like the prophets, was a day that was 'last' or final (an *eschaton*) for the people of his time. It was the harvest that could have come for those who were sowing and planting at that time. It did not come because the people of his time did not respond in sufficient numbers to the favourable historical conditions of that time.

Today, whatever we may believe about the last day and the

next world, the day of salvation that should be our primary concern, our *eschaton*, must be related to the particular sinfulness and evil that we are experiencing at this time and in this place. Are there any signs that a time of salvation is near for us in South Africa today?

The religious symbol of the kingdom or reign of God has now been so overlaid with apocalyptic associations that it is very difficult in practice to rework it and to give it the meaning that Jesus had in mind. What I would like to attempt therefore is a reworking of our current concept of *salvation*, in terms of what Jesus said and did and in the spirit in which he reworked the concept of the reign of God in his time, but on the basis of our experience of the work of God in South Africa today.

7
The Signs of Hope

The Signs of the Times

It is by reading the signs of our times that we discover what kind of time we are living in. We have already seen that our time in South Africa is characterised by a barbarous excess of suffering. We have also seen that this suffering is caused by a sinful system that has infiltrated and permeated every aspect of our lives. Our time and our country are dominated by the monster that we call apartheid. And it was in analysing these signs in the light of our faith that we discovered God crushed, crucified and trampled upon by the powers of evil.

If that were all, our times would indeed be sad times – a time for mourning and tears, a time for sackcloth and ashes. Our time would then be qualitatively the same as the time of Amos or Jeremiah or John the Baptist – the prophets of doom. And our response would have to be similar to their response. Indeed many South African Christians do see our time in this way and do respond with prophecies of doom. But Jesus read the signs of his times differently. He saw what John the Baptist saw, a society plunging headlong to its destruction; but he also saw *signs of hope*. That is why Jesus, unlike John, preached a gospel, a message of joyful good news.

We need to examine more closely this difference between John's time and Jesus' time, between John's reading of the signs of the times and Jesus' reading of them. This is important if we, as Christians, are to discover the great and powerful signs of hope that finally and definitively characterise this moment of time in our country.

John the Baptist saw the sinfulness and perversity of his

generation and condemned it in no uncertain terms. In the spirit of the apocalyptic thinking of his time, John prophesied the coming wrath of God, an imminent day of judgment. The only hope that John could see was that some individuals might be saved from the catastrophe. These would be the individuals who repented and were purified by baptism.

The people John attacked in his preaching were the upholders of the system: the Sadducees (the priestly aristocracy), the Pharisees and Herod. It was he who first called them 'a brood of vipers' (Mt 3: 7). On the whole they simply treated him as a madman. But some of the people on the periphery of the system who were neither poor nor very wealthy or powerful were converted by his preaching. They were the people who had two coats and enough food, relatively wealthy people like tax-collectors and soldiers. Their conversion entailed personal sharing and economic justice. This is made very clear in Lk 3: 10–14:

> 'What must we do then?'
> John answered, 'If anyone has two tunics, he must share with those who have none, and the one who has something to eat must do the same.'
> There were tax collectors too who came for baptism, and these said to him, 'Master, what must we do?'
> He said to them, 'Exact no more than your rate.'
> Some soldiers asked him in their turn, 'What about us? What must we do?'
> He said to them, 'No intimidation. No extortion. Be content with your pay.'

This was clearly not addressed to the poor. Nor was it addressed to the rich and the powerful. We might call the people John is speaking to here the middle classes (Hollenbach 1979: 869ff). The individual conversion of a small number of these people was not going to change the system. But at that time John could not see any other hope, although he did expect someone to come after him who would achieve much more. John's reading of the signs of his times, then, was somewhat pessimistic. Jesus described John's message as a 'funeral dirge' (Mt 11: 16–19 par). He was basically a prophet of doom – a doom from which a few individuals might be rescued.

Jesus saw what John saw and at first he followed John, was baptised by him and participated in a ministry of baptism alongside of him (Jn 3: 22–26; 4: 1–3). But then Jesus began to see the signs of hope, signs of an approaching day of salvation, signs that the reign of God was near. In their search for the signs of the times the great difference between Jesus and John was that Jesus looked not only at the sins of the rich and the powerful and all their collaborators, but also at what was happening amongst the poor and the oppressed. There amongst the outcasts and 'sinners', amongst the 'lost sheep of the house of Israel' (Mt 15: 24), amongst 'the rabble who know nothing of the law' (Jn 7: 49) and even amongst pagans who were totally outside of the law, Jesus found something that was a powerful sign of hope. He found faith.

Faith

It seems as if Jesus himself was surprised to find so much faith *and* such a lively and powerful faith outside of the system of purity and holiness, especially when he found it in pagans too. He does not seem to have anticipated the strong faith of the Canaanite woman (Mt 15: 28) or the Roman centurion (Mt 8: 10). 'Nowhere in Israel have I found faith like this' (Mt 8: 10). God was at work outside of the system.

The first and most obvious manifestations of this faith were the cures, healings and exorcisms. People were being healed, saved and put on their feet again by their faith. It was the work of God, and Jesus was instrumental in bringing it about, but as he says after almost every healing: 'Your *faith* has saved [or healed] you' (Mk 5: 34, 36; 10: 52; Mt 8: 10; 9: 22, 29; 15: 28; Lk 8: 48, 50; 17: 19; 18: 42; Nolan 1976: 31). Thus when John the Baptist sends his disciples to find out what Jesus was up to, why he has changed from baptising to healing (Hollenbach 1982: 177ff) and whether he is still 'the one who is to come', Jesus simply points to the signs. 'Go back and tell John what you *hear* and *see*; the blind see again and the lame walk, lepers are cleansed and the deaf hear and the dead are raised to life, and good news is proclaimed to the poor' (Mt 11: 2–5). Jesus does not point to the fact that *he* is doing these things. What matters is that these things are happening. They are the signs that God is at work through the faith of the people. And if this is the 'finger of God' then the day of salvation is near: 'If it is through the finger of God that I cast out devils, then know that the kingdom [or rule] of God has overtaken you' (Lk 11: 20 par).

However it was not only in the cures, healings and exorcisms that Jesus found a lively and genuine faith. One of the signs that are included in the list that Jesus gives to John's disciples is that 'good news is proclaimed to the poor' (Mt 11: 5). The faith of the poor, the faith of those who were regarded by the system as 'mere children', was also manifested in their ability to hear and welcome the news of God's salvation as good news. 'I thank you, Father, for hiding these things from the learned and the clever and revealing them to mere children' (Mt 11: 25 par). Those who did not benefit from the system, those who suffered under it and were rejected by it, and those who felt overburdened by all its prescriptions (Mt 11: 28; 23: 4) were in the best position to accept what Jesus had to say about sin and salvation. The conditions for faith were present in this social group rather than in 'the learned and clever', the upholders of the system. But why?

Jesus lived in a time of considerable 'unrest'. This conclusion is confirmed by all scholarly research. Although the causes of this 'unrest' and the forms that it took were considerably different from what we are experiencing in South Africa today, there was a situation of crisis, conflict, chaos and social upheaval in the time of Jesus. The poor were becoming poorer and more numerous, while the rich were becoming richer. Small farmers had had their land expropriated and sold to wealthy landowners (Stegemann 1984: 19). Taxes had become a crushing burden. There had been droughts and famines and unemployment was increasing (Schottroff and Stegemann 1986: 40ff). Peasants and dispossessed farmers were flocking to the towns and cities to become either beggars or robbers (Theissen 1978: 34–35, 47ff). There was a general situation of what Theissen calls 'social rootlessness'. At the same time there was a chronic political crisis because of the tensions between the different structures of government (Roman procurators, Herodian kings and the Jewish Sanhedrin), not to mention the cultural identity crisis of the ruling Jewish elite (Theissen 1978: 76, 93).

In such circumstances it should not be surprising to discover that there were uprisings and demonstrations by the poor and especially the impoverished peasants. The interesting thing, though, is that it took a religious form. It took the form of popular prophetic movements (Horsley 1985: 161ff). These should not be confused with the more literate and middle-class movements like those of the Essenes, the Zealots and the followers of John the Baptist (*Catholic Biblical Quarterly* 47, 1985: 444f). The poor had their own leaders and prophets. The contemporary historian Josephus, who had no time for such prophets, described them as 'impostors and demagogues [who] under the guise of divine inspiration provoked revolutionary actions and impelled the masses to act like madmen' (*Jewish War* 2.259).

Whatever one may think about the eccentricities of some of these uprisings (searching for sacred vessels or waiting to cross the Jordan or expecting the walls of Jerusalem to collapse), they clearly demonstrate that 'the yearning for liberation had reached a fevered pitch' and that there was an underlying trust in God (Horsley 1985: 162–164). It was this yearning and this trust or faith that made the poor so ready to hear the good news. It was this too that made Jesus so excited and hopeful about the future. He could depict the scene as crowds and crowds of people forcing their way (Lk 16: 16 NEB) into the community of God from which they had previously been excluded. They were coming from east and west (Mt 8: 11) and taking the city (or kingdom) of God by storm (Mt 11: 12) while those who were supposed to be the people of God ('sons of the kingdom') were left outside (Mt 8: 12). 'Prostitutes and tax-collectors were making their way in' instead of the chief priests and elders (Mt 21: 31, 23). The rich, the powerful, the scribes, and the Pharisees had been offered a baptism of repentance by John. They had refused it (Lk 7: 30; Mt 21: 32). So now they were being left out while 'the poor, the crippled, the blind and the lame' were coming in from 'the highways and the byways' (Lk 14: 15–24). 'Blessed are you who are poor,' Jesus exclaims, '*yours* is the kingdom of God' (Lk 6: 20; compare Lk 12: 32).

This, then, was the great sign of hope: God was at work in an unexpected place, outside of the system of purity and holiness. It was a new time, a time for dancing, singing, rejoicing and celebrating because God's victory over sin and evil was not far off (Lk 7: 31–35 par; Nolan 1976: 79).

And in South Africa today? Are there signs of hope in unexpected places? The mood of this book so far has been somewhat like the harsh and mournful tones of the prophets of doom. But if we dig deeper and look in the right places, we shall find, as Jesus did, abundant reason for dancing, singing and rejoicing.

Hope against Hope

South Africa is a land of hope and despair, a land that paradoxically gives birth to hope while it tries to destroy all hope. So many of us have been through the experience of having our hopes and expectations crushed overnight by a blind and ruthless regime. I am thinking of the false hopes that so many Christians have entertained, the hope that real change might come from the top, that members of the 'government' might actually have a change of heart or that the white electorate might develop a conscience and vote against apartheid. At least we now know that such hopes are illusions.

I am thinking also of the hopes that some black people have had, the hope that whites would begin to see their folly, the hope that with enough protest and explanation whites would begin to see reason and act like rational human beings. What an illusion that has proved to be! But I am also thinking of the hopes and expectations of some of the township youth in recent years. They had hoped that with all the pressure of boycotts, strikes, stayaways and sanctions the regime would be toppled in a matter of months. Not everyone in the townships shared such unrealistic hopes and especially not the political leadership, but there *were* people who entertained them for a while. They were due for a rude awakening.

The South African system must be the world's greatest destroyer of illusionary hopes and expectations. But that precisely is its weakness, that precisely is how it gives birth, unintentionally, to real hope. There is an extraordinary amount of real hope in South Africa, hope that has been stripped of all illusions. Paradoxically it has been the system itself that has stripped our hope of its illusions. We now know that we cannot base our hopes upon individual conversions at the top. Not only do they generally not happen but even when they do happen, even when some individuals are converted or half-converted, the only result is that they must immediately opt out of the system, or at least, out of the system's corridors of power. I do not wish to sneer at such conversions but they do make it quite clear that personal conversions at the top or anywhere near the top make no difference to the system itself. The system just co-opts others and rolls on as before. There are no individuals who control the system, the system controls them, and if they dissent, the system will simply spew them out.

The white electorate has even less chance of making any real changes. The 1987 white election made that abundantly clear. All the system had to do was frighten whites with scare stories and they all came running to the polls to vote for the continuation of the same old system with a few gradual adaptations or reforms.

We have now reached the stage in South Africa when anyone who is searching for signs of hope must realise that these cannot be found within the system itself. Many have known this for a long time. They were stripped of their illusions many years ago. But now everyone who is serious about change knows that we must look outside and beyond the system to what we call extra-parliamentary politics. Hence the visits by representatives of business, Churches and students to Lusaka and by Afrikaner academics to Dakar. But much more important than that has been the phenomenal growth of extra-parliamentary movements and organisations over the last ten years. The system now recognises this as a threat to its very existence. Hence the clampdown upon all extra-parliamentary movements and the systematic attempt that is being made to eliminate all forms of political organisation outside of the system, outside of the tricameral parliament and homeland governments.

What we are up against are not some unreasonable leaders or misguided individuals whom we might hope to convert. What we are up against is not 'flesh and blood' (Eph 6: 12) but the powers of evil embodied in the system. Nothing that really threatens the system will be allowed to develop. Where, then, is the hope for the future? Can extra-parliamentary politics survive? And if it does survive, can it ever become powerful enough to change the system? Yes, it can and it will. And one of the first and most fundamental reasons for saying this is that the system is its own worst enemy. The system has now become so evil, so manifestly evil, that it is in danger of breaking its own back. This will not happen without a great deal of pressure from outside of the system itself but the paradox or irony is that the system is busy creating and strengthening its opposite, its enemies and eventually its own downfall. And what is more it can no longer avoid this.

Somewhere here is the beginning of our hope for the future but it requires some explaining. It has to do with the dynamics of social change, the way in which a system can begin to give rise, unintentionally, to its opposite.

Non-Racial Unity

Racism has been taken to such lengths by the system that it has produced a deep thirst for its opposite: non-racialism. The people who have suffered so much for so long under a system that classifies everyone according to race, colour or ethnicity will no longer tolerate any such distinctions. Even multiracialism is now rejected. Multiracialism is not the same as non-racialism. A multiracial society or a multiracial government is one in which all the racial or ethnic groups are supposed to be equal. But the non-racial ideal that has developed and spread and really taken root among the people of South Africa, in opposition to the system, is an ideal of a society in which race, colour or ethnicity is totally irrelevant. According to the Freedom Charter, 'South Africa belongs to all who live in it, black and white' and in the future 'the rights of the people shall be the same regardless of race, colour or sex'; in fact 'the preaching and practice of national, race or colour discrimination and contempt shall be a punishable crime'. (For the full text of the Freedom Charter see Appendices.)

It is amazing that so many whites are simply unaware of this. They imagine that blacks want to become the dominant group in order to reduce whites to an oppressed minority – a reversal of roles within the same system. Most whites do not understand that it is the system itself that is being rejected, the system of classifying people according to their race. There may have been a time in the past when some blacks thought freedom meant throwing whites into the sea or telling them to go home to Europe. But those days are long past. Everybody now knows that it is the system that must change and not the colour of the faces at the top. If anything more was needed to convince people of this, the system has provided it in the form of homeland leaders, community councillors, a tricameral parliament and black policemen. For the people it is now a fact of everyday experience that one can be oppressed and exploited by people of any colour or race. It is not even necessary to be told about those African countries where nothing changed with independence except the colour of the faces on top – the change from colonialism to neo-colonialism. In South Africa it is the system itself that has provided the necessary contrast experience.

A contrast experience enables one to see what is right and what is needed as the contrast or opposite of what one is presently experiencing (Schillebeeckx 1979: 621ff). The Freedom Charter is an excellent example of this. It was adopted at a huge gathering of representatives of the people from all the so-called race groups in Kliptown near Johannesburg in 1955. The preparation of the Charter took the form of a wide consultation of the people about two things: their grievances and their demands (Suttner and Cronin 1985: 25ff). The grievances were what the people were experiencing; the demands were formulated as the contrast or opposite of these grievances. The ideal for the future would be the opposite of racism, inequality, discrimination, domination and exploitation. My point is that it is the excesses of the system itself that have given rise to these strongly held ideals, and the more the system tries to entrench itself, the more it deepens and clarifies these ideals.

Thus the ideal of one nation or one unitary state has been deepened since the writing of the Freedom Charter. This ideal is present in the Charter but it is weakened by a reference to 'the equal status of national groups and races'. Since then the system has gone to such bizarre lengths to separate people, to re-tribalise them, to force them into homelands, to insist on ethnicity and multiracialism, that the people have deepened their aspiration not only for non-racialism but also for one undivided nation. The more the system tries to destroy this, the more determined the people become to build it.

One day we will be a thoroughly non-racial and unified nation. The system is forcing us, quite unintentionally, in that direction, and more and more whites are beginning to accept this as our only possible future. As a firm basis for hope this is not enough, but there are other signs too.

Participation

The process of dialectical change is not merely a matter of developing values and ideals that are opposed to the values and ideals of the system. There is also a process whereby the system itself conscientises and politicises the people.

There are political organisations that try to make the people aware of what is happening and of the need to resist the system. By itself that would be a long, slow process that reaches only a small number of people. But in South Africa there is more hope than in most other countries because the system does what no people's organisation could ever achieve alone. When the system, in its frustration, sends its police and its army into the townships to beat people up, to shoot, maim and kill, to rape, rob and imprison them indiscriminately and ruthlessly, thousands and thousands of people are conscientised and politicised overnight. Who needs so-called 'agitators' when the system itself makes it so clear that it is the enemy of the people? Those who are treated badly in so many ways do not need to be told that the system is evil or that its propaganda is all lies.

Because the system has generated so much alienation and so unashamedly treated people as mere *objects*, it provokes a very powerful reaction on the part of those who do not benefit from such perversity. They rebel, assert their humanity and become determined *subjects* of their own history and destiny. This is happening in South Africa today to such an extent that whites find it quite bewildering. People who had been previously regarded as mere labour units are standing up, asserting themselves and, to make quite sure they will be heard, throwing stones and burning buildings. They cannot be pacified with minor concessions or promises or the scrapping of some laws. What the regime and most whites and their collaborators simply cannot understand is that the people are not demanding more and more concessions or privileges or benefits, they are demanding a say – participation in the whole process of decision-making in South Africa. They do not want to be objects who receive concessions, they want to be subjects who decide with others what is to be done or not done. The regime cannot even bring itself to consult the people. Now the people no longer want to be consulted, they want full participation, they want to be subjects of their own destiny and in many ways they have already become the agents of their own future.

A massive change is taking place for more and more people, in a deeper and deeper way, every day: the change from being passive objects to becoming active subjects and co-creators with one another of our common future. In many other parts of the world this is something that one can read about in books: theological, philosophical and political books that deal with the need to overcome alienation. In South Africa it is a fast-growing reality. Millions of oppressed people in South Africa are determined to have a say with others in the future of our country.

The reason why this is such an enormously hopeful sign is that we can be quite sure that our future will not be oppressive and alienating. In other words the one thing we need not fear for the future is the kind of take-over whereby another group of people simply replaces the present rulers and maintains the same type of system so that people (of whatever colour) are manipulated as objects. That possibility is gone forever. Our people will no longer let anyone of any shade of colour treat them as mere objects. Any future government will have to be answerable to all the people otherwise it will simply not be allowed to govern.

The only problem is that most whites and a good number of their collaborators do not yet understand this. Most of them indeed do not know what it means to be the subject of one's own history. They are quite happy to be objects as long as they can keep their privileges and their possessions and as long as they can control the masses of the people. They cannot understand what the people are asking for, because they imagine all that people want is money and privileges and power over others. Most whites still have much to learn but perhaps there is more hope of their learning these things in South Africa, where they have to share the same country with the people they have colonised, than is possible for other imperialist peoples who never even come into contact with the people they are exploiting.

Organisation

It has often been pointed out that the power of the poor and the oppressed lies in their ability to make their demands in unity and solidarity through the creation of their own organisations. The excessive individualism of the sytem, its policy of 'divide and rule', and its attempts to destroy extra-parliamentary politics, have made the people all the more determined to create and expand their own organisations. The best example of this is trade unionism.

The growth of trade unions over the last ten years or so in South Africa has been phenomenal. The trade-union movement has had a long history of successes and failures. There was the initial success of Clements Kadalie who formed the ICU (Industrial and Commercial Workers' Union) in the 1920s. This did not last very long. During the 1940s a number of African trade unions were formed and strike activity resumed. The most important event was the African miners' strike of 1946. Mineworkers' wages had actually decreased since 1890. The strike was crushed by the police and union leaders were arrested. Again there was a lull, especially after 1948. 'Africans were excluded from the definition of employee, and thus were statutorily excluded from the process of industrial negotiation'

(Stadler 1987: 173).

But then in the 1970s strikes began to occur on a scale never seen before. The system had to find a way of controlling this. The method of control up to this point had been 'parallel unions', an arrangement whereby African grievances had to be communicated to employers via white-controlled unions. The state then made provision for the establishment of 'liaison committees', half of whose members were nominated by the employer. Some workers rejected these 'puppet bodies' immediately, others by participating in them soon discovered that proper independent trade unions were necessary. In 1981 the state legalised African trade unions while applying certain conditions and restrictions. The legal space thus provided was taken up immediately and trade-union organisations began to flourish. The conditions and restrictions (such as racially separate unions, non-political unionism and conditions for official registration) were hotly debated by workers and unionists, gradually ignored and eventually superseded by the formation in November 1985 of a massive, united, non-racial and overtly political alliance of trade unions called COSATU.

COSATU was and still is an organisational miracle. The fact that it all happened so quickly, so effectively and with such carefully laid plans for the future is a great witness to the level of worker consciousness and worker leadership in South Africa today. Now on almost any day of the year you will find that there are several small or large strikes going on at the same time throughout the country – not to mention numerous talks and negotiations around industrial disputes. Decades of worker exploitation originating in the need for very cheap labour on the mines have given rise to a consciousness and an organisation that can no longer be stopped or controlled by the system. It is one of the great signs of hope for the future.

Another organisational miracle has to do with students and youth in South Africa. University students have been organised for some time in NUSAS. During the black consciousness period there was the powerful SASO on black campuses. Since the intensification of protests and boycotts in the late 1970s, most black students have been organised by AZASO (now called SANSCO) and white students by NUSAS. Both are non-racial organisations and affiliated to the United Democratic Front (UDF). But the miracle has been the organisation of high-school students and youth in the urban townships and the rural areas.

Soweto 1976 was the beginning of one of the most remarkable features of the struggle against the apartheid system: the rebellion of school children and their use of the school boycott. This required a considerable amount of organisation. The first national organisation of school students was COSAS. In 1985 it was banned. Since then and under the very restrictive conditions of a state of emergency two new national organisations have been formed: one body for school students and another for youth. What is most striking and most hopeful about these two organisations is that they have been built up from below. The students' representative councils (SRCs) from different schools come together in a township and with other townships form a regional organisation and then a national one. The youth do the same. The fact that such national organisations can be built up by the youth, despite continual harassment and numerous setbacks, is a remarkable sign of hope.

The development of civic associations in almost every township in South Africa has been no less remarkable. In one way or another they have been responsible for community campaigns: bus boycotts, consumer boycotts, rent boycotts and stayaways. It is becoming more and more difficult to organise such boycotts, although successful stayaways do still take place and in some townships the residents have not paid their rent for years. The latest development in this area of community organisation is the street committee. In some ways this was a spontaneous reaction on the part of neighbours in a street who discovered that the only way to survive the chaos of township life, especially when the troops or police are fighting the 'young comrades' on the streets, is to become organised. Problems that no individual could do anything about, can be sorted out by street committees.

The organisation of women in South Africa has also been very important and very powerful. Because of the many ways in which women in particular suffer under the system and because their cause is seldom appreciated by men, it has been necessary for women to develop their own campaigns and their own organisations. The most famous of their demonstrations involved the 60 000 women who marched to the Union Buildings in Pretoria to protest against the pass laws in 1956.

As early as 1954 the women in the struggle had formed a national federation (FEDSAW) and adopted the Women's Charter (see Appendices). Like most other bodies, the various women's organisations have had their ups and downs over the years, and yet in recent times they have gone from strength to strength, and FEDSAW has in fact been revived as a national federation. The organisation of women has been a distinctive feature of the South African struggle.

There are numerous other people's organisations and more in the making. Democratic lawyers, doctors, teachers and academics are developing their own bodies. There are also Church or religiously based organisations in the struggle, not to mention the End Conscription Campaign for white conscripts. Although not all these bodies are affiliated to UDF, there are now some 700 organisations within UDF alone. And then there are the groups that have ideological differences with UDF, for example, AZAPO, AZASM and NEUM. One could go on and on but enough has been said to establish my point that oppression in South Africa has given rise to a phenomenal growth in people's organisations and that this must be regarded as one of the principal signs of our times.

Democracy

What is even more significant than widespread organisation as such is the ideal and reality of democracy that pervade these organisations. The system's abuse of power has been so autocratic, authoritarian and undemocratic, in fact so tyrannical, that the people who suffer under it have learnt to appreciate the value of democracy. I never cease to be amazed at the lengths to which people will go, even in the most repressive situations, to ensure that every decision at every level is as democratic as possible. The principle of democracy is now so deeply entrenched that the whole struggle against the system is frequently called the democratic movement or the national democratic struggle and those who participate in it (black and white) are simply called democrats.

The opposite of apartheid is democracy. The undemocratic system whereby a small minority of whites have the vote while the majority of the people are excluded has led to the obvious demand for one-person-one-vote. Everyone who has any understanding of what is happening in South Africa knows that there will be no peace in our country until we have one-person-one-vote in an undivided general election. But democracy has come to mean much more than being allowed to vote in general elections every few years. A form of grassroots democracy is being developed in the organisations of the people. People are learning to make democratic decisions at every level and in every sphere of life. People who have never had any part in the decision-making processes of the system are being given a say in how the struggle against the system is to be conducted. This has a powerful effect upon them and produces a quite extraordinary sense of responsibility.

Again one of the problems here is that generally speaking whites do not appreciate the value of democracy, at least not at every level of society. They are generally content with voting every few years and don't mind having no active say in all the other authoritarian institutions to which they belong. Most whites are apathetic and do not want to take responsibility for the way they are governed or the way things are run in any institution as long as their interests are being cared for. One even gets the impression that some whites would be quite happy with an overt dictatorship as long as their interests were protected by the dictator. That such people should have the vote while others who have developed a sense of democracy and responsibility are denied it is one of the great contradictions of apartheid.

There is also a problem here with the Churches. On the whole (there are exceptions) the Churches are not democratic institutions. There may or there may not be good reasons for that and we shall have to discuss the role of the Church in our last chapter, but when church people get involved in the struggle one of the first things they have to learn is how to participate in democratic decision-making.

The development of grassroots democracy in South Africa is an important sign of hope for the future. It is one of the ways in which our country has an advantage over other colonised countries especially in Africa. In many of these countries independence was gained after a brief struggle and frequently after an armed struggle that did not involve all the people, or, at least, did not involve all the people in grassroots organisations over many years. Popular organisation is now happening in some Latin American countries and in the Philippines, but in Africa as a whole there has not been the same contrast experience and the same long, democratically organised struggle. Thus when independence came most of the people were unconscientised, unpoliticised and unprepared for a fully participatory democracy.

South Africa is different and will be different when liberation comes.

People's Education

One final example of a contrast experience that augurs well for the future of South Africa is people's education. The present education crisis is facilitating a new understanding of the whole meaning of education. In the 1970s the regime tried to impose Afrikaans as the medium of education in some township high schools. The blindness that made them even contemplate such a move is astonishing, although in essence it was no different from all the other forms of manipulation and social engineering whereby people, especially young blacks, are treated as mere objects. The students protested. They were ignored, so they came out onto the streets of Soweto in their thousands for a peaceful march. On that fateful day, 16 June 1976, the police began to shoot school children. For days and weeks they continued in Soweto and elsewhere to shoot them, until hundreds of pupils had been killed and many thousands injured.

The students reacted by throwing stones and burning buildings. They boycotted school and continued to do so periodically until the end of 1986. Their demands changed from having English as a medium to the abolition of corporal punishment, free textbooks, better teachers, elected SRCs and equal education with whites in one education department. An organisation was formed to promote these aims: COSAS. The system refused to listen, had more students detained and introduced more regulations to control them. The crisis reached such proportions that parents became concerned and in Soweto organised themselves into the SPCC (Soweto Parents' Crisis Committee). This gradually became a national organisation, the National Education Crisis Committee (NECC).

By now the students had come to see the weaknesses of the white system of education and they began to demand a new approach to education, an approach that would allow them to have a say in their own education. At the NECC conferences the demand was made by students, parents and teachers for what they called 'people's education'. Amidst boycotts, continual harassment, fighting on the streets and the banning of COSAS, NECC began to prepare for people's education. New syllabuses were being prepared, new and more progressive ideas about education were studied and new textbooks were in the making. Each school was to have a PTSA (Parent-Teacher-Student Association) and these would be linked regionally and nationally to make the NECC more thoroughly democratic. Some students were already busy re-organising themselves into a new student organisation based upon the elected SRCs at each school, people's education was already being implemented in some circles, and by the beginning of 1987 all boycotting students would return to school. While all of this was going on the system in its usual authoritarian and repressive manner, clamped down. The national executive of the NECC was detained and people's education was outlawed.

Of course this did not end the process. It simply brought about a more clandestine way of operating. The students went back to school, formed a new national students' organisation, and the preparations and plans devised for people's education continued.

The learning process for parents, teachers and students was enormous. Everyone has learnt more about the real meaning of education, co-operation, democracy and organisation than they could have learnt in any other circumstances. The education crisis is but one example of how the system's stupidity and blindness have enabled the people to become subjects and creators of their own future. We can look forward to a remarkably progressive and democratic form of education in the future.

The Crisis of the System

One cannot deny that the organisations of the people have encountered very severe setbacks since the state of emergency and sustained repression. The system is determined to crush all people's organisations and to discredit extra-parliamentary politics of any kind. Thousands upon thousands of political activists from these organisations are either in prison or in hiding. Many have had their homes bombed or set alight and some have been killed. Thousands are on the run and have not been home for years. They have become internal refugees. Nevertheless the work of organising goes on.

What fills some people with despair, though, is the power, the strength and the desperate determination of the system to survive. But this 'no surrender', 'over my dead body' or 'to the last man' bravado should not be mistaken for real strength. It is a display of forcefulness or *kragdadigheid* that hides a feeling of weakness and a sense that change is inevitable. While we should not underestimate this power and determination, we should also recognise that the system is going through a desperate crisis which it simply cannot survive.

The point has now been reached where, no matter what tactics the system uses to perpetuate itself, its every effort will prove to be counterproductive in terms of its own aims. The system cannot but create more and more of its opposite: the struggle for total liberation. But that is not all. Because of the unprecedented pressure from the townships and from the international community in the last few years, the system has been forced to find some way of adapting or reforming itself. But if it promises more reforms it will lose the support of its right-wing conservatives; while if it does not keep its promises and is also not able to keep the peace it will lose the support of its left-wing.

Whites themselves are becoming more and more polarised. And that is a sign of hope.

Christians tend to abhor polarisation and division. But the tendency to look for peace, unity and reconciliation at all costs and in all circumstances is simply not Christian (Kairos Document 1986: 9ff). Jesus foresaw that his practice and preaching would cause dissension and even divide families (Lk 12: 51–53 par). The present polarisation among whites can be constructive. It weakens the system and creates division in its ranks. It also facilitates more debate and more questioning and more constructive doubt. It may even help people to have their eyes opened.

One of the signs of hope must surely be that the system is losing credibility. Apart from a diminishing number of fearful whites who want change without change or, rather, without sacrificing their privileges and their power, nobody really believes that the regime can bring peace and justice for all. I suspect that even in the corridors of power they know that it is only a matter of time before we have one-person-one-vote. In the townships the system has never had any credibility and now it is simply regarded as an illegitimate government. The question of the moral legitimacy of an apartheid government is now being widely debated. It is also on the agenda of some Churches. 'An increasing number of people are beginning to realise that white minority rule is doomed. It is only a question of time and manner, when and how this rule will be replaced.' 'This', says Charles Villa-Vicencio, 'is a sign of hope' (SACC 1986a: 34).

Of course there are those who do not want any change at all, who actually want to turn the clock back. This is inevitable in any society. It is part of the dynamics of change and it can even have an indirect influence upon the process of change. The AWB, at the extreme right, is proving to be a real thorn in the side of a system that wishes to survive. It is rumoured that a large percentage of the white police force in the Transvaal is associated with the AWB. I do not know if this is true. But even if it were only half true, the system must be faced with an insuperable problem about how whites are going to be controlled in the future – let alone blacks. And if the tricameral parliament collapses? If members of the 'Coloured' and 'Indian' chambers cannot produce enough for their voters and cannot afford to take all the insults? Will we end up with a more explicit, and perhaps even a military, dictatorship? That will plunge the system into a yet deeper crisis.

Many fear this; not because they agree with the system but because they fear chaos. But chaos is here with us already, at least for the majority of the people. The hope is not that there will be yet more chaos but that as the crisis deepens for the system, the present rulers will be forced to the negotiating table for open and honest negotiations about a totally new constitution and a one-person-one-vote election.

The Work of God

We have only begun to read the signs of our times, but already we can see the finger of God. And *if* it is by the finger of God that these things are happening, then know that the day of salvation must be near (Lk 11: 20).

In the Bible the saving activities of God are called the *mirabilia Dei*, that is to say, the wonderful works of God. These wonderful works of God are not miracles, at least not in the sense in which the word 'miracle' is generally understood today. They are not magical interventions that upset the laws of nature (Nolan 1976: 33–36) or the laws of social change. The works of God are called wonderful *(mirabilia)* because they are unexpected or surprising, they make us wonder. Of course when we say they are wonderful we also mean that they are good, that they come as a pleasant surprise.

In religion the recurring temptation is to start looking for magical interventions. Jesus himself knew this temptation. In the desert he was tempted to test God by trying to produce a sign from heaven (Mt 4: 6–7 par). Later the scribes and the Pharisees would ask him for a sign from heaven. He refuses and points them instead to the signs that are on earth, the signs of the times (Mk 8: 11–13 par; Lk 11: 16). The signs of the times, insofar as they are signs of hope, are the *mirabilia Dei*.

What makes the work of God so unexpected and so pleasantly

surprising is God's tendency to bring good out of evil, life out of death, something out of nothing, victory out of defeat, or, as Augustine once said, God writes straight with crooked lines. In his *Enchiridion* Augustine could even argue that 'God decided it was better to allow good to come from evil than to allow no evil' (27). Paul presents the same paradox in another way: 'Where sin increased, grace abounded all the more' (Rm 5: 20 RSV; compare Rm 6: 1; 11: 32).

Is this not precisely what is happening in South Africa today? Are we not experiencing a classic example of good coming out of evil? We have seen how racism has given rise to non-racialism, separation to a desire for unity, authoritarianism to democracy, alienation to human responsibility, repression to consciousness, a gutter education to people's education, and so forth. Insofar as the dynamics of social change are paradoxical, unexpected and surprising and insofar as these dynamics work for the good of human beings, they must be seen as the finger of God. They are just as much wonderful works of God as anything we read about in the Bible. Of course some of the works of God, like the resurrection of Christ from the dead, have a very special and unique significance, but that does not detract from the reality of what God is doing in our country today.

Nor is this all that God is doing. The fact that the system tends to give rise to its opposite and to create its own enemies is not by itself and alone a firm basis for hope. It establishes the necessary social conditions for change but it does not guarantee that people will take the opportunity of building an alternative to the system. There are social forces moving us in a certain direction but if people in large numbers were not consciously responding to the favourable conditions of the moment, there would be very little reason to be hopeful about the near future. To base one's hopes only upon the dynamics of social change would be to take a deterministic view of life. It would leave no room for human responsibility. Change does not happen automatically and inevitably and no matter how people respond or don't respond. Nor should we expect to find God in some kind of iron law of social determinism. That would be just another form of absolute predestination that leaves no room for human responsibility.

Fortunately, as we have already begun to see, the people of South Africa are responding in great numbers to the favourable conditions created quite unintentionally by the system. But the struggle is not perfect. The people's organisations are not perfect. There are divisions and differences of opinions, rivalries and factions. There are mistakes and miscalculations. What is remarkable is how people learn from their mistakes and how they gradually overcome divisions and transcend differences, although that too does not happen automatically. The struggle has a long history as we shall see later. It has been, among other things, a history of learning from experience, a process of political education second to none. We still have much further to go and much more to learn. Nobody has all the answers and nobody is satisfied with the struggle as it now is. We are a people on the move.

The signs of hope then are the favourable conditions and the human response. And God is present in both. In order to make this visible, in order to gain a deeper understanding of the signs of hope in South Africa today, we must now take a closer look at the quality of the human response, namely the spirit of the struggle. Is there anything there that would correspond to the faith that Jesus discovered outside of the system of purity and holiness?

8
The Struggle

'The quest for freedom and the yearning for liberation are among the principal signs of our times.' This is not an assertion of some liberation theologian. It is a quotation from a Vatican document, 'Instruction on Christian Freedom and Liberation' (SACBC 1986: 5). This same document goes on to state that it is 'perfectly legitimate that those who suffer oppression . . . should take action . . . to secure structures and institutions in which their rights will be truly respected' (75). Apart from the paternalism of conceding that this is 'legitimate', the Catholic Church can be said to have recognised the yearning for liberation as among the principal signs of our times and the action that follows from it as a good thing. In South Africa the yearning for liberation has been translated into action and we call it the *struggle*.

The struggle is the opposite of the system. In the townships what people are concerned about is not your ancestry or the colour of your skin but whether you are on the side of the system or on the side of the struggle. There is no grey area in-between. You are either with us or against us (Mt 12: 30 par). You cannot serve two masters (Mt 6: 24 par). Within the struggle there is room for differences about how it should be conducted and furthered, just as there seems to be room for differences within the system about how it should be maintained or adapted, but no compromise between the two is possible.

The struggle in South Africa today is a particular historical practice. It is a human work, a particular kind of project and it has a spirit of its own. Our concern will be to search, in all honesty, for signs of the *practice* of Jesus, the *work* of God, the *project* Jesus called the reign of God and the *spirit* that is known to us as the Holy Spirit.

The Experience of Struggle

For those whose only source of information about the struggle is television, the radio and the daily newspapers, the characteristic feature of the struggle must appear to be violence. I remember how on one occasion after a talk that I had given to a largely white audience of church people the discussion developed into an argument in which we seemed to be at cross-purposes with one another. At first I could not understand why. Then suddenly it struck me that the word 'struggle' which I had been using all evening meant, for most of that audience, fighting on the streets and planting bombs in shopping centres. I laughed. What else could I do? How does one even begin to explain what the struggle means to people who have been so profoundly influenced by the propaganda of the system?

If one were to try to pinpoint the most visible and most characteristic manifestation of the struggle, then it must surely be not violence but *singing and dancing*. At meetings, conferences, rallies, funerals and church services the experience of struggle manifests itself not only in speeches and slogans, but above all in the joyful and spontaneous outburst of liberation songs and tireless dancing – African-style. Dancing while you sing is typically African. Everyone in the struggle, no matter what his or her cultural background might be, has learnt to sing (mainly in African languages) and to dance while they sing.

Singing and dancing are a way of celebrating the struggle. What they express and confirm most of all is the joy of hopefulness, the indestructible conviction that victory is certain. I doubt whether the faith and hope, the yearning for liberation, that Jesus discovered in the popular movements and in the poor generally in his time were as strong and as indestructible as the hope that is celebrated in the struggle in South Africa today.

The experience of struggle is an experience of hope. One cannot *talk* a person into being hopeful. One has to be involved in the struggle and experience its joyful celebrations to know what hope really means. The theologian Dorothee Soelle captures this insight in a few bold and emphatic sentences. 'Struggle is the source of hope. There is no hope without struggle. There is no hope that drops from heaven through the intervention of God. Hope lies within the struggle.' (1984: 161)

The singing and dancing are more than a celebration of hope, they are also a celebration of solidarity or unity in struggle. The struggle rescues people from alienation, isolation and individualism. It restores *ubuntu* (humanness) and the experience of being a living member of a living body. Hence the slogan: 'An injury to one is an injury to all.' I can only presume that this is derived from the statement of Paul in I Corinthians: 'God has arranged the body . . . so that each part may be equally concerned for all the others. *If one part is hurt, all parts are hurt with it.* If one part is given honour, all parts enjoy it' (12: 24–26). I am also reminded of Jesus saying, 'Whatever you do to the least of my brothers and sisters, you do to me' (Mt 25: 40).

Nor is this merely a slogan. In the struggle it is a lived reality. Nobody can fail to be impressed by the way in which thousands upon thousands of workers will risk their precious jobs by going on strike because of an injury to one. Strikes in South Africa, like boycotts and stayaways, are acts of enormous self-sacrifice. A bus boycott means walking many miles to and from work or paying for a taxi. A consumer boycott means doing without things you need or paying higher prices. A school boycott means sacrificing one's education or chances of passing an examination. A stayaway may lose you your job or at least part of your already low wages. But of all the organised actions or campaigns in the struggle that require self-sacrifice, the strike must surely be the most heroic. The willingness to forfeit one's wages, sometimes for weeks or months on end, and the willingness to risk losing one's job with practically no hope of ever finding employment again, never cease to amaze the 'bosses' who are seldom prepared to make any sacrifices at all, least of all financial sacrifices. The individualism of the 'bosses' makes it very difficult for them to understand such dedicated solidarity. That is why they so easily believe that there must be a great deal of intimidation going on. Nothing else would ever induce the bosses themselves to take such risks. No doubt there is some intimidation at times. The struggle is not perfect and standing together in a boycott or a strike is so crucial for its success. The leaders in the struggle are strongly opposed to intimidation and on the whole it simply isn't necessary. That an injury to one is an injury to all is becoming more and more entrenched as a basic value. What an impressive sign of hope that is!

The experience of struggle is an experience of *total commitment*. People give of themselves unstintingly – their time, their energy, their freedom, their lives. In their organisations and campaigns people work extraordinarily hard, travelling hundreds of kilometres through the night after a full day's work to attend a meeting which can go on and on no matter how tired and hungry people might be. There is a sense of dedication and commitment here that is the very opposite of the apathy that one finds in white and middle-class circles.

To participate fully in the struggle you need something more than commitment, you need *heroic courage*. There is always the risk that you will be detained, interrogated, beaten up and tortured. There is also the real danger that you might be killed. People are so angry with a system that is merciless and unreasonable that they become highly motivated to do something about it. But it is the struggle that helps them to overcome their natural fears. The experience of solidarity and support together with the example of others gradually enables a person to overcome fear and to act with confidence and courage.

The struggle is very demanding. Among other things it demands a great deal of self-discipline and organisational discipline. Again this is not always achieved in everyone or in every organisation but it is an ideal that everyone strives for. The temptations of the system have to be constantly guarded against. But there are also the temptations to do one's own thing, to boost one's own ego, to impose one's own opinions on others, to rival and compete with others. The struggle has its own hazards. What is amazing is that there is so much discipline and that problems of discipline do get sorted out eventually.

The struggle has a kind of religious aura about it. The celebration of hope, the experience of community, the self-sacrifice, the total commitment, the courage, the discipline and the willingness to live and to die for the struggle, are things that we would normally associate with religion. Is that why the struggle can feel so at home in a church and why the funerals of those who have died in the struggle are always associated with a church or a mosque? What could be more religious than the way people stand in motionless respect and reverence while they sing the anthem, the great hymn of the struggle, *Nkosi Sikelel' iAfrika*?

When Jesus discovered great faith outside of the system, as we have already noted, he exclaimed: 'Nowhere in Israel have I found faith like this' (Mt 8: 10 par). Would it be an exaggeration to say of the struggle in South Africa today: 'Nowhere in the Church have I found faith like this'? Perhaps we need to dig still deeper to find out whether this is true or not.

The Memory of Struggle

The struggle in South Africa has a long history. We can trace it back to the colonial wars or even further back to the struggles of the Khoikhoi and the San in the early days of colonial settlement in the Cape. But the struggle as we know it today, as a national struggle, began in 1912 with the formation of the South African Native National Congress, which was the forerunner of the African National Congress or ANC. This must make our struggle for national liberation one of the longest in history. In terms of suffering and oppression it is of course a bitter thought that liberation has been delayed for so long, but it also has its advantages. Ours is a struggle with a very long memory, with many years of experience.

The memory of struggle is the memory of what we have learnt over the years. There have been mistakes and successes. There have been adaptations to new circumstances and many new insights. The history of the struggle has been a learning process. Very important lessons have been learnt from the mistakes of the past as well as the successes. There have been times when the past had been forgotten and had to be recovered. The young students who rose up in 1976 did not know about the struggles and campaigns of the 1950s. Many of them thought they were the first generation to rise up against the system. But they soon began to hear about the struggles of the past, often enough from their own parents who had been silent for years. One suspects that some of the very young and very militant youth of today still have much to learn from the experience of the past.

One of the ways in which the memory of the past is kept alive today is by commemorative events. The successes and turning points of our history are commemorated each year with celebrations on 16 June, Sharpeville Day, Women's Day, Freedom Charter Day and so forth. The struggle has its own alternative calendar. To forget the past is not only to lose contact with our roots but also to lose contact with the wealth of experience that has been gained over the years.

It is not possible or necessary for me to trace the whole history of the struggle in a book of this nature. But some examples of the memory of struggle might be helpful at this point.

To go right back, there is the memory of pre-colonial times. We do remember that there was a time before apartheid and before colonialism, when people were treated as people and when they worked the land and had enough to eat. There was a time when a person could walk tall, when the ancestors were respected and people lived in peace with one another. There were occasional disruptions of that peace as during the time of the *Mfecane* (or *Difaqane*) but on the whole they were times of peace and harmony – the time of *khotso*. That is a powerful memory. We can never again go back to those times but we can go forward to a new era of peace.

1912 is remembered as the beginning of an African national struggle. Until then each chiefdom or community had struggled alone against the colonisers. In 1910 the white colonisers came together to form the Union of South Africa. The black view of this is expressed by Albert Lutuli:

The Act of Union virtually handed the whole of South Africa over to a minority of whites, lock, stock and barrel. . . . As far as whites were concerned the matter was settled: they had become the owners of the new state. The members of other races who found themselves handed over officially, entirely without their consent, were the livestock which went with the estate, objects rather than subjects. (Quoted in Villa–Vicencio 1987: 90.)

In 1912 people from different African communities came together to petition for a place in the new country as persons rather than as objects. They were simply ignored.

The 1940s saw the beginning of the Africanist tradition or vision of the future, the realisation that incorporation into a European-dominated state would not bring true liberation to Africans. What was needed was a completely new society, a truly African society.

With the Congress Alliance and the Freedom Charter in 1955, we remember the beginnings of a united non-racial struggle. The Congress of the People brought together organisations or congresses of the African, Indian, 'Coloured' and white communities to declare that 'South Africa belongs to all who live in it'.

And so we could go on with the violent suppression of the nonviolent campaigns of the ANC and the PAC, their banning in 1960, the rise of the Black Consciousness movement, the uprising of 16 June 1976 and the subsequent development of widespread organisation, the trials, the martyrs, the massacres, the victories. But enough has been said to show how the struggle has changed over the years, adapted to new circumstances and developed new insights. This is a sign of hope for the future. The struggle in South Africa is not based upon a fixed and predetermined ideology that has been imposed upon people regardless of the circumstances. It is based upon the memory of the past and the lessons that have been learnt in and through the struggle itself. Our struggle is fluid, flexible and practical. It will continue to adapt itself to whatever the future brings.

The Struggle and Power

The singing and dancing, the speeches and slogans, the unity in action and the spirit of hope, the commitment and the courage, together with the memory of the past, have engendered in the people a deep sense of *power*. It finds its most emphatic expression in the clenched fist salute and the acclamation, *Amandla*!, with the response, *Ngawethu*! This frightens many whites and others who are outside of the struggle. It needs to be analysed and properly understood.

We have had occasion to talk about power and salvation and to distinguish between the abuse of power and the right use of power, between 'power over' and 'power with'. *Amandla* is decidedly 'power with' rather than 'power over'. The response *Ngawethu* makes this abundantly clear. It means 'power is ours, yours and mine'. In fact the acclamation and its response are not unlike the liturgical exchange: 'The Lord be with you / And also with you.' In other words the wish or entreaty is that power should be shared as in the slogan, 'Power to the people'. What we are dealing with, then, is not the power of domination and oppression but people's power.

Among other things this concept of power has deep African roots. In traditional African thinking, which still has an influence today and often enough, through the struggle, on people who do not have an African ancestry, everything in the world has its *umthunzi* or *seriti*. Literally the Nguni and the Sotho words mean shade or shadow, but the shade or shadow of a thing or a person is their dignity, their influence, their power. It is almost impossible to translate the concept into English but perhaps we come close to its meaning when we speak of the vital force of a thing or a person or a community, that is to say, its energy or power. People's power is the *umthunzi* or *seriti* of people working together in harmony for the good of all.

To those who can only think in terms of an authoritarian power that controls the selfishness of individuals in a society, people's power sounds like chaotic mob rule. In fact it is even feared that people's power might be the power of anger, hatred and revenge. For the sake of Christians who might be mistakenly concerned about these things and therefore unable to find God in the events of our time, we must say something about these fears.

People's power is not mob rule, it is another word for grassroots democracy. In any true democracy there are elected leaders who represent the people at every level of society and in all its institutions. When the Freedom Charter says, 'The people shall govern', it means quite obviously through elected or delegated representatives as the next sentence makes clear: 'Every man and woman shall have the right to vote and stand as a candidate for all bodies which make laws.' That is people's power.

The militancy of the struggle and its emphasis upon power are in no way an expression of hatred for whites. Why is it that so many Christian documents associate struggle and particularly class struggle with hatred? Is it because those who think this way feel that they are being attacked or struggled against and therefore hated? There is simply no evidence from the side of the struggle itself to warrant any such conclusion. People's power is not aimed against any particular people, it is aimed against a system that abuses its power. If anything is hated it is an inhuman system, not people. It is of course true that anyone would find it difficult to distinguish between a person as an individual human being and as the representative of a system, so as to love the sinner while hating the sin. But what must surely strike any Christian who has any experience of the struggle is the amazing absence or infrequency of hatred, bitterness and resentment in the midst of an angry determination to rid the country of this evil system.

One of the most persistent misconceptions about the struggle is that it is bent upon revenge. I can only imagine that this arises out of a projection onto others of one's own perverted feelings. As a white man once said to me: 'I am sure blacks want revenge; if I were black I would certainly want to take revenge for what whites had done to me.' Nothing could be further from the truth. There is no spirit of revenge in the struggle. It is bent upon setting right what is wrong and not upon imitating the spirit of the oppressor.

There is a quite extraordinary fear amongst some church people that the struggle will simply repeat the sins of the present oppressor and introduce new forms of oppression in a spirit of revenge. Let us be quite clear about the fact that in the ethics of the gospel there is no place for revenge. That is made abundantly clear in the New Testament. 'Never repay evil with evil . . . . never try to get revenge' (Rm 12: 17, 19). Instead of demanding 'an eye for an eye and a tooth for a tooth . . . . turn the other cheek . . . . and love your enemies' (Mt 5: 38–39, 44; compare Lk 6: 27–35; I Pet 2: 23). This principle is adhered to in the struggle just as much as it is adhered to in the Church – if not more so! But in the struggle it is never used as an excuse for apathy and weakness. The power of the people that is manifested in the struggle is indeed the power of God. There are individuals who sometimes misuse this power and imitate their oppressors, but whenever this happens we should see it as a betrayal of the spirit of the struggle.

People's power like the power of God is invincible. Nowhere is this more apparent than in the power of people who are willing to suffer and die for the liberation of others. Nothing can destroy such power. The attempt to destroy the power of Jesus by killing him was a failure. The attempts of the Roman Empire to destroy Christian faith by persecution and martyrdom were a failure. You can kill the body but you cannot kill the spirit. When a person is willing to die, he or she has nothing to lose. You can no longer tempt them, bribe them, fool them or threaten them. They are free and their captors are cornered.

In South Africa today the system has everything to lose and the struggle has nothing to lose. As Charles Villa–Vicencio puts it: 'Those who have suffered least are able to bear the least suffering and those who have most to lose are less inclined to lose everything than those who have already lost virtually everything' (SACC 1986a: 33). What the system is up against now is not 'flesh and blood' but the almighty power of God, because the struggle against the system is 'an unquenchable thirst for freedom' (Villa–Vicencio 1987: 92).

The Struggle and Violence

There can be no doubt that violence in any circumstances is a problem, not only for us as Christians but for anyone who has any feeling of moral responsibility. The reason for this is quite simple: *violence causes suffering*. However, we also know that in extreme circumstances, in order to prevent far worse violence or in order to put an end to an intolerable excess of suffering, some people may be called upon to resort to measures that cause a certain amount of suffering. The best example of this is the surgeon's knife. Surgery causes pain and suffering, but we regard it as justified when its purpose is to prevent far worse suffering and hardship. We could also cite the example of violence that is used in self-defence or in defence of others who are threatened by some far greater form of violence. In such circumstances we face the agonisingly difficult ethical question about when it has become necessary to impose some measure of suffering in order to prevent far worse suffering.

But the gospel is more than just a matter of ethics. Our concern in these chapters has been to read the signs of the times in our country. What is God saying to us through the particular violent conflict in which we find ourselves in South Africa today?

One way of introducing our answer to this question would be to try to imagine how Jesus would react to South Africans who condemn the struggle as godless and evil because of its violence. Taking into account the passionate concern and compassion that Jesus had for people, I can only conclude that Jesus would react by saying something like this: 'You hypocrites! You whited sepulchres! You brood of vipers and blind guides! Why do you rave about the speck in someone else's eye while there is this great beam of wood in your own eye? Why do you want to throw the first stone at these people while there is so much blood on your own hands?'

It is simply intolerable that a system which has been responsible for so much violence and bloodshed should self-righteously condemn a peace-loving people for now resorting to violence. I am not saying that there isn't a problem here. There is and we need to be very sensitive to it. But when the upholders of the system rant and rave about 'necklace murders' and refuse to talk to people until they give up all violence, we must know that we are dealing with downright hyprocrisy.

For those who rely upon the propaganda of the media for their information this may not be immediately obvious. Official newsreports on violence these days are extremely misleading. We are told that people are killed or houses petrol-bombed but we are seldom told who did it and whose side they were on. The general impression given is that some 'radical' black youths are going around killing people indiscriminately and that the police are trying very hard to stop them from doing so. But is that true? We ask this not in order to justify anyone but in order to find out what is really happening.

Because of the tight control over information it is not easy to find out what is going on in the townships today. Indeed some of you who read this book may know far more than I do about what is really happening. I could simply relate what I have seen myself or have been told, especially by priests and ministers who work in these areas; but I think it would be more helpful to quote from a scientific study made by the Unrest Monitoring Project of the Department of Town and Regional Planning at the University of Natal. While the study is limited to one province (Natal) and one period of time (1 January 1986 to 31 March 1987) and relies mostly on published reports of violence, its conclusions confirm what the people of the townships are saying.

What are the conclusions of this study? 'Quite clearly, the incidents of unrest are predominantly attacks on what are perceived to be progressive individuals by groups of people, often Inkatha supporters or conservative vigilantes. . . . The major initiators of unrest appeared to be Inkatha, the security forces and vigilantes. . . . In contrast to those initiating the unrest, people from youth groups, UDF and COSATU appear to be the major targets of the unrest. . . . Security forces, Inkatha and vigilantes were the targets in respectively only 8%, 9% and 3% of all incidents. . . . Inkatha initiated about seven times as many attacks on people than [*sic*] the youth did.' (*Ecunews* April 1987: 21, 24–26) And this is a study based upon the *reported* incidents of so-called 'unrest'!

If we are to read the signs of our times, what we must face is the reality of an exceptionally violent and *uneven* conflict between, on the one hand, the forces of apartheid with its massive military machine willing to kill anyone who gets in its way, and, on the other hand, millions of defenceless people who are demanding their rights peacefully and nonviolently, while an extremely small number use weapons of some kind. It is the story of David and Goliath writ large, and whoever said that God dissociated himself from David because he used the violence of a sling-shot!

It would be difficult to exaggerate the violence of the system. We have seen the barbarous excess of suffering that it causes – its institutional violence. We have seen how it brutalises whites as well as blacks. We have seen how it kills political activists directly or through its 'puppets'. On the other hand it would be equally difficult to exaggerate the nonviolence of the struggle. At least 90 per cent of the struggle at present is nonviolent – a few years ago I could have said 99 per cent. Our struggle in South Africa must rate as the most sustained, long-lasting, comprehensive and extensive use of nonviolent strategies in the history of human struggles. Somewhat to his surprise, the American protagonist of direct nonviolent action, Walter Wink, discovered this when he visited South Africa recently. He writes of his experience:

> When I pressed these same people [students] to identify the tactics that had proved most effective in the past two years, they produced a remarkably long list of nonviolent actions: labor strikes, slow-downs, sit-downs, stoppages, and stayaways; bus boycotts, consumer boycotts, and school boycotts; funeral demonstrations; non-cooperation with government appointed functionaries; non-payment of rent; violation of government bans on peaceful meetings; defiance of segregation orders on beaches. . . . This amounts to what is probably the largest grassroots eruption of diverse nonviolent strategies in a single struggle in human history (1987: 4).

What surprised Walter Wink even more and what he was quite unable to understand, was why 'these students, and many others we interviewed, both black and white, failed to identify these tactics as nonviolent and even bridled at the word' (1987: 4). Violence has a different meaning in South Africa. Violence tends to mean any strong and forceful uprising of the people whether weapons are used or not. Thus nonviolence tends to mean passive acquiescence or mere talking.

This unusual use of words is best illustrated by the way in which both the oppressor and the oppressed in South Africa might refer to the destruction of property, such as the burning down of a building, as violence! To complicate matters still further the system will report any such event as an act of violence on the part of the youth who did it and as an act of peacekeeping on the part of the police who killed some of the youth involved. Is this because property is more valuable than people? People can be killed at no great expense. Property might cost millions to replace.

I am not trying to imply that there is no violence against human beings on the part of some people in the struggle, I am simply trying to put things into perspective. We must now begin to look at some of the other things that might count as violence. For example, what are we to think of the Defence Committees? It seems that in some townships there are groups of young people who have taken up arms to defend themselves and others from attack by police or vigilantes. Frank Chikane tells of his dilemma when, after his house and family were attacked with petrol bombs and while he was preaching nonviolence, the community organised a group of armed youth committed to preserving his life and the lives of his family (Villa–Vicencio 1987: 303). Is that violence?

The fundamental question, of course, is not what counts as violence or as nonviolence; the fundamental question is who is the aggressor and who is the defender. Would anyone want to deny people the right to defend themselves from attack? Of course, the system maintains that it is defending South Africa from attack. By whom? We have no foreign enemies who would dare to attack us. Then why does South Africa need such a huge and sophisticated military machine? Because this has become the only way the system can subjugate the people of South Africa.

But what about the armed struggle? What about 'necklacing' and bombs in shopping centres? To understand the armed struggle we need to make a distinction between disciplined and undisciplined violence. The armed struggle is, or is supposed to be, an ordered and disciplined use of a measure of violence for the explicit purpose of putting an end to all violence. Moreover, the purpose of the armed struggle in South Africa is not to overthrow the present system by winning a military victory. That is totally out of the question. There is no way that a few guerilla fighters or even a large number of them could ever gain a military victory over the SADF. Those who think this could happen have not applied their minds to the matter. The purpose of the armed struggle is to add another form of pressure to the many forms of pressure that are being used to force the system to come to the negotiating table.

But the armed struggle has yet another purpose: to prevent chaotic, undisciplined and mindless violence. Mandela spelt this out at his trial when he explained why the ANC had decided that it was necessary to initiate an armed struggle alongside the nonviolent struggle. In his speech from the dock he said:

> As a result of government policy, violence by the African people had become inevitable and unless responsible leadership was given to canalise and control the feelings of our people, there would be outbreaks of terrorism which would produce an intensity of bitterness and hostility between the various races of this country which is not produced even by war (Extract from Court record of trial held in Pretoria from 15 October to 7 November 1962).

The ANC has managed to control possible outbursts of chaotic and undisciplined violence for many years, but it seems that now neither the ANC nor the 'legal' organisations of the people are able to do this in all cases. Perhaps this is because most of the leaders are in prison, detention or exile. In any case, court records show that at least some of the young people who planted bombs in shopping centres or on busy streets were not instructed to do so and even felt that they would be disciplined by the ANC for doing so. There is no evidence that the ANC or any of the people's organisations ever instructed the youth to 'necklace' anyone. (According to newspaper reports published after this was written, the ANC has now distanced itself from the practice of 'necklacing'.) Whatever the truth of the matter may be, this kind of chaotic and undisciplined violence does not accord with the spirit of the struggle. One can understand why and how it happens, but, apart from any ethical considerations, I cannot see how it really promotes the struggle and *I cannot find God in it*.

Finally, in order to understand the significance of this reality, it needs to be made quite clear that the system is not only the source and origin of all this suffering and violence, but its upholders and leaders are the only ones who could stop it all tomorrow. All they have to do is release all political prisoners, unban political organisations and go to the negotiating table to draw up a truly democratic constitution. As long as they refuse to do this, they must be held responsible for the perpetuation and escalation of violence on all sides.

The Struggle and Revolution

The word 'revolution' means such different things to different people. In its 150 years as a nation, Bolivia is said to have had more than 150 revolutions. I was once in Peru during a revolution but I didn't even notice that anything was happening. One general had simply taken over from another. In the USA 'the glorious American Revolution' is celebrated every year while many Americans rant and rave about the revolutionary government of Nicaragua. We would all be worried about the prospect of something like the mob violence and the reign of terror that are associated with the French Revolution of 1789, but the French celebrate that revolution every year on Bastille Day. Most of us were brought up to think of the Industrial Revolution in Britain as one of the great achievements of human progress, but what about the incredible violence it did to men, women and children in the mines and the factories? And then, of course, there was the Russian Revolution – glorified by some and totally condemned by others.

In the final analysis a person's attitude to revolution does not seem to be determined by the amount of violence involved or by the total lack of violence as in a bloodless coup, but by *whether one approves of the change or not.* Those who disapprove of any kind of anti-capitalism, socialism and especially Communism would disapprove of any revolution, violent or not, that moves in that direction, and approve of any revolution, violent or not, that moves in the other direction – and vice versa for those who oppose capitalism. The problem is not revolution but the nature of the change envisaged by the revolution.

In general the word 'revolution' means a radical change, a change in the basic structures of a society or an institution. As such it must be clearly distinguished from the word 'reform', which means changes that merely adapt the present structures to changing circumstances. P. W. Botha in South Africa and Gorbachev in Russia are not revolutionising their respective systems but reforming them. In the time of Jesus the great reformers of the system were the Pharisees. They were trying very seriously to adapt the system to changing circumstances. On the other hand the kind of change that Jesus had in mind can only be described as revolutionary. He and his disciples 'turned the world upside down' (Acts 17: 6).

A revolutionary change does not necessarily involve violence. Much depends upon whether the system resists this kind of change with violence or not. Nor does revolutionary change always happen by means of a military victory. In any case, as we have already seen, this is totally impossible in a country like South Africa. Revolutionary change could only come about here, as in Zimbabwe, through pressure that brings the system to the negotiating table so as to agree to a wholly new constitution. You could call this pressure revolutionary because its aim is to dismantle apartheid and replace it with true democracy. In that case the revolution is the process of struggle that is now going on and not some future coup that would put the ANC in power (Stadler 1987: 7–8, 33). If the ANC ever does come to power it would have to be through a general election. It is this election that will produce a revolutionary change in South Africa, as it did in Zimbabwe and as it will in Namibia.

The system now knows this and that is why it is trying to avoid a one-person-one-vote election at all costs. It is also interesting to note that the propaganda of the system speaks about the pressure from below as a 'revolutionary onslaught' and the aspirations of the people as a 'climate of revolution'. But in the struggle itself, although the word 'revolution' is now being used more frequently, the sacred word that describes what the people are doing is still the word 'struggle'.

The Struggle and Communism

But what is the relationship between the struggle and Communism? Numerous Christians in South Africa are asking that question and demanding a straight answer. But how can you give a straight answer with a crooked word? 'Communism' as a word is even more slippery than 'violence' or 'revolution'. The extreme right might call P. W. Botha a communist. If Communism means a dictatorial and authoritarian regime which oppresses the people, then we might say that the present regime is communist, although that is clearly not what the extreme right-wingers would mean. Or is Communism simply a form of militant atheism that persecutes religion? Or are we talking about a system that denies its citizens the right to any private ownership? We might agree that Russia and the Eastern European nations are communist, but is Zimbabwe to be regarded as a communist country? It is clearly impossible to say anything about Communism without defining exactly what you mean.

If Communism is defined as an undemocratic, totalitarian and dictatorial system that deprives people of their rights, then the struggle is without doubt anti-communist. We have seen that what the people are striving for is democracy. They are not about to exchange one form of oppression for another. Nor are they likely to be fooled by any person or any ideology that is not thoroughly democratic. The people have suffered too much for too long.

On the other hand if you define Communism very broadly as anti-capitalism, then one must say that the struggle is definitely moving in that direction. In itself that should not be very surprising. Capitalism today is coming under heavy fire from many quarters throughout the world and not least of all from Christians. What is becoming clearer and clearer today is that, as the Bible says, 'the love of money is the root of all evil' (I Tim 6: 10). The social encyclicals of the Catholic Church are becoming increasingly critical of capitalism and although there is still a kind of tacit alliance between the Church and capitalism, more and more Christians in the most surprising places would like to see the Church dissociating itself completely from this ideology.

However, what is much more pertinent to our struggle for

freedom in South Africa is that apartheid is regarded as a total system, a form of racial capitalism. The capitalist 'bosses' are seen to be just as much part of the system as the leaders of the National Party. It is frequently said that if it were possible to remove all racism and leave the system of 'free enterprise' unaltered, the people would continue to suffer poverty and degradation. There has to be some way of redistributing the wealth of the country. The people are very aware of that. As the Freedom Charter declares: 'The people shall share in the country's wealth. The mineral wealth beneath the soil, the banks and monopoly industry shall be transferred to the ownership of the people as a whole; *all other industries and trade* shall be controlled to assist the well-being of the people; all people shall have equal right *to trade* where they choose, to manufacture and to enter all trades, crafts and professions' [emphasis added].

Strictly speaking, this is not Communism. It isn't even socialism, although the implicit nationalisation of mines, banks and monopoly industry and the control of other industries is what one may call a 'socialist orientation' (Suttner and Cronin 1985: 143–146). I suppose some people would call it a mixed economy. What is certain is that it is anti-capitalist, and this is indeed the general orientation of the struggle at the present stage. The people are not afraid of socialism but they know what they want and what they don't want. There is a kind of ideology here but it is not a fixed, predetermined and dogmatic ideology. In politics it is impossible (and quite unnecessary) to avoid all ideology. What matters is that the ideology is not absolutised but remains open and practical (Leatt 1986: 281–4, 301).

Of course, in the end the type of society we shall have and the way the economy is to be structured will be decided by a general election. What most of the people will be concerned about is that we continue to generate wealth, that this is not done at the expense of a genuinely human life and that the wealth is evenly distributed. The political parties that contest the election will have to explain how they plan to achieve this. Voting in that case will not be along racial lines.

This brings us back to the question of whether you can do

away with apartheid or racism and leave the capitalist system intact. Once you allow everyone to vote, you will have a majority of working-class voters and *they* are not going to vote for more capitalist exploitation.

Finally, if Communism means an atheistic philosophy that rejects all belief in God and persecutes religion, then the struggle in South Africa is not communist. However, the matter is not as simple as that. While the majority of the people involved in the struggle are believers (Christian, Muslim, Jewish or Hindu) and some of them are very staunch believers, there is a visible shift away from any regular attendance at church services, especially where black youth are concerned. Most church services these days are attended by women, children and elderly men. The African Independent Churches can still attract middle-aged men but the youth are definitely drifting away from all the churches. I do not know whether this is also true of the mosque, the synagogue and the Hindu temple but any Christian priest or minister (with some remarkable exceptions) will tell you that the youth no longer come to church.

Recently I was discussing this with a group of Catholic priests. One of them suggested that the youth were being influenced by 'communist agitators' who told them not to go to church. The others disagreed. 'It is our fault,' they confessed. 'Our churches are simply irrelevant to the concerns of the youth.' Several of these priests had been told by the youth that they stopped coming to church because during the services not even once had there been any mention of the struggle. Who is betraying God here?

The system professes belief in God. But what does that mean in practice? Is it not possible to say that we also have practical atheists, that is to say, people who say they believe in God but deny that in practice? And do we not find them on the side of the system rather than on the side of the struggle. Then there are the theoretical atheists who say they no longer believe in God or those who simply don't go to church anymore. What if their practice is closer to the practice of Jesus?

The God of the Bible cannot possibly be identified with capitalism. Nor can every alternative to capitalism be regarded as atheistic. If the struggle is moving away from capitalism it is not moving away from the worship of God, it is moving away from the worship of Mammon.

The Practice of Faith

Faith is not primarily a way of thinking, it is a way of living. We talk about the practice of our faith, but in a very important sense this practice *is* our faith. It implies certain convictions or beliefs. What people really believe cannot be ascertained, with any degree of certainty, by listening to what they profess to believe. You can see without doubt what they really believe by observing what they do in practice. You judge a tree by its fruit. Faith, then, is a particular kind of practice.

When Jesus found faith in the lost sheep of Israel and even in pagans, he found it in the way they acted or reacted to him or to his message or to the situation in which they found themselves – illness, poverty, oppression. He did not have to ask them to make an explicit profession of faith in God or to recite some kind of creed. He did not expect them to confess that he was the Messiah or Son of God before he could declare that their faith had saved them. In the parable of the last judgment (Mt 25: 31–46) people are judged on their practice and not on their profession of faith. 'Lord, when did we see you hungry?' They did not realise that when they fed the hungry they were doing this to God. But they did it and that is what counts.

What Jesus found in the scribes and the Pharisees was not faith but 'works'. These 'works', as Paul calls them, were observances, that is to say, the practices of the law or the system of purity and holiness. For Jesus (and for Paul) what these 'works' proved conclusively was that the scribes and the Pharisees believed in the law rather than in God. They had the 'works of the law' but they had no real faith in God. That is why Paul could conclude that we are not saved or justified by the 'works of the law' but by faith.

On the other hand James is equally emphatic about the fact that faith without 'works' is dead (2: 14–26). But what James is referring to is not the 'works of the law' but 'the works of faith' or what we would call the practice of faith. He makes this abundantly clear by the example he gives of 'works': helping those who are in need of clothes or who do not have enough food to live on (2: 15–16). 'Pure, unspoilt religion', says James, 'is this: coming to the help of orphans and widows when they need it' (1: 27). This is the practice that proves conclusively that one has faith in God: 'I will prove to you that I have faith by showing you my works' (2: 18).

The faith is there if the practice is there, even if that faith is not made explicit in a profession of belief in Jesus Christ. The conditions for such a profession of belief are there in the 'works of faith'.

I hope that by now I have made it quite clear that the practice of the struggle is the practice of faith even when it is not accompanied by an explicit profession of faith in God or in Jesus Christ. In reading the signs of our times in South Africa today we have been able to discover what Jesus discovered in his time: signs of hope. God is at work in the struggle. The 'works of faith' are there and the conditions for an explicit belief in the good news can be found in the spirit, the commitment, the courage and the hope of the struggle. As Steve Biko once expressed it: 'The revolutionary seeks to restore faith in life amongst all citizens of his [or her] country, to remove imaginary fears and to heighten concern for the plight of the people' (quoted in Villa–Vicencio 1987: 93). If this is what is happening, then the Spirit of God, the Holy Spirit, is moving quietly and invisibly in the struggle, like the yeast in the dough.

Nor can one try to deny this by pointing to the flaws, the faults, the mistakes or even the sins of the struggle. As we have said before, the struggle is not perfect. But that does not negate the presence in the struggle of a practice that is Christian in spirit and far closer to the practice of Jesus than the practice one finds in Christian circles outside of the struggle. I do not wish to deny that the practice of Jesus can be found in the Church too. *But the Church has never claimed that its practice was perfect. If* the Church points fingers at the struggle and *if* it denies that the practice of Jesus can be found there because of the faults of some people, the Church is being shamelessly hypocritical.

All we need to do is read Jesus' own account in Luke 4: 18 of the practice he felt called to, and then ask ourselves where this practice is being lived most conspicuously in South Africa today:

> He has sent me to give good news to the poor, to proclaim liberty to captives, and to the blind new sight, to set the downtrodden free, to proclaim the Lord's year of favour.

9
The Good News of Salvation

The reading of the signs of our time enables us to see not only the kind of time we are living in and the degree of similarity it has with the time of Jesus, but also, and more important, the reading of the signs enables us to see the uniqueness and singularity of what God is doing in our country today. This would be the gospel or good news for us.

On the basis of our investigations so far, it is now possible to put together a *report* on what God is doing and saying. It will be necessary to follow this up with some checks and controls in order to make quite sure that our reporting of the good news tallies with the Christian tradition about salvation and about the way God acts and works. We shall then be in a position to spell out the challenge of the good news for South African Christians in general (Chapter 10) and for the Church as an institution (Chapter 11).

The Good News

God is angry about the intolerable suffering that is being inflicted upon so many human beings by a system which God abhors and detests. It is God who is being crucified and sinned against. The tragic blindness, hypocrisy and apathy of some people must be a cause of great sadness and disappointment to God. Consequently, in South Africa today, God is exceptionally busy laying the foundations for a new future. As of old, we are now witnessing the wonderful works of God as we see good coming out of evil and life out of death. The powers of evil are being outwitted by God and used for purposes they would never have dreamt of. With an extraordinary sense of urgency and a life-and-death seriousness, God is preparing the conditions for salvation and bringing people together in solidarity and commitment, fearlessness and hopefulness, excitement, celebration and power. At the same time God is shaking up the white establishment in order to give new sight to the blind. Something miraculously new is happening in South Africa today and God is behind it working for the good of all. 'I know the plans I have in mind for you – it is Yahweh who speaks – plans for peace, not disaster, reserving a future full of hope for you' (Jer 29: 11).

We can therefore say of our time, as Jesus and some of the prophets before him said of their time:

> The time has come;
> the day of salvation is near.

That is the good news.

Such direct God-talk frightens some people. It makes them think of the way the Nazis used God to promote their cause or the way the Voortrekkers saw themselves as God's chosen people. It is reminiscent of the way some so-called 'sects' claim that God is with them and everyone else is damned, or the way some Christians seem to imagine that they have a hotline to God who speaks to them every day. However, such manifest abuses of God's name should not lead us to treat God as abstract and remote. To treat God as absent from human affairs because of the danger of identifying him with some unworthy cause amounts to a denial of *everything* that we read in the Bible. The fact that in recent times some people have been mistaken about where God is to be found and what God is doing, does not invalidate the very vivid God-talk that characterises the whole Bible. Nor is there any suggestion in the Bible itself or in the Christian tradition that after the last events recorded in the Bible God went into retirement.

God is not dead. Those who treat God as an abstract entity who is absent from human affairs, do so in order to close their ears to the good news about what God is doing and saying in South Africa today.

The Day is Near

I have a very vivid childhood memory of people singing and

dancing on the streets of Cape Town. It was the end of the Second World War. They called it VE (Victory in Europe) Day. Europe had been finally liberated from the scourge of Hitler and the Nazis. Cape Town was a long way from Europe, but we had felt the effects of this war and now there was the most remarkable outburst of rejoicing, merriment and relief. It was the first time that I had ever seen such spontaneous singing and dancing on our streets. I can just imagine what it must have been like on the streets of Europe. But even that would not be comparable to the superabundance of joy and happiness that will bring millions of people out onto the streets dancing and singing inexhaustibly when South Africa's day of liberation comes.

The sheer relief! No more apartheid! Freedom at last! Amandla!

The people of South Africa, on the whole, are convinced that victory is certain. This is what is preached not only at political rallies but also in churches and mosques. Archbishop Tutu brings this certainty into most of his sermons (Tutu 1983: 11, 13, 44, 56, 66, 72, 85, 87, 104, 121). Speaking on the topic of 'Evangelism in Situations of Deprivation and Extremity' at a recent conference, Wesley Mabusa makes the same point: 'Not even Reagan with all his American might and dollars, or the present Government with its armies, vigilantes, deceits, dirty tricks and stubbornness can ever stop this country from getting justice for all in a united and new South Africa. This should be . . . the message of the Church of God in situations of deprivation and extremity' (SACC 1986b: 96). This is indeed the good news that is being preached in an ever-increasing number of church communities.

Victory is certain but can we really say that it is *near*? The struggle has been going on for such a long time. Is it not likely to drag on for many more years?

When Jesus announced that the rule of God was near, he did not mean that he knew the date or the hour. In fact he denied quite emphatically that he or anyone else could calculate the date or the hour (Mk 13: 32 par). As we pointed out in Chapter 6, the nearness of the day of salvation is not a matter of chronological time or calendar dates. It is a statement about the quality and uniqueness of the time in which we are living. Our time is overshadowed by a forthcoming victory. Our time is qualified, determined and shaped by the imminence of liberation. Our time is different and special because things are coming to a head in a way in which they have not done before. Revolutionary changes could break in upon us at any time. We don't know the date or the hour, but salvation is in the air. You can feel it. It is near. All the signs are there. 'As soon as you see the trees bud, you *know* that summer is near' (Lk 21: 31).

Things could go wrong. Something unexpected could happen. There could be a major setback and everything could be delayed. But there is no indication of that at present. We live in a time of unprecedented expectancy and hope. And that is why we say: 'The time is now.' The day of liberation is *near* but the time or *kairos* is *now*.

Our Kairos

South African theology in recent years has been dominated by the debate on the Kairos Document. It shook the foundations by announcing that South Africa's *kairos* had come. As the document explains the *kairos* is 'the moment of truth . . . the moment of grace and opportunity, the favourable time in which God issues a challenge to decisive action' (1986: 1).

The limitation of the Kairos Document, however, is that it does not provide us with sufficiently plausible reasons for believing that our time is a *kairos*. There can be no doubt that our time is experienced by many Christians as a *kairos*, but the document does not explain why, or at least not adequately and rigorously. The impression is given that our time is a *kairos* simply because there is a serious crisis and conflict in the country and especially because the Church is in crisis on account of the divisions in its ranks. That is true, but it is not the fundamental reason why our time is experienced as a *kairos*.

The *kairos* or moment of truth has come *because the day of liberation is near*. Throughout the Bible a *kairos* is determined and constituted by the imminence or nearness of an *eschaton* (Nolan 1976: 86; and in *Missionalia* 1987: 61ff).

An *eschaton*, as we explained in Chapter 6, is a future event that is in some way final, definitive and determinative for our present time. In other words it is final and ultimate in relation to our time, our sins, our problems, our need for salvation. As we have seen, in the Bible the *eschaton* or day of salvation or rule of God does not refer (at least not exclusively) to the last day of all time, for all people and in relation to all struggles for liberation. It refers first and foremost to the particular victory of God that is demanded and required at this time and in this particular place, the victory of God that is now imminent.

Our *eschaton*, then, is the day of liberation which is already in the air, which we are already celebrating with singing and dancing, and that gives our time its very special character as a *kairos*, as 'the Lord's year of favour' (Lk 4: 18).

What are we saying then? Are we saying that the good news of salvation in South Africa is simply the struggle for political liberation under another name? To say that would be to make the mistake of what theologians call reductionism – reducing the gospel to nothing more than. . . . There *is* a difference between salvation and liberation.

Salvation and Liberation

The final document of the meeting of Latin American bishops at Puebla in 1978 acknowledges that the clarification of the relationship between historical liberations and salvation in Jesus Christ is 'the great challenge, the original imperative of this divine hour' (*Puebla*, 90, 320, 774, 864). Volumes and volumes have been written about this question and a range of different models for understanding the relationship have been proposed (see for example L. and C. Boff 1984: 56–64). I am tempted to give an outline of all the different theories, to say why I think each of them is inadequate, and to end up with my own theory. This is the way that academic theology usually proceeds, but I am not at all sure that most of my readers would find it particularly helpful. Let me simply say what seems clear to me on the basis of our experience, our reflections and our study in South Africa and then comment briefly on some of the theological theories.

In South Africa we have the memory, and for some the present reality, of traditional African religion. One of the most striking features of the African concept of religion, in comparison with Western Christianity, is that there is no separation whatsoever between religion and life. There is no 'sacred' apart from the 'secular'. 'All aspects of life are spheres of divine activity in all its intensity – and one ignores this at one's own risk', says Setiloane (Mosala 1986a: 77). 'Salvation', he continues, 'is a situation, in which harmony and peace prevail in community life' (82). The memory of a time when there was no 'apartheid' between religion and life has not been lost.

Moreover in South Africa there is the awareness that the system, for its own purposes, has tried to drive a wedge between religion and politics, or, more accurately, between religion and the politics of resistance. Any attempt to find divine salvation in political liberation is rejected as heresy, liberation theology and Communism. It is in reaction to this that many Christians (and people of other faiths) try to integrate religion and politics.

For a people who have been told to wait for 'pie in the sky when you die' or to wait for the coming of God's kingdom, it has become imperative to assert that *we* are building the kingdom now. The youth are no longer clear about where God fits into this, but they are quite convinced that if *they* don't do it, nothing will ever change.

It is against this background that we have to ask about the relationship between salvation and liberation. Salvation says something more than liberation. Everyone is agreed about that. The problem is to define what this 'something more' might be. It seems clear to me that it cannot mean something more of the same thing. Salvation cannot simply mean more liberation, extra liberation, additional liberation. In other words the relation between salvation and liberation cannot be a relation of total and partial, as is so often maintained by theologians. The 'something more', as far as I can see, must be another dimension, another angle or perspective on the same concrete reality. This I call the religious dimension. Simply speaking, it means introducing God into the picture. 'The eye of faith . . . discerns the divine dimension in the ordinary events of human history' (Tutu 1983: 59).

We shall have to try to indicate what that means in practice (on the basis of what we have already pointed out in this book), but I should like to state now that introducing God into the picture *makes a world of difference*, not only to our picture but also to our practice. However, this difference, as we have said, is by no means, in theory or in practice, an extra dose of liberation.

What we need to be clear about from the beginning is that the comparison we are making between salvation and liberation is a comparison between two ideas or notions. This comes across clearly in the following statement from a papal encyclical: 'The Church links human liberation and salvation in Jesus Christ but she never identifies them because she knows . . . that not every *notion of liberation* is necessarily consistent and compatible with the vision of the gospel . . .' (*Evangelii Nuntiandi* 35, emphasis added). This is perfectly true but it is also true that not every notion of salvation in Church circles is necessarily consistent and compatible with the vision of the gospel either. Both salvation and liberation might be adequately or inadequately conceived. That is not the difference between them.

The same is true of the practice of salvation and the practice of liberation. Here it is particularly clear that one cannot talk about salvation as total and liberation as partial. The practice of salvation has very frequently been partial and limited, especially when it was reduced in practice to the salvation of souls or when it ignores the liberation of women. On the other hand, the practice of liberation can also be partial and limited, for example, when it leaves out the need for liberation from personal guilt. If we add the guilt-factor to liberation we don't thereby turn it into salvation. Both salvation and liberation can be partial and limited in practice and both should be striving to be total.

The difference between salvation and liberation is frequently thought of in terms of time. Liberation is seen as temporal and salvation as eternal. Liberation is confined to a particular time and a particular place whereas salvation encompasses all times and all places including the last day and the afterlife. I do not want to deny this, but I should like to point out that the real difference here has nothing to do with the idea that one can 'universalise' the concept of salvation but cannot 'universalise' the concept of liberation. As we have seen, salvation in the Bible refers to a particular time and a particular place: the day of salvation. As Leonardo Boff rightly points out, this tendency to 'universalise' and 'dehistoricise' salvation 'runs the risk of evaporating in pure phraseology, in words without substance' (L. and C. Boff 1984: 44). Moreover there is no reason why someone should not do the same with the notion of liberation, 'universalise' and 'dehistoricise' it. That would not turn liberation into salvation.

The difference arises when we introduce God into the picture and this does not have the effect of 'totalising' or 'universalising' the picture. It enables us to see our concrete reality *in terms of transcendence*.

Transcendence

There are few words that mystify the situation more thoroughly than the word 'transcendence'. I hesitate to use it. But I can find no better word to describe the experience and practice of bringing God into the picture.

Transcendence means going beyond something, going beyond some boundary or limitation. This is a very concrete, everyday experience. Love, for example, is an experience of transcendence because it means going beyond myself and my own selfish interests. The experience of hope is the experience of reaching out beyond the status quo, the given situation (Soelle 1984: 160). The experience of being freed or liberated from something that was closed, fixed, frozen or narrow is an experience of transcendence. The struggle itself is an experience of going beyond the straitjacket of the system with its blindness, alienation, separation, racism, individualism and apathy.

All these experiences of going beyond some limitation or restriction are experiences of God, because God *is* transcendence. God's voice is the call of transcendence that challenges us to go further, to do more, to try harder, to change our lives, to venture out into new areas and into the unknown. It is a liberating experience. God is out there calling us to move beyond the system, beyond sin, beyond suffering, beyond our narrow and limited ideas of what is possible. The trouble with the Pharisees, like the upholders of the system today, is that they want to lock God up within the confines of their system. But God is beyond the system, out there with those who suffer under the system, as the almighty power of transcendence.

Another of the great temptations of religion is to turn transcendence into a thing, an object, another parallel world, the world of the supernatural. It then becomes detached from this world and develops a separate existence of its own on the other side of death or beyond history. Transcendence is not a fixed, definable thing. It is more like an horizon. We are always moving towards it but we never reach it because 'it moves along with us and invites us to press further ahead' (Moltmann 1967: 125). When we say that the horizon 'invites us', we are speaking about it in personal terms. Although the horizon is not a thing, a world or a person, we can speak about it in such terms provided we do not become too literal-minded. The horizon does not literally 'move' or 'invite'.

In a similar way, although transcendence is not a thing or another world or a person, the most revealing way to speak about it is in personal terms – as God. God is not *a* person alongside of other persons. Any theologian will tell you that (see, for example, Schillebeeckx 1979: 626ff). If we talk about God in personal terms rather than in terms of abstract nouns, then it is because transcendence is above all the experience of becoming a person or subject rather than being an object. We have seen how this is happening in South Africa today. Those whom the system treats as mere objects or labour units are becoming human persons who want to be subjects of their own history. This is an experience of transcendence. It is God calling us to personhood, to *ubuntu*.

Transcendence, we said, means going beyond something. However, we cannot go beyond everything at the same time. We cannot transcend boundaries that we have not even reached yet. At this moment of time we are called to transcend the particular sinfulness and evil that dominate life in South Africa today, and we are called to do this personally and collectively.

When we reach that goal we shall have other boundaries and limitations to break through. But *at this moment* our horizon, our *eschaton*, our salvation is the liberation of South Africa from this particular system of slavery and sin.

What the concept of salvation enables us to do is to discover the transcendence that is in our midst and to keep alive the call to transcendence both now and in the future. When we introduce God into the picture, our minds and our hearts are opened up to think not only beyond ourselves and beyond the system, but also beyond the present limitations of the struggle and beyond death and beyond history at the same time as we are deeply involved in the urgency of this moment and of our present horizons. Faith is the attitude of mind and heart that will enable us to cross those other bridges when we come to them.

Dorothee Soelle sums it up well: 'The dignity of human beings is the capacity for going beyond what exists. We are only truly alive when we transcend' (1981: 68).

God's Grace

Introducing God or transcendence into our picture of what is happening in South Africa today provides us with yet another insight: the reality of what we call 'grace'. Grace is a religious word. It means a gift from God. When we experience liberation as salvation, we experience it as God's grace. But what does that mean?

We know that the concept of God's grace has been misinterpreted to mean that we can do nothing about our own salvation but sit back, pray and wait for God to send it to us as a free gift. If we could do anything about it ourselves, salvation would no longer be a grace or free gift. But that is a distortion of the meaning of grace.

A genuine gift is something that comes to us from outside of any system of buying and selling, bartering or bargaining, paying the price, duties and obligations or any other form of exchange. A genuine gift has no strings attached. It is free. In other words it *transcends* all the restrictions of an exchange of one thing for another. It does not arise out of the system and there is no place for it within the system. In fact a totally free gift, a totally voluntary giving, contradicts the system and transcends it.

Now this is precisely how we experience the struggle. It is a grace. The struggle for liberation is a completely voluntary undertaking. It has nothing to do with the obligations and duties of the system. It transcends all the rewards and benefits that are offered to us in exchange for conformity. In comparison with the system, the struggle is experienced as free, voluntary and spontaneous. It is true that the struggle challenges us and is extremely demanding, but it does not bribe us, buy us or coerce us into conformity. When we enter into the struggle there are no strings attached and the liberation it offers us is free.

Grace is not a thing alongside of other things. It is not a commodity or a private possession that can be bought or sold. But when things come to us in life freely and spontaneously we say they have the *quality* of grace or a gift. There is a well-worn cliché that nevertheless expresses a profound truth: 'The best things in life are free.' That is the quality of things we are talking about. Thus love is a grace. The hope, the commitment, the solidarity, the courage and the discipline we find in the struggle cannot be bought with money or with any other form of exchange. They are free. Above all, our particular *kairos* in South Africa today is a grace. As the Kairos Document declares, 'the *kairos* [is] the moment of grace' (1986: 1). I would interpret this to mean that 'a *kairos* is a privileged time that not everyone is called to witness or to participate in' (Mosala 1986a: 134). That is why Jesus could say of his *kairos*: 'Happy the eyes that see what you see, for I tell you many prophets and kings wanted to see what you see and never saw it' (Lk 10: 23-24). There is a sense in which we are fortunate to be living in these times.

This is the experience that the Christian tradition calls grace. It is a sign of the presence of God, the giver of all grace. We can be grateful and thank God for it, but that would not be the end of the story. The grace of God challenges us to transcend our present limitations and to reach out to greater heights. Every moment of transcendence will be another grace. To live in privileged times like ours is to be faced with gigantic challenges.

Salvation from Below

To say that salvation comes from God is to say that salvation comes *from below*. We are accustomed to thinking about God as somewhere above, and of salvation as coming from above. The Bible does sometimes speak about God and salvation in this way, but the idea of God being above us is easily manipulated by the system in a way that is unbiblical. What we have above us are 'bosses' and oppressors. If God is further above them, then he is the 'big boss' and the super-oppressor. This is indeed how most people think of God, but it is not the God of the Bible.

Why is it that in Western Christianity so much emphasis has been laid upon God as a king or monarch with royal majesty and absolute sovereignty? This God has been made in the image and likeness of the kings and emperors of Europe. This God may indeed be similar to the God who was made in the image and likeness of King Solomon, but it is not Yahweh, the God of the Hebrew slaves or the Father of Jesus or the Crucified One. As Metz puts it: 'The God of the Christian gospel is, after all, not a God of conquerors, but a God of slaves' (1980: 71).

In our search for God, throughout this book, we have discovered someone who is down below with the crucified people of South Africa in their struggle for liberation. God is outside of the system and beyond the cycle of sin and guilt, amongst those who are sinned against. It is from there that we must expect divine salvation to come.

However there is a sense in which God may be said to be above. The almighty power of God is above all other powers and authorities, not because it is *like* the powers and authorities in their royalty, majesty and sovereignty, but because, like people's power, God's power is above and beyond all that. In fact it is something better or superior, although in the present order of things it seems to be below. One day 'the first shall be last and the last first' (Mk 10: 31 parr) and God shall rule from above, albeit in a very different way from those who rule from above today.

Something similar needs to be said about Jesus. Too many Christians in our country have made him into an idol. He has become for them a kind of dictator who makes his followers into servile dependants and passive objects who escape all responsibility by leaving him to do everything for them (Soelle 1981: 85-86). That is not the Jesus of the gospels who washed the feet of his disciples, suffered and died in disgrace on a Roman cross, challenged his disciples to read the signs of the times and to follow him.

Jesus saves us not by doing everything for us but by challenging us to imitate his practice. We meet the living Christ and accept Jesus as our personal saviour when we recognise the *practice of Jesus* in people and especially in the struggle, and are challenged by it. A Jesus who doesn't challenge us is a dead or lifeless idol.

Nor should we be surprised to find the practice of Jesus *in* the struggle and *outside* of the system. It is by no means perfect, but it is there, because 'Jesus suffered outside the gate' (Heb 13: 13). If we want to share his perspective on the world, then we must 'go to him outside the camp and bear the abuse he endured' (Heb 13: 16), in order to view the world from below. As Bonhoeffer discovered: 'There remains an experience of incomparable value. We have for once learnt to see the great events of world history from below, from the perspective of the outcast, the suspects, the maltreated, the powerless, the oppressed, the reviled' (quoted in English by T. R. Peters in *Concilium* 1979: 80).

Salvation comes from the cross and not from some heavenly throne. God and Jesus are transcendent not because they are on the pinnacle of the system but because they are below or beyond the system.

It is hardly necessary to point out that this is good news for the poor. The challenge that it presents to the rich and the not-so-rich, and indeed in another way to the poor themselves, will have to be spelt out in the next chapter.

'Something More'

Our conclusion, then, is that the good news of salvation from sin in South Africa today is *not* just another way of talking about the struggle which adds nothing new and makes very little difference to the struggle itself. It makes a world of difference.

Not because it necessarily adds some new forms of liberation or because it provides us with some extra scientific knowledge or novel explanations of what is happening. The purpose of the gospel is not to explain the world but to save it. The difference has nothing to do with the *quantity* of what we know or do but with the *quality* of it. A totally new quality is achieved when we *name* the divine dimension in human events.

When we introduce God into the picture, or rather when we discover God already there in our world, it takes our breath away. When we begin to see God as the one who is sinned against and crucified in South Africa today, it makes us shudder. We are struck with the full impact of the crisis, the conflict, the struggle and the day of liberation, when we see them as the wonderful works of God. We appreciate what is happening more fully, when we experience it as grace. Understanding the events of our time in terms of transcendence makes them much more challenging. We feel confirmed, strengthened and overcome with a sense of awe and reverence. In short, the religious dimension engages the whole of one's being – body, soul, mind, will, heart and feelings.

We are trying to pinpoint the *difference* between a religious and a non-religious experience of life in South Africa today. But in the concrete we do not experience only the element of difference, we experience life as a whole in a religious manner. We experience everything that everyone else experiences in the struggle, only we experience it in a religious or Christian mode.

A simple example from the gospels might serve to illustrate this. In the parable of the sheep and the goats (Mt 25: 31-36), those whose practice included feeding the hungry, giving drink to the thirsty and clothes to the naked, and visiting the sick and the imprisoned, are told that whenever they did these things, they did them to God. They are surprised. They had not realised this. But they got their reward just the same. However, the reader of the parable now realises where God fits into the picture. He or she will now start doing the same things or continue doing the same things (or whatever is required by their circumstances), but they will do them with a new sense of the all-importance, transcendent value and religious meaning of what they are doing or should be doing.

Last but not least, there is a form of liberation that, in some cases and perhaps in most cases, can *only* be achieved by a correct or more accurate preaching of the gospel. And that is liberation from the alienation of false religion. Much of this book has been taken up with an attempt to liberate people from the alienating forms of religion or Christianity that are an obstacle in the way of God's plans and purposes for peace in South Africa. This, after all, is one of the most important things that Jesus has taught us to do. He tried to liberate the scribes and the Pharisees and all who were influenced by them from an alienating and false form of religion. And what world-shaking consequences that had!

The gospel or good news in South Africa today is the religious meaning or significance of what is happening in our country. We are experiencing a divine visitation. God in Christ, who is being crucified by the system, is rising up from below in a powerful struggle against the powers of evil that will end soon in victory and peace. God is doing a new thing. We are experiencing a very special moment of grace because the boundaries, limitations and chains of the past are being transcended, and now we have, as never before, the promise of a day of salvation when the evils of apartheid will have been transcended and overcome. The time is now and the day of salvation is near. It is the work of God and we can already rejoice with singing and dancing.

This is the religious and prophetic meaning of the struggle for liberation in South Africa today. We can speculate about the religious meaning of other things like death, life after death, the end of the world, nuclear warfare or whatever. But the good news for us is concerned with the signs of our times in our country. That is the source of our hope for now. That is what challenges us today. That is what the Spirit is saying to the Churches in South Africa. That is God's news for us and without doubt it is good news.

10
The Challenge

Hope and Challenge

The effect upon us of the good news of what God is doing in our country today is captured by these two words: hope and challenge. God is the basis of our hope *because* it is the good news of God's wonderful works that gives us hope. God is the one who challenges us – to believe the good news, to be hopeful and to transcend our present limitations.

Hope and challenge always go together. They are dialectically related because they depend upon one another and are fed by one another. Without hope for the future of South Africa it is impossible to feel challenged to do anything about the situation. On the other hand, it is only when we begin to take up the challenge that we begin to feel hopeful. We find hope in the struggle. The more we become involved in the process of salvation, the more hopeful we become. And the more hopeful we become, the more deeply do we feel challenged to further and further transcendence. Any attempt to preach a gospel that leaves everything to God is doomed to failure, because it is an attempt to have a gospel of hope that does not challenge us to 'work out our own salvation in fear and trembling' (Phil 2: 12). Similarly, any attempt to preach a gospel that challenges us to work for the liberation of our country without providing us with a firm basis for hoping that South Africa will be saved, is also doomed to failure. Hope and challenge belong together – they begin together and develop together. That is the covenant.

The dialectic of hope and challenge takes place not only in the individual but also in the community. We generate hope in one another. We create together an atmosphere of hopefulness. I am challenged by the hopefulness of other people and by the way they have taken up the challenge. I become hopeful when I see what God is doing in and through other people, and they are no doubt affected by my hope and my commitment. We need one another.

There is also a danger here. If the challenge is not sustained and broadened to more and more people, hope can begin to wane. If hope weakens, the challenge and the commitment weaken too. I have absolutely no reason to believe that this is going to happen. But it remains a danger and we continue to be responsible for one another and for the future.

The challenge that we must now try to spell out in greater detail is addressed to *all* Christians. (The same challenge or at least a similar challenge can no doubt be formulated in other terms and addressed to others who are not Christians.) My concern is that the challenge of the good news should not be seen as addressed *only* to white Christians or to Christians who actively or passively support a sinful system and are therefore not on the side of the struggle. It is true that for the unconverted or half-converted the challenge might need to be spelt out in greater detail, but the good news is addressed in the first place to the poor and to all who side with the cause of the poor. The good news is not supposed to bring hope to the poor and challenge to the rich. It is supposed to bring hope and challenge to everyone, by first of all encouraging *and* challenging the poor. The gospel is good news for the poor because salvation comes from below. It is the poor and the oppressed who are being challenged to take up their own cause as the cause of God or who are being confirmed and strengthened in the cause they have already taken up. Others will then be challenged to turn to God by supporting the cause of the oppressed and their struggle because it is God's struggle.

It should also be emphasised that for a Christian the challenge comes from God and not from me or anyone else. Being the author of this book does not make me the author of the challenge. Both you and I are challenged by the *kairos* in which we find ourselves and by the good news of what God is doing and saying in this moment of truth. The preacher of the gospel is not its author but its servant and messenger.

Repentance

Every gospel or prophetic message includes a call to repentance. The English word 'repentance', however, is misleading. It does not say enough. The Greek word that it translates, *metanoia*, means a change of mind and heart with the consequent change of behaviour or practice. The Hebrew word *sub* means to turn and in this context it means turning to God. What we are being challenged to do is to turn to God.

The God to whom we must turn, however, is the God who is alive and active in South Africa today. Repentance is not a general turning to an abstract God on the basis of his eternal commandments or general ethical principles. The call to repentance is an urgent call in the here and now, and it is based upon the belief that this is a moment of grace. The *kairos* is now. The time is ripe. God is challenging us by offering us a unique opportunity that may not be offered again or, at least, not in the same way. We must decide one way or the other now.

Turning to God means a conversion. It means turning from sin to salvation. But to be more specific, it means turning from sin as we experience it today in South Africa – the cycle of sin, the system and our active or passive involvement in it. Conversion means turning away from our possible apathy or sins of omission. On the other side it means turning to the whole process of salvation as God is working it out in South Africa today. Repentance or conversion does not mean trying to dissociate ourselves from the system so that we can say we are now all right. Turning to God in our context means committing ourselves to structural change because that is the struggle for salvation going on at this moment.

We should not try to separate and oppose the change of heart and the change of structures. They belong together and both are part of God's saving work. Personal conversion and structural change are dialectically related. Structural change takes off when some people begin to respond personally and communally to the material conditions of oppression in which they find themselves. Personal conversions are influenced by the social conditions and structural changes that are taking place. Some will probably only be converted later when the structural changes have taken root. Personal conversions only happen when the social conditions for them are right and ripe. It is through these social conditions that God calls us to repentance. On the other hand social conditions are also made ripe and developed into structural changes by people who have been converted to the need for structural change. The two are inextricably bound together because we are social beings.

Some people, of course, are in a much better position to accept the challenge and to oppose, resist, unmask and transcend the system. They are the ones who do not benefit from the system but suffer under it – those who are being sinned against. It is much easier for them to see the sinfulness of the system, to be conscientised and to have their eyes opened. That is a grace and it is the reason why Jesus could say: 'Blessed are you who are poor.'

However, not everyone who is oppressed will necessarily unmask the system and transcend it. If an oppressed person does not realise that he or she is being oppressed by a system, but thinks that it is simply some individuals at the top who are responsible, he or she might be tempted to try to move up to the top in order to join or replace those who are up there. The system would remain intact but the individual who reached the top would now begin to benefit from it. This is the individualist option for upward mobility. It is a rejection of God's grace.

Beyond Compromise

For many of us the great temptation is to compromise. We hear the call to turn to God and we try to make a half-turn. The ideological excuse for this is that we must avoid extremes and adopt a more moderate or balanced view of things. We can see this at work in those who hesitate about, or even balk at, the clear-cut distinction between the oppressor and the oppressed or between the system and the struggle. This, they say, is an oversimplification. Life in South Africa is much more complex than that. We must take a more balanced view that leaves room for nuances, qualifications and exceptions to the general rule –

for compromise.

We could discuss some of the complexities of the situation and possible exceptions and identify individuals who are oppressors in one respect and oppressed in another respect, but I am not sure that this would help. What we really need to look at are the motives of people who raise such objections and the interests that are served by dwelling upon them. Is the motive not to avoid the challenge and its far-reaching implications? Are the interests being served not the interests of the status quo and the system?

The way of compromise and moderation is not the way of God. The message of a true prophet is always direct and to the point. The Biblical prophets did not indulge in qualifications, complications and exceptions. The same is true of Jesus. 'Anyone who is not with me is against me' (Mt 12: 30 par). You cannot serve two masters. You must choose between God and Mammon – now. There is no third way.

This is an extreme position. But then God's position is an extreme one. What Jesus fought against was the moderation of the scribes and the Pharisees. Their cautiousness and false prudence led to compromise and hypocrisy. In the Book of the Revelation the Spirit says to the Church in Laodicea: 'Since you are neither hot nor cold but lukewarm, I will spit you out of my mouth. . . . Look, I am standing at the door, knocking. Repent *in earnest*' (3: 16, 19–20). For Aristotle, *virtus stat in medio*, virtue is constituted by moderation. But this is not true of the Bible. We are not called to love God or to love one another with moderation. We are called to transcendence.

In practice this means taking sides and not sitting on the fence (Bruggemann 1978: 24f; Soelle 1981: 51ff; Nolan 1985: *passim*; Kairos Document 1986: 9ff, 28). Those who stand on the sidelines and observe the struggle between good and evil from a distance or take a mere academic interest in how it is going to work itself out, are giving their support, by omission, to the aggressor. In the townships those who stand by and watch like spectators are called *Izethameli*, television viewers (Villa-Vicencio 1987: 95). We are called to transcend such compromises and such apathy, because nobody can in fact be neutral. As Metz says, 'following Christ never takes place in a vacuum; it is not something that happens in isolation from society or apart from a particular political situation, so as to be spared the antagonisms and sufferings of the world and to be granted the ability to maintain its own innocence by not being a participant' (1978: 43).

However, taking sides does not mean abandoning all criticism and becoming the slave of another ideology. The struggle is not perfect. It is flexible and adaptable, and it thrives on the constructive criticism of those who are committed to it. To be effective the struggle does require solidarity, unity, commitment, discipline and loyalty, but it can do without blind and slavish adherents. The spirit of the struggle against sin is a spirit of critical loyalty. Everyone in the struggle needs to cultivate this critical spirit, *not only Christians.*

New Life

The gospel is not a call to renewal but to new life. To re-new is to go back to a time when something that is now old was still new – to make it (or ourselves) 'like new again'. But the challenge of the good news is to transcend the past, not renew it, to make a fresh start, to be born again. We are called to new life because we live in a new time with new challenges and new hopes. The times have changed and God is doing a new thing (Is 43: 18–19). It is the surprising newness of the good news about what God is doing today that challenges us to begin a transcendently new life.

New life comes after death, that is to say, after we have died to the old ways, to our former selves and our old securities. As Paul says, we must die to sin and to the law (or the system), so as to rise up with Christ to a new life (Rom 6: 2–11; 7: 4–6). But the real importance of this is that we are being challenged to die, as Christ died, so that others may have new life. The ultimate challenge is the challenge to martyrdom for the sake of the struggle. James Cone says it with unusual directness: 'only those who are *prepared to die* in the struggle for freedom will experience *new life* in God' (in *Christianity and Crisis* 1973). We only find life when we are prepared to lose it (Mk 8: 35 parr).

It is here that we reach the most profound depths of the spirit and the challenge of the struggle. Here, more than anywhere else in our society today, we come face to face with God. People, especially young people, are willing to die, and are dying, so that others may have life, and have it in abundance (Jn 10: 10). Thousands have died, and who knows how many thousands more will die in the struggle for new life. When the workers go out on strike, especially when they are workers in the 'strategic' industries of mining and transport, they know that some of them will be killed. When the youth face the Casspirs and the riot police, they know they are facing death. They are prepared to die and that is why they already have new life. The struggle has become a matter of life and death for everyone involved.

Hence the extraordinary importance of funerals. Funerals are celebrations of new life. Those who have died in the struggle must be honoured. They are heroes and martyrs. *Hamba kahle*, go well, comrade. We shall carry on the struggle until we die too.

Less dramatic but even more challenging is the danger that every political activist faces: the danger of long imprisonment, solitary confinement and torture. Death must sometimes seem preferable to rotting in prison or going mad in solitary confinement, not to mention the horrors of interrogation and torture.

How pathetic in comparison are those who opt for half-measures and compromises. How pathetic are those who want renewal but would not be willing to risk anything, least of all their own lives, so that others may have new life. And we who are Christians and profess belief in the death and resurrection of Jesus Christ, can we face the challenge of death and resurrection in the struggle against the powers of evil?

Many of us will have to start with small steps. We shall have to learn to walk before we try to run. Perhaps we can begin to risk some other things before we try to risk our lives. For those of us who come from a white middle-class background we shall have to begin by overcoming or transcending our individualism.

Beyond Individualism

The people who came to John for baptism asked the question that is typical of their class: 'What must I do?' John told them, and doing what he suggested no doubt made them better people, but it would not have shaken the foundations of the system. The individual feels so powerless in the face of such an almighty system. 'The feeling of powerlessness', says Dorothee Soelle, 'is the deepest form of estrangement which our civilisation produces' (1981: 44). What can I do about it? I am only one person.

But Jesus seems to have had another idea. Alone you can do nothing. 'As a branch cannot bear fruit all by itself, but must remain part of the vine, neither can you unless you remain in me. I am the vine, you are the branches. . . . Cut off from me [the vine], you can do nothing' (Jn 15: 4–5). The vine as a living organism is the image of a human organisation that works together in harmony and solidarity to achieve what no individual can achieve alone. We are being challenged to become part of the body that incorporates the spirit and the practice of Jesus – in order to be effective.

We have seen the power of organisation and solidarity in the struggle. We have seen how salvation needs to be structured in organisations like the Church and political bodies. The question then is not, 'What must I do?', but 'Which organisation or group or community should I join?'

Those of us who suffer from this disease of individualism can do nothing until we begin to transcend it. The challenge to turn to God is a challenge to turn to the community, to learn to work *with* people instead of working *for* them. It takes time to overcome our individualism and to become truly democratic. For those of us who were not brought up to think things out with others, trying to work with others in a team is a heavy discipline. Even those who have not been brought up with the cult of individualism, or who are already involved in democratic organisations, need to resist the temptation of relying upon their own wisdom, doing their own thing, ignoring the decisions of the group and dominating others. We all need to be challenged again and again to overcome our individualism. That is the true meaning of love in social relationships. And God is love.

A person can have no greater love and reach no greater heights in transcending individualism, than to lay down his or her life for others (Jn 15: 13).

Action

The problem is not that we Christians have not loved one another. We can even claim to have loved our enemies. The problem is that our love has not been sufficiently active and effective. Protestations of love and concern that do not bear fruit in action are no longer credible in South Africa. The house (or organisation) that is built upon professions of faith without an active practice of faith will collapse when the storm comes (Mt 7: 26–27 par). Love without concerted action is simply an excuse for sins of omission – for apathy, passivity and cowardice. It has nothing to do with the practice of Jesus Christ.

Why is it, then, that in many Church circles in South Africa the term 'activist' is used as an accusation? The feeling still lingers that if you call someone a political activist, you are accusing them of sin or at least of some kind of human weakness, rather than praising them for their virtue and their courage. Nor is this because the activist is involved in politics. More and more Christians now see that we cannot avoid politics. But to become an activist is another matter. The word seems to imply agitating, causing trouble, making a fuss, staging walkouts or boycotts and generally taking militant action against what is wrong. But is that not precisely what we ought to be doing when faced with sin and evil? Or are we supposed to acquiesce with a few mild words of protest or even with many strong words of protest, in order to avoid 'activism'?

On the other hand, many Christians in South Africa have now discovered that love means action and that the only way to follow Jesus Christ in our circumstances is to become an activist. In fact this is the only way to minimise the violence. Sins of omission based upon apathy, timidity and fear will be one of the principal causes of any future or present escalation of violence and bloodshed. The challenge of our *kairos* is to act, to act effectively and to act together.

It is not possible for everyone to become an activist or even to join one of the people's organisations. There are sometimes 'circumstances beyond our control' that prevent a person from becoming fully involved in the mainstream of the struggle. But there is nothing to prevent any Christian from accepting the challenge to identify with the struggle and to find ways and means (at home, at work, in Church or amongst friends) of furthering the struggle against sin.

Reflection

Action without reflection degenerates into mere 'activism'. An active love cannot become an effective or efficacious love without reflection. A mindless frenzy of activity only produces mindless results. Sometimes we simply must stop to reflect upon what we are doing, why we are doing it and what it is supposed to achieve. Moreover, it is absolutely essential for us to reflect *together*. Alone we would probably only find more reasons for doing what we have always done and in the manner that we have always done it.

We learn from our practice or actions. There is no better teacher. It is in the actions and campaigns of the struggle that people have learnt the meaning of commitment, solidarity, democracy, hope and courage. Involvement in actions for justice and liberation is the only way of transcending alienation and becoming a subject of one's own history. However, it is one thing to have had the experience; it is another thing to have learnt from it, especially when it comes to learning from one's mistakes. Without reflection we shall not be able to learn all the lessons that action can teach us.

The challenge of the hour is not only a challenge to action but also to reflection. This is already happening. It is part of the spirit of the struggle. But the challenge remains. We all need to be challenged again and again to avoid mere 'activism', to learn from our mistakes, to transcend our present limitations and to consolidate the lessons of the past, by reflecting more deeply upon what we are doing, what we hope to achieve and how we hope to achieve it. Without continuous reflection there is always the danger that we shall lapse into dogmatism and ideological rigidity.

There are other things, apart from our own actions, that we need to reflect upon. We should never cease to reflect upon the latest strategies of the system, the new forms of co-option, the present dangers of compromise. Christians will want to reflect upon the ever-changing signs of the times to discover what God is doing now. We also need to look at the direction that the struggle is taking and assess it in terms of the spirit and aims of the struggle, and in the light of the practice of Jesus. And then there is the question of strategies and tactics. Any idea that we can succeed against the powers of evil by just being kindhearted and dedicated without a carefully thought-out plan or strategy is plain foolishness. We Christians have been taught to be suspicious of anything that looks like a manoeuvre, a plot or a conspiracy. We seem to have forgotten that Jesus told us to be as cunning as serpents (Mt 10: 16) and to learn from the astuteness of crooks such as the dishonest steward (Lk 16: 1–8). It seems that even in those days 'the children of light' were not as astute or cunning (same word in the Greek) as 'the children of this world' (Lk 16: 8). But how else are we ever going to deal with the 'wolves' of this world (Mt 10: 16)?

Jesus himself had to adopt the tactic of outwitting his opponents in argument (e.g. Mk 12: 13–17), of going into hiding at night and of making clandestine arrangements for the last supper (Nolan 1987: 105). Jesus' action in the Temple courtyard was a premeditated strategy to put his opponents on the spot (Nolan 1976: 103). The early Christians seem to have shown a good deal of cunning in their ability to run an underground Church in the tunnels of the catacombs that could not be detected by their persecutors because of 'false doors' and 'secret exits' (Lesbaupin 1987: 20). When the ancient Israelites outwitted their enemies, they attributed their success to God. The genius of Jesus was his ability, in dealing with wolves, to combine the cunning of the serpent with the gentleness of the dove (Mt 16: 10). Strategy and tactics are indispensable in the work of salvation.

There is yet another matter that requires deep and honest reflection. It is our *motives* for involvement in the struggle or for wanting to get involved in the struggle. Wrong motives begin to catch up with us sooner or later. It is better to detect them in ourselves and in others before they begin to have a harmful effect upon the struggle. The wrong motives which might creep in and to which we ought to pay attention, would include: the desire to be popular and admired, the desire for power over others, an attitude of rebelliousness against all authority and leadership, deep resentment or nursed anger, guilt or paternalism. It would be quite wrong and counterproductive to expect everyone in the struggle to have perfect motives. Nor should we become scrupulous about our own motives. But if we never even reflect upon these things, wrong motives could creep in by the back door and destroy much of the good work that has been done. We need to find a way of transcending our imperfect motivation, for the sake of the struggle.

The struggle against sin will not succeed without reflection. It is part of the challenge.

Prayer

For the Christian this kind of reflection moves over very quickly and easily into prayer. Prayer means making contact with the living God. And because God, in the Christian tradition, is discovered and spoken about as a person, prayer is experienced as contact with a person. The challenge of the good news and the call to transcendence are experienced as the voice of God. Whenever we hear that voice and respond to it we are praying.

Prayer is a typically religious way of expressing what we feel and think about the situation in which we find ourselves. It can give expression to what we long for – both for ourselves and for others. In prayer the hopes and the fears, the commitment and the frustration, the courage and the cowardice, the love and the selfishness that we find within us, can be made explicit and brought to consciousness before God. The full horror of the suffering and the powers of evil in South Africa can be faced in prayer; while the good news, the opportunity of the moment and the transcendent glory of what we are being called to, can be articulated and verbalised in prayers of praise, worship and thanksgiving. Prayer can be a way of celebrating our hope and making our commitment to transcendence.

Prayer *can* be all these things and much more. In practice it is all too often used or misused for other purposes. Prayer is sometimes used as a form of escape, as a substitute for action. Prayer without action, as Jesus says, is like saying 'Lord, Lord' but not doing the will of God – which is like building a house on sand (Mt 7: 21–27 par).

Prayer can also be hypocritical. This is the prayer of the Pharisee who stands up and prays in public so that others might see him, admire him and praise him for being a 'man of prayer' (Mt 6: 5–6). This is no prayer at all. It is a pretence. It is a sin of hypocrisy.

And then there is the prayer of the Pharisee who in the parable 'went up to the Temple to pray' (Lk 18: 9–14 RSV). His prayer is simply an expression of his arrogance, his grand illusion of being superior to other people: 'I am not like other people.' He stands before God and boasts about his fasting and other 'good works'. As Jesus says in the parable, this man was 'not justified in the eyes of God'. His pretence at prayer is simply a sin of insufferable pride and arrogance.

There was yet another kind of false prayer that Jesus rejected outright. He called it 'babbling'. 'In your prayers do not babble', he says, like those who 'think that by using many words they will make themselves heard' (Mt 6: 7). Babbling prayer is superstition. It treats prayer as a kind of magic. In all religions we find this temptation to reduce prayer to superstition and magic.

Prayer is not a matter of closing one's eyes and going into a trance. Prayer means opening one's eyes and facing reality. Nor is it a matter of adopting a servile attitude towards Jesus, which then enables us to escape our responsibilities. To hear the voice of God in prayer is to hear the call to take responsibility with others for sin and salvation in South Africa today. Genuine prayer heightens our awareness of what God is doing in our part of the world and challenges us to respond.

Prayer, like action and reflection, is most effective and powerful when it is done together with others in a spirit of solidarity. There may be times when we have to act alone. There is certainly value in sometimes reflecting alone. And there is a definite place for private prayer. But we are much more likely to experience the power of Christ's spirit 'when two or three are gathered together in my name' (Mt 18: 20). Prayer together in community is called liturgical prayer or divine worship – and that brings us to the role of the Church.

11
The Role of the Church

The Church and the Gospel

The Church is defined and constituted by the gospel. Put quite simply, the role of the Church is to preach the gospel. This involves considerably more than preaching sermons from a pulpit on Sundays. Evangelisation or preaching the gospel is more than just communicating a message. The purpose of a church service is to put people in touch with the living God. That is why the services of the Church are sometimes called divine worship, and that is why they include ritual or liturgical prayer and symbolic acts like the celebration of the sacraments. In the Catholic tradition the emphasis has been upon the sacraments, while in the Protestant tradition it has been upon the word. Today both traditions recognise the importance of sacrament and word alike for proclaiming, celebrating and bringing to life the good news about the living God (see, for example, *Evangelii Nuntiandi* 10, 26).

The gospel can also be preached by means of public statements. The Church comments on current events in terms of the good news, denouncing sin and announcing the hope of salvation, protesting about what is wrong and supporting what is right.

And finally the Church preaches the gospel by its witness. The witness of the Church is its activity of practising what it preaches. On the one hand, this is done by gathering together a community of believers that can be an example, a sign or sacrament of the salvation we are hoping for. On the other hand, the Church practises what it preaches by actions or campaigns and by social services such as feeding the hungry or running hospitals and schools. In themselves these actions, campaigns and social services are not the specific task of the Church. The Church becomes involved in running hospitals, schools and other social services only when the State is neglecting its social duties or is simply unable to do these things alone. Similarly, actions and campaigns for justice are not the specific task of the Church. These are the things that ought to be done by political organisations, but in times of crisis the Church might need to witness to what it believes to be right by taking some action. All of this is done by the Church, in certain circumstances, in order to preach the gospel by example.

The specific task of the Church, then, is to make known, by whatever means, the good news of how God is involved through Jesus Christ and the Holy Spirit in the events of our time. That, at least, is the theory. In practice in South Africa today there is considerable confusion about what the Churches are in fact doing and also about what the Churches are supposed to be doing. Much of this confusion centres around the meaning of the gospel. Many different and even contradictory versions of the gospel are being preached and celebrated. Among other things this leads to a bewildering variety of opinions about the role or mission of the Church (see SACC 1986b: 39–50). Everyone agrees that the Church is supposed to preach the gospel but everything depends upon which gospel you are talking about. If the gospel is defined too narrowly then some people are led to believe that the Church ought to be involved in other activities alongside the preaching of the gospel. Others will have different opinions. An institution that is so divided and speaks with so many different voices begins to lose its credibility.

A Divided Church

It is not without reason that I have left this discussion of the role of the Church until last. The Church is defined by the good news. It has therefore been necessary to grapple with the shape and the contents of this good news before trying to outline the role of the Church or Churches in South Africa. In theory it is the Church that should interpret and define the good news for our time. But when the Church is so divided (not only into thousands of different denominations but also within any one denomination or tradition) and when so many different gospels are actually being preached, it becomes quite impossible for the Church *as a whole*, or even one Church denomination *as a whole*, to determine what the good news is for us today. We may regret this, but it is a fact about our situation which cannot be ignored and which calls for explanation.

Hopefully what I have written in this book about the gospel is not just another personal opinion that will add more confusion to an already confused situation. My intention has been to give expression to the gospel that is emerging from the experience and the practice of a *part of the Church* in South Africa today. I should therefore like to think that I speak with the authority of that part of the Church, and that I have been able to show that the good news we preach does not contradict the Bible or the Christian tradition, but that it is the only way of making sense of this tradition in our present circumstances.

The part of the Church that I am referring to is the oppressed part, the poor and oppressed Christians of South Africa and all other Christians who have recognised the cause of the oppressed as the cause of God. This cuts across all our Church denominations and includes Church leaders from various traditions. In fact, this part of the Church must now be, far and away, the majority of Christians in South Africa.

What we are talking about, then, is a gospel that emerges from below, from the practice of faith and the instinct of faith of those who are oppressed. That is its authority and that is the sense in which this gospel *is* being preached by the Church – even if it is not the whole Church.

The Church in South Africa is divided. Apart from the divisions that arose historically because of controversies which took place in Europe a long time ago, the effective dividing line for us today is between Christians who actively or passively support the system and Christians who actively support the struggle. It is this division that prevents the Church from speaking with one voice, and it is this division that undermines, in practice, the authority of the Church as a whole. The result is what I want to call 'taking refuge in abstractions'.

Abstraction

We take refuge in abstractions when we divorce faith from life, or preach a 'universal' gospel and, most of all, when we engage in a ritual, liturgy or sacramental celebration that is separated off from the hard realities of daily life. There is nothing new about this. All religions face the danger of degenerating into mere rituals, formulas and formalities that are divorced from life. The Old Testament prophets had to confront the religious establishment of their own time with the irrelevance, emptiness and even the blasphemy of their sacrifices and ceremonies. Condemnations of the attempt to rely upon Temple rituals without the practice of justice can be found in several of the books of the prophets (Is 1: 11–17; 58: 1–12; Jer 6: 19–20; Amos 5: 21–24). To make the point clear, we quote from two of these passages.

> What are your endless sacrifices to me?
> says Yahweh.
> I am sick of holocausts of rams
> and the fat of calves.
> The blood of bulls and of goats revolts me.
> When you come to present yourselves before me,
> who asked you to trample over my courts?
> Bring me your worthless offerings no more,
> the smoke of them fills me with disgust.
> New Moons, Sabbaths, assemblies –
> I cannot endure festival and solemnity.
> Your New Moons and your pilgrimages
> I hate with all my soul.
> They lie heavy upon me,
> I am tired of bearing them.
> When you stretch out your hands [in prayer]
> I turn my eyes away.
> You may multiply your prayers,
> I shall not listen.
> Your hands are covered with blood,
> wash, make yourselves clean.
> Take your wrong-doing out of my sight.
> Cease to do evil.

> Learn to do good,
> search for justice,
> help the oppressed,
> be just to the orphan,
> plead for the widow.
> (Is 1: 11–17)

A more devastating indictment of a form of divine worship that is divorced from the practice of justice has never been written. It would not be difficult to translate it into modern terms and relate it to many a Sunday service in some of our South African churches (see, for example, Cassidy 1980: 154ff).

This is what I call abstract religion. It does not touch the realities of life. It enables the oppressor to carry on oppressing and exploiting and it presents no challenge to the apathy of those who sin by doing nothing (Balasuriya 1977: 6, 12ff).

Further on in the Book of Isaiah we have a passage that highlights the hypocrisy of those who side with oppression while they try to please God with the practice of fasting.

> Look, you do business on your fastdays,
> you oppress all your workers;
> look, you quarrel and squabble when you fast
> and strike the poor person with your fist.
> Fasting like yours today
> will never make your voice heard on high.
> Is not this the sort of fast that pleases me:
> to break unjust fetters and undo the thongs of the yoke,
> to let the oppressed go free
> and break every yoke.
> (Is 58: 3–6)

Jesus faced the same problem with the worship, the prayers and the other religious practices of the system of purity and holiness.

The role of the Church is to bring God into the picture. The trouble with an abstract gospel or liturgy is that it brings God in but leaves out the picture – the events and struggles of our time. When a Church preaches and celebrates a gospel that does not challenge anyone to *transcend* the status quo with all its sinfulness, that Church has lost contact with the transcendent God in our midst and is worshipping an idol.

We have seen how the youth are leaving the Church because its services and sacraments make no mention of the struggle. We have seen how the tendency to universalise and generalise about salvation makes it good news for neither the rich nor the poor. But we have also seen how powerful the good news can be when it is understood as good news about what God is doing and saying in South Africa today. If this were the good news that was preached and celebrated at Sunday services and at funerals, weddings and baptisms, the effect upon our country would be immeasurable. What would be released upon South Africa would be something more than the power of religious symbols. It would release the almighty power of God.

Church people today often ask: but what more can the Church do? The assumption here is that the Church, or at least some Churches, have made strong statements, have made representations to the government and have even given support to some of the campaigns of the people, and there is little more of this kind of thing that those Churches can do. I am not sure about that. Perhaps there is more of this kind of thing that these Churches can do; *but*, before we even begin to think about that, we should be asking about the transformation of what the Kairos Document calls, the Church's :'own specific activities': its regular preaching and its liturgical celebrations (1986: 29). This is the specific role of the Church and this is the role in which the Church can make a unique, an incalculable and indeed a transcendent contribution to the future of South Africa.

A Site of Struggle

If the Church, or part of the Church, were to begin to relate its preaching and its sacraments directly to the concrete realities of life in South Africa today in a way that is honest, bold and consistent, the immediate result would be division and dissension. This is already happening, precisely because there are some Church communities and some Church leaders or priests and ministers who have not hesitated to take this course. But the Church as a whole hesitates. It hesitates because it wants to preserve its denominational *unity* at all costs. In South Africa today, taking refuge in abstractions is the only way of preserving the unity of the Church. But the role of the Church is not to preserve its unity at all costs but to preach the gospel at all costs – even at the cost of unity (compare Kairos Document 1986: 11).

Jesus was not concerned to preserve the unity of Judaism at all costs. In fact he was very well aware of the fact that the good news he was preaching cut to the bone and would divide Judaism down the middle, right through the unity of the family itself. That is why Jesus says:

> Do you suppose that I am here
> to bring peace on earth?
> No, I tell you, but rather dissension.
> For from now on a household of five will be divided:
> three against two and two against three;
> the father divided against the son,
> son against father,
> mother against daughter,
> daughter against mother,
> mother-in-law against daughter-in-law,
> daughter-in-law against mother-in-law.
> (Lk 12: 51–53)

Jesus made Judaism itself into a site of struggle. For the sake of the good news and the urgency of its challenge to us today in South Africa, the Church will have to become a site of struggle.

A site of struggle is a place in society where, in one form or another, the struggle for liberation takes place. The factory, the mine, the school, the university and the community can be called sites of struggle. That the Church should become a site of struggle is regrettable, but the fact of the matter is that we are not all on the same side and we do not all believe in the same gospel. What we have in common is a longing to be faithful to Jesus Christ and perhaps a loyalty to the same Church tradition, such as Catholicism or the Reformed tradition. For the rest, we are divided and we shall have to confront one another and struggle against all the forms of 'worldliness' and blindness that have crept into the Church because of the system.

There is no point in trying to pretend that we are not a divided Church. Nor is there any point in entertaining the illusion that the whole Church can become, at this stage, a prophetic

Church. Part of the Church has already become prophetic and that part will increase as more and more Christians respond to the unprecedented opportunity that God is offering us in this *kairos*. But others will resist – strongly and forcefully. Some will probably leave the Church, or at least leave one denomination to join another more conservative one. Others will search for a compromise and do everything in their power to stem the tide of defections. It will be indeed a struggle and sometimes it might split families. But it will be part of God's struggle against sin and evil and against the powers that cause so many millions to suffer in South Africa today. What is at stake here is not just the reform or purification of the Church but the salvation of millions of people from sin, from suffering and from death.

The Church has a very important role to play in South Africa today. Its role is to introduce God into the picture – for the sake of everyone. But because this will be resisted by those who want to cling to an abstract God or neutral God or even a God who sides with the system, the Church can only play its invaluable role by becoming itself a site of struggle.

The Church and Politics

The Church is not a political organisation and it should not try to play the role of a political organisation or party. That would be a disaster both for the Church and for politics. It has happened before in the history of the Church and it is happening again today – whether the politics concerned are progressive or conservative. The only result is that the Church ceases to be the Church, the gospel is no longer preached and politics becomes confused.

To understand this we need to be clear about the distinction between the Church as an *institution* and the Church as the *people* who belong to it. Up until now we have been talking about the Church as an institution. We have seen that its role as an institution is to preach the gospel, to bring God into the picture. The picture is political, and bringing God into it has far-reaching political consequences, but that does not make the Church (as an institution) into a political organisation.

The role of a political organisation or party (one that is

opposed to the system) is to restructure the society by political means, that is to say, by mobilising and organising to put political pressure on the system, by taking part in negotiations, by contesting an election, by canvassing for votes and then by participating in the government of the country. Not every political organisation will do all of this but this is the aim of politics and political organising. The Church may want to see this happen, encourage people to do it, support the organisations that are doing it and even give a helping hand, *but* the aim of the Church as an institution is not to contest an election or take its place in a new parliament or share in any way in the governing of the country.

However, the *people* who are members of the Church must do this. They are also members of society. The *same people* who come to Church to celebrate what God is doing in the country will go to a political organisation to do God's will in trying to dismantle apartheid and set up a new government. There need be no contradiction here, but there is a difference of role. Both the Church and the political organisations are involved (or should be) in the same struggle against sin or injustice, but not in the same way.

Problems arise when the Church as an institution begins to offer its own solutions to political problems. To formulate one's own political policies and to mobilise people around them: this is to play the role of a political organisation. The role of the Church is to comment on political policies, to name the sin and the salvation, to criticise what is wrong, to praise what is right, to pray for salvation, to praise God for what is good, to support, to protest and even to propose new ways of acting, but not to formulate political or economic policies. We have already seen that the Church itself is a site of struggle. That makes it difficult enough for the Church to preach the gospel; if it were to start formulating its own political policy we would find ourselves with some kind of compromise – *a third way*.

The great temptation of the Church as an institution is to promulgate a third way of some kind or another, a political policy that is neither that of the system nor that of the struggle but somewhere in-between. Quite apart from the fact that there is no viable third way, any Church that proposes it and tries to mobilise its members around it is playing the role of a political organisation. If any such middle-of-the-road policy is to be proposed to the people and tested in the political arena, it should be done by a political organisation or party.

It is a pity that Walter Wink chose to entitle his book on South Africa, *Jesus' Third Way*. He does not seem to realise how that will be understood in South Africa and what confusion it will sow about the role of Jesus in the struggle. The third way for Walter Wink (and others in South Africa) is the way of nonviolent militant action which is set between flight and fight, where flight means doing nothing and fight means the violence of revenge and retaliation (1987: 23). But this is not the choice with which we are faced at the moment. The choice is between the system and the struggle. The author realises that most of the struggle is nonviolent (4, 45) and he does not wish to sit in judgment over those who resort to violence (68) nor does he wish to compromise with mere reforms (10). All he wants to do is propose some tactics which are not violent and which are similar to the tactics used by Jesus in his circumstances. To call this 'Jesus' third way' is to confuse the issue no end. In South Africa the third way is the way of compromise and that is how his book will be understood.

The Calling of the Church

The Church in South Africa today, or at least that part of the Church which is on the side of the struggle, has a unique prophetic calling or vocation. The *role* of the Chuch may be the same in all circumstances or in all circumstances of conflict, but in South Africa the Church also has a special, if not unique, *calling* because of the particular *kairos* in which we find ourselves.

From the point of view of the struggle itself, the Church, or at least a part of it, has an irreplaceable role to play. The other religious faiths also have an important and irreplaceable role to play, but the specialness of the role of the Christian Churches is based upon the very large numbers of people on both sides of the struggle who claim to be Christians. The struggle itself is a human project that proposes to build a truly human community, but, because by far the majority of the people involved believe in God, the project will not succeed unless God is brought into the picture explicitly and by name.

God is at work in the world even if we fail to preach and celebrate this reality. But when people do believe in God and when God is named and when the wonderful works of God are preached and celebrated, the effect upon the outcome of human struggles can be transcendently powerful. That is the role of organised religion. In the case of Christianity, it is the role of the Church, and it is the reason why the Church *must* find a prophetic way of preaching and celebrating the good news of what God is doing in our time.

There are considerable similarities between the calling of the Church in South Africa and the calling of the Church in places like Latin America or the Philippines, but there are also very challenging differences. There is the challenge that is presented by the enormous variety of Christian Churches and traditions in South Africa, including the traditions of the African Independent Churches. There is the challenge of racially divided Churches and the fact that there are strong Christian traditions on both sides of the struggle. There is the challenge of being a Christian in a country where there are other religious faiths such as Islam, Hinduism and Judaism, not to mention African traditional religion and atheists. There is the challenge of Marxism. And then there is the challenge of the struggle itself and a repressive regime that has no legitimacy in the eyes of most of the people, and the challenge of possible future compromises. And what of the challenges presented to the Church by millions of starving people, an armed struggle and a possible bloodbath?

How does the Church preach the gospel and speak about God in such circumstances and in such a time of crisis and conflict? As I have said, we cannot expect the whole Church to speak with one voice. But challenges are opportunities and I am convinced that at least part of the Church, if not the major part, will rise to the occasion, to speak of God and Jesus Christ and to develop a practice of the faith that will be an example, at least in some respects, to the rest of the world. This is already beginning to happen. God has given the Church in South Africa an opportunity and a calling that is special, if not unique, in the history of the Christian faith.

South Africa is remarkably different. God is doing a new thing here. We who are privileged to be South Africans, painful as that may be at the moment, have a calling or vocation that is of historical significance for Africa and indeed for the whole world. One day we shall be a united nation that is thoroughly non-racial, democratic at every level, liberated from political oppression and economically independent, a nation that develops new forms of economic justice, new cultural values, new forms of music and so forth. The liberation of South Africa will have an enormous impact upon the whole of Africa, particularly because of the economic wealth and industrial development here in the South. In many ways Africa will not be truly free until South Africa is free. The liberation of South Africa will also be of vital importance to North–South relationships in the world. If we can overcome the so-called First World–Third World oppression within our country, we can make a valuable contribution to the liberation of the rest of the Third World.

The implications for the Church are immeasurable. God has called us to be the Church of Jesus Christ at this time and in this place. If we can measure up to the challenge, we can make a significant contribution to Christian practice and Christian theology in the world of tomorrow.

Appendix I

The Freedom Charter

as adopted at the Congress of the People on 26 June 1955

Preamble

We, the people of South Africa, declare for all our country and the world to know: That South Africa belongs to all who live in it, black and white, and that no government can justly claim authority unless it is based on the will of the people; That our people have been robbed of their birthright to land, liberty and peace by a form of government founded on injustice and inequality; That our country will never be prosperous or free until all our people live in brotherhood, enjoying equal rights and opportunities; That only a democratic state, based on the will of the people, can secure to all their birthright without distinction of colour, race, sex or belief; And therefore, we the people of South Africa, black and white, together equals, countrymen and brothers, adopt this FREEDOM CHARTER. And we pledge ourselves to strive together, sparing nothing of our strength and courage, until the democratic changes here set out have been won.

The People Shall Govern!

Every man and woman shall have the right to vote for and stand as a candidate for all bodies which make laws; All the people shall be entitled to take part in the administration of the country; The rights of the people shall be the same regardless of race, colour or sex; All bodies of minority rule, advisory boards, councils and authorities shall be replaced by democratic organs of self-government.

All National Groups Shall Have Equal Rights!

There shall be equal status in the bodies of state, in the courts and in the schools for all national groups and races; All national groups shall be protected by law against insults to their race and national pride; All people shall have equal rights to use their own language and to develop their own folk culture and customs; The preaching and practice of national, race or colour discrimination and contempt shall be a punishable crime; All apartheid laws and practices shall be set aside.

The People Shall Share in the Country's Wealth!

The national wealth of our country, the heritage of all South Africans, shall be restored to the people; The mineral wealth beneath the soil, the banks and monopoly industry shall be transferred to the ownership of the people as a whole; All other industries and trades shall be controlled to assist the well-being of the people; All people shall have equal rights to trade where they choose, to manufacture and to enter all trades, crafts and profession.

The Land Shall Be Shared Among Those Who Work It!

Restriction of land ownership on a racial basis shall be ended, and all the land re-divided amongst those who work it, to banish famine and land hunger; The state shall help the peasants with implements, seed, tractors and dams to save the soil and assist the tillers; Freedom of movement shall be guaranteed to all who work on the land; All shall have the right to occupy land wherever they choose; People shall not be robbed of their cattle, and forced labour and farm prisons shall be abolished.

All Shall Be Equal Before the Law!

No one shall be imprisoned, deported or restricted without a fair trial; No one shall be condemned by the order of any government official; The courts shall be representative of all the people; Imprisonment shall be only for serious crimes against the people, and shall aim at re-education, not vengeance; The police force and army shall be open to all on an equal basis and shall be the helpers and protectors of the people; All laws which discriminate on the grounds of race, colour or belief shall be repealed.

All Shall Enjoy Human Rights!

The law shall guarantee to all their right to speak, to organise, to meet together, to publish, to preach, to worship and to educate their children; The privacy of the house from police raids shall be protected by law; All shall be free to travel without restriction from countryside to town, from province to province, and from South Africa abroad; Pass laws, permits and all other laws restricting these freedoms shall be abolished.

There Shall Be Work and Security!

All who work shall be free to form trade unions, to elect their officers and to make wage agreements with their employers; The state shall recognise the right and duty of all to work, and to draw full unemployment benefits; Men and women of all races shall receive equal pay for equal work; There shall be a forty-hour working week, a national minimum wage, paid annual leave, and sick leave for all workers, and maternity leave on full pay for all working mothers; Miners, domestic workers, farm workers and civil servants shall have the same rights as all others who work; Child labour, compound labour, the tot system and contract labour shall be abolished.

The Doors of Learning and Culture Shall Be Opened!

The government shall discover, develop and encourage national talent for the enhancement of our cultural life; All the cultural treasure of mankind shall be open to all, by free exchange of books, ideas and contact with other lands; The aim of education shall be to teach the youth to love their people and their culture, to honour human brotherhood, liberty and peace; Education shall be free, compulsory, universal and equal for all children; Higher education and technical training shall be opened to all by means of state allowances and scholarships awarded on the basis of merit; Adult illiteracy shall be ended by a mass state education plan; Teachers shall have all the rights of other citizens; The colour bar in cultural life, in sport and in education shall be abolished.

There Shall Be Houses, Security and Comfort!

All people shall have the right to live where they choose, to be decently housed, and to bring up their families in comfort and security; Unused housing space to be made available to the people; Rent and prices shall be lowered, food plentiful and no one shall go hungry; A preventive health scheme shall be run by the state; Free medical care and hospitalisation shall be provided for all, with special care for mothers and young children; Slums shall be demolished and new suburbs built where all shall have transport, roads, lighting, playing fields, crèches and social centres; The aged, the orphans, the disabled and the sick shall be cared for by the state; Rest, leisure and recreation shall be the right of all; Fenced locations and ghettos shall be abolished and laws which break up families shall be repealed.

There Shall Be Peace and Friendship!

South Africa shall be a fully independent state, which respects the rights and sovereignty of all nations; South Africa shall strive to maintain world peace and the settlement of all international disputes by negotiation not war; Peace and friendship amongst all our people shall be secured by upholding the equal rights, opportunities and status of all; The people of the protectorates Basutoland, Bechuanaland and Swaziland shall be free to decide for themselves their own future; The right of all the peoples of Africa to independence and self-government shall be recognised, and shall be the basis of close cooperation.

Let all who love their people and their country now say, as we say here: 'These freedoms we will fight for, side by side, throughout our lives, until we have won our liberty.'

Appendix II

The Women's Charter

as adopted by the Federation of South African Women on 17 April 1954

Preamble

We, the women of South Africa, wives and mothers, working women and housewives, hereby declare our aim of striving for the removal of all laws, regulations, conventions and customs that discriminate against us as women.

A Single Society

We do not form a society separate from men. There is only one society, and it is made up of both women and men. As women we share the problems and anxieties of our men, and join hands with them to remove social evils and obstacles to progress.

Women's Lot

We women share with our menfolk the cares and anxieties imposed by poverty and its evils. As wives and mothers it falls upon us to make small wages stretch a long way. It is we who feel the cries of our children when they are hungry and sick. It is our lot to keep and care for the homes that are too small, broken and dirty to be kept clean. We know the burden of looking after children and land when our husbands are away in the mines, on the farms, and in the towns earning our daily bread. We know what it is to keep family life going in pondokkies and shanties, or in over-crowded one-room apartments. We know the bitterness of children taken to lawless ways, of daughters becoming unmarried mothers whilst still at school, of boys and girls growing up without education, training or jobs at a living wage.

Poor and Rich

These are the evils that need not exist. They exist because the society in which we live is divided into poor and rich, into black and white. They exist because there are privileges for the few, discrimination and harsh treatment for the many. We women have stood and will stand shoulder to shoulder with our menfolk in a common struggle against poverty, race and class discrimination.

National Liberation

As members of the National Liberatory movements and trade unions, in and through our various organisations, we march forward with our men in the struggle for liberation and the defence of the working people. We pledge ourselves to keep high the banner of equality, fraternity and liberty. As women there rests upon us also the burden of removing from our society all the social differences developed in past times between men and women, which have the effect of keeping our sex in a position of inferiority and subordination.

Equality for Women

We resolve to struggle for the removal of laws and customs that deny African women the right to own, inherit or alienate property. We resolve to work for a change in the laws of marriage such as are found amongst our African, Malay and Indian people, which have the effect of placing wives in the position of legal subjection to husbands, and giving husbands the power to dispose of wives' property and earnings, and dictate to them in all matters affecting them and their children. We recognise that the women are treated as minors by those marriage and property laws because of ancient and revered traditions and customs which had their origin in the antiquity of the people and no doubt served purposes of great value in bygone times. There was a time in the African society when every women reaching marriageable stage was assured of a husband, home, land and security. The husbands and wives with their children belonged to families and clans that supplied most of their material needs and were largely self-sufficient. Men and women were partners in a compact and closely integrated family unit.

Women Who Labour

Those conditions have gone. The tribal and kinship society to which they belonged have been destroyed as a result of the loss of tribal land, migration of men away from the tribal home, the growth of towns and industries, and the rise of a great body of wage-earners on the farms and in the urban areas, who depend wholly, or mainly on wages for a livelihood. Thousands of women are employed in factories, homes, offices, shops, on farms and in professions as nurses, teachers and the like. As unmarried women, widows or divorcees they have to fend for themselves often without assistance of a male relative. Many of them are responsible for their own livelihood but also for that of their children. Large numbers of women are in fact the sole breadwinners and heads of their families.

Forever Minors

Nevertheless, the laws and practices derived from an earlier and different state of society are still applied to them. They are responsible for their own person and their children. Yet the law seeks to enforce upon them the status of a minor. Not only are African, Coloured and Indian women denied political rights, but they are also in many parts of the Union denied the same status as men in such matters as the right to enter into contracts, to own and dispose of property, and to exercise guardianship over their children.

Obstacles to Progress

The law has lagged behind the development of society; it no longer corresponds to the actual social and economic position of women. The law has become an obstacle to progress of the women, and therefore a brake on the whole of society. The intolerable condition would not be allowed to continue were it not for the refusal of a large section of our menfolk to concede to us women the rights and privileges which they demand for themselves. We shall teach the men that they cannot hope to liberate themselves from the evils of discrimination and prejudice as long as they fail to extend to women complete and unqualified equality in law and in practice.

Need for Education

We also recognise that large numbers of our womenfolk continue to be bound by traditional practices and conventions, and fail to realise that these have become obsolete and a brake on progress. It is our duty and privilege to enlist all women in our struggle for emancipation and to bring to them all realisation of the intimate relationship that exists between their status of inferiority as women and their inferior status to which people are subjected by discriminatory laws and colour prejudices. It is our intention to carry out a nation-wide programme of education that will bring home to all the men and women of all national groups the realisation that freedom cannot be won for any one section or for the people as a whole as long as we women are kept in bondage.

An Appeal

We women appeal to all progressive organisations, to members of the great National Liberatory movements, to the trade unions and working-class organisations, to the churches, educational and welfare organisations, to all progressive men and women who have the interests of the people at heart, to join with us in this great and noble endeavour.

Our Aims

We declare the following aims.

This organisation is formed for the purpose of uniting women in common action for the removal of all political, legal, economic and social disabilities. We shall strive for women to obtain:

(1) The right to vote and to be elected to all state bodies, without restriction or discrimination.

(2) The right to full opportunities for employment with equal pay and possibilities of promotion in all spheres of work.

(3) Equal rights with men in relation to property, marriage and children, and for the removal of all laws and customs that deny women such equal rights.

(4) For the removal of all laws that restrict free movement, that prevent or hinder the right of free association and activity in democratic organisations, and the right to participate in the work of these organisations.

(5) For the development of every child through free compulsory education for all; for the protection of mother and child through maternity homes, welfare clinics, crèches and nursery schools, in countryside and town; through proper homes for all and through the provision of water, light, transport, sanitation, and other amenities of modern civilisation.

(6) To build and strengthen women's sections in the National Liberatory movements, the organisation of women in trade unions, and through the people's varied organisations.

(7) To cooperate with all other organisations that have similar aims in South Africa as well as throughout the world.

(8) To strive for permanent peace throughout the world.

Bibliography

Journals

Catholic Biblical Quarterly.

Christianity and Crisis.

Concilium.

Ecunews.

Journal of Theology for Southern Africa.

Missionalia.

Union Seminary Quarterly Review.

Books

Abesamis, Carlos H.: *Where are We Going: Heaven or New World?* Foundation Books (Manila), 1983.

Anderson, B. W.: *The Eighth Century Prophets: Amos, Hosea, Isaiah, Micah.* SPCK, 1979.

Balasuriya, Tissa: *Jesus Christ and Human Liberation.* SCM, 1977.

Banana, Canaan: *The Gospel According to the Ghetto.* Mambo Press (Gweru), 1980.

Banana, Canaan: *Theology of Promise: The Dynamics of Self Reliance.* College Press (Harare), 1982.

Baum, Gregory: *Religion and Alienation: A Theological Reading of Sociology.* Paulist Press, 1975.

Belo, Fernando: *A Materialist Reading of the Gospel of Mark.* Orbis, 1981.

Bloch, Ernst: *Man on his Own: Essays in the Philosophy of Religion.* Herder, 1970.

Boesak, Allan: *Farewell to Innocence: A Socio–Ethical Study on Black Theology and Power.* Orbis, 1977.

Boesak, A. & Villa–Vicencio, C. (eds.): *When Prayer Makes News.* Westminster Press, 1986.

Boff, Clodovis: *Theology and Praxis: Epistemological Foundations.* Orbis, 1987.

Boff, Leonardo: *Liberating Grace.* Orbis, 1979.

Boff, Leonardo and Clodovis: *Salvation and Liberation: In Search of a Balance Between Faith and Politics.* Orbis, 1984.

Brown, Delwin: *To Set at Liberty: Christian Faith and Human Freedom*. Orbis, 1981.

Brueggemann, W.: *The Prophetic Imagination*. Fortress, 1978.

Caird, G. B.: *Principalities and Powers: A Study in Pauline Theology*. Clarendon Press, 1956.

Campbell, Alastair V.: *The Gospel of Anger*. SPCK, 1986.

Casalis, Georges: *Correct Ideas Don't Fall from the Skies: Elements for an Inductive Theology*. Orbis, 1984.

Cassidy, Sheila: *Prayer for Pilgrims*. Collins, 1980.

Charles, R. H.: *Eschatology: The Doctrine of a Future Life in Israel, Judaism and Christianity*. Schocken, 1963.

Clévenot, Michel: *Materialist Approaches to the Bible*. Orbis, 1985.

Cloete, G. D. and Smit, D. J. (eds.): *A Moment of Truth: The Confession of the Dutch Reformed Mission Church 1982*. Eerdmans, 1984.

Cole, Josette: *Crossroads: The Politics of Reform and Repression 1976–1986*. Ravan, 1987.

Cone, James: *God of the Oppressed*. Orbis, 1975.

Cone, James: *A Black Theology of Liberation*, 2nd ed. Orbis, 1986.

Cox, Harvey: *God's Revolution and Man's Responsibility*. SCM, 1969.

Cox, Harvey: *On Not Leaving It to the Snake*. SCM, 1968.

Croatto, J. Severino: *Exodus: A Hermeneutic of Freedom*. Orbis, 1981.

CTA–CCA (Commission on Theological Concerns of the Christian Conference of Asia): *Minjung Theology: People as the Subjects of History*. Orbis, 1983.

de Gruchy, John W.: *The Church Struggle in South Africa*. David Philip, 1979.

de Gruchy, John W. (ed.): *Cry Justice: Prayers, Meditations and Readings from South Africa*. Orbis, 1986.

de Gruchy, John W.: *Theology and Ministry in Context and Crisis: A South African Perspective*. Collins, 1987.

de Gruchy, John W. and Villa–Vicencio, C. (eds.): *Apartheid is a Heresy*. David Philip, 1983.

de Kiewiet, C.: *South Africa. A History Social and Economic*. Oxford, 1941.

de la Torre, Edicio: *Touching Ground, Taking Root: Theological and Political Reflections on the Philippine Struggle*. SPI (Quezon City), 1986.

de Santa Ana, Julio: *Good News to the Poor: The Challenge of the Poor in the History of the Church*. WCC, 1977.

Desmond, Cosmas: *Christians or Capitalists? Christianity and Politics in South Africa*. Bowerdean, 1978.

Douglas. Mary: *Purity and Danger*. Routledge, 1978.

Dumas, André: *Political Theology and the Life of the Church*. SCM, 1978.

Durand, J. J. F. *Die Sonde: Wegwysers in die Dogmatiek*. NG Boekhandel, 1978.

Echegaray, Hugo: *The Practice of Jesus*. Orbis, 1984.

Ela, Jean–Marc: *African Cry*. Orbis, 1986.

Elliot, Charles: *Comfortable Compassion? Poverty, Power and the Church*.

Hodder & Stoughton, 1987.

Fierro, A.: *The Militant Gospel: An Analysis of Contemporary Political Theologies*. SCM, 1977.

Foster, Don with Davis, Dennis and Sandler, Diane: *Detention and Torture in South Africa*. David Philip, 1987.

Gardavsky, V.: *God is Not Yet Dead*. Penguin, 1973.

Gibellini, R. (ed.): *Frontiers of Theology in Latin America*. Orbis, 1979.

Gottwald, Norman K.: *All the Kingdoms of the Earth: Israelite Prophecy and International Relations in the Ancient Near East*. Harper & Row, 1964.

Gottwald, Norman K.: *The Tribes of Yahweh: A Sociology of the Religion of Liberated Israel 1250–1050 B.C.E.* Orbis, 1979.

Gottwald, Norman K. (ed.): *The Bible and Liberation: Political and Social Hermeneutics*. Orbis, 1983.

Gutierrez, Gustavo: *A Theology of Liberation*. Orbis, 1973.

Gutierrez, Gustavo: *We Drink from Our Own Wells: The Spiritual Journey of a People*. Orbis, 1984.

Hanks, Thomas D.: *God So Loved the Third World: The Bible, the Reformation and Liberation Theologies*. Orbis, 1983.

Hechanova, L. G.: *The Gospel and Struggle*. CIIR, 1986.

Hellwig, Monika K. *Jesus the Compassion of God*. Glazier, 1983.

Hinkelammert, F. J.: *The Ideological Weapons of Death: A Theological Critique of Capitalism*. Orbis, 1986.

Hollenbach, Paul: 'Social Aspects of John the Baptizer's Preaching Mission in the Context of Palestinian Judaism' in *ANRW II 19.1*, ed. by W. Haase: Berlin & New York, 1979.

Hollenbach, Paul: 'The Conversion of Jesus: From Jesus the Baptizer to Jesus the Healer' in *ANRW II 25.1*, ed. by W. Haase: Berlin & New York, 1982.

Horsley, R. A. and Hanson, J. S.: *Bandits, Prophets and Messiahs: Popular Movements at the Time of Jesus*. Seabury, 1985.

ICT (Institute for Contextual Theology): *Speaking for Ourselves*. ICT, 1985.

Jennings, W. (ed.): *The Vocation of the Theologian*. Fortress, 1985.

Jeremias, Joachim: *Jerusalem in the Time of Jesus*. Fortress, 1969.

Kairos Document: *Challenge to the Church*, revised edition. Skotaville, 1986.

Kinghorn, Johann (ed.): *Die N.G. Kerk en Apartheid*. Macmillan, S.A., 1986.

Koch, K.: *The Rediscovery of Apocalyptic*. SCM, 1972.

Lash, Nicholas: *A Matter of Hope: A Theologian's Reflections on the Thought of Karl Marx*. Darton, Longman & Todd, 1981.

Leatt, J., Kneiffel, T., Nürnberger, K. (eds.): *Contending Ideologies in South Africa*. David Philip, 1986.

Lelyveld, Joseph: *Move Your Shadow: South Africa Black and White*. Jonathan Ball, 1986.

Lesbaupin, I: *Blessed are the Persecuted: Christian Life in the Roman Empire*. Orbis, 1987.

Metz, J. B.: *Faith in History and Society: Towards a Practical Fundamental Theology*. Burns & Oates, 1980.

Metz, J. B.: *Followers of Christ: Religious Life and the Church*. Burns & Oates, 1978.

Mofokeng, Takatso: *The Crucified among the Crossbearers: Towards a Black Christology*. de Kok, 1983.

Moltmann, Jürgen: *Theology of Hope*. SCM, 1967.

Moltmann, Jürgen: *The Crucified God*. SCM, 1974.

Moltmann, Jürgen: *The Experiment Hope*. SCM, 1975.

Mosala, I. J. and Tlhagale, B. (eds.): *Hammering Swords into Ploughshares: Essays in Honour of Archbishop Mpilo Desmond Tutu*. Skotaville, 1986a.

Mosala, I. J. and Tlhagale, B. (eds.): *The Unquestionable Right to be Free: Essays in Black Theology*. Skotaville, 1986b.

Nolan, Albert: *Jesus before Christianity*. David Philip, 1976.

Nolan, Albert: *Taking Sides*. Catholic Truth Society, London, 1985.

Nolan, A. and Broderick, R.: *To Nourish Our Faith: Theology of Liberation for Southern Africa*. Cornerstone Books, 1987.

Oosthuizen, D. C. S.: *The Ethics of Illegal Action and Other Essays*. Sprocas, Ravan, 1973.

Prior, Andrew (ed.): *Catholics in Apartheid Society*. David Philip, 1982.

Rahner, Karl: *Foundations of Christian Faith: An Introduction to the Idea of Christianity*. Seabury, 1978.

Riches, J.: *Jesus and the Transformation of Judaism*. Darton, Longman & Todd, 1980.

Russell, D. S. : *The Method and Message of Jewish Apocalyptic*. SCM, 1964.

SACBC (South African Catholic Bishops' Conference): *The Last Affidavits*, 1987.

SACBC (South African Catholic Bishops' Conference): *Evangelization in the Modern World Pope Paul VI*, 1975 (Pastoral Series 6).

SACBC (South African Catholic Bishops' Conference): *Instruction on Christian Freedom and Liberation, Sacred Congregation for the Doctrine of the Faith*, 1986 (Pastoral Series 43).

SACC (South African Council of Churches): *Hope in Crisis: National Conference Report 1986, ed.* by Sol Jacob. 1986a.

SACC (South African Council of Churches): *The Relevance of Evangelism in South Africa Today: Seminar Papers*. 1986b.

Schillebeeckx, E.: *Jesus: An Experiment in Christology*. Collins, 1979.

Schillebeeckx, E.: *Christ: The Christian Experience in the Modern World*. SCM, 1980.

Schoonenberg, P.: *Man and Sin. A Theological View*. Notre Dame, 1965.

Schottroff, L. and Stegemann, W.: *Jesus and the Hope of the Poor*. Orbis, 1986.

Schottroff, W. and Stegemann, W. (eds.): *God of the Lowly: Socio–Historical Interpretations of the Bible*. Orbis, 1984.

Schüssler–Fiorenza, E.: *Invitation to the Book of Revelation*. Image Books,

1981.

Segundo, J. L.: *Evolution and Guilt*. Gill & Macmillan, 1980.

Sobrino, J.: *Jesus in Latin America*. Orbis, 1987.

Soelle, D.: *Choosing Life*. SCM, 1981.

Soelle, D.: *To Work and to Love: A Theology of Creation*. Fortress, 1984.

Stadler, Alf: *The Political Economy of Modern South Africa*. David Philip, 1987.

Stegemann, W.: *The Gospel and the Poor*. Fortress, 1984.

Sunter, Clem: *The World and South Africa in the 1990s*. Human & Rousseau, 1987.

Suttner, R. and Cronin, J. (eds.): *Thirty Years of the Freedom Charter*. Ravan, 1985.

Tamez, Elsa: *Bible of the Oppressed*. Orbis, 1982.

Theissen, Gerd: *The First Followers of Jesus: A Sociological Analysis of the Earliest Christianity*. SCM, 1978.

Tutu, Desmond Mpilo: *Hope and Suffering: Sermons and Speeches*. Skotaville, 1983.

Villa–Vicencio, Charles: *Between Christ and Caesar: Classic and Contemporary Texts on Church and State*. David Philip, 1986.

Villa–Vicencio, Charles (ed.): *Theology and Violence: The South African Debate*. Skotaville, 1987.

Villa–Vicencio, C. and de Gruchy, J. W. (eds.): *Resistance and Hope: South African Essays in Honour of Beyers Naudé*. David Philip, 1985.

Von Rad, Gerhard: *The Message of the Prophets*. SCM, 1968.

Von Rad, Gerhard: *Old Testament Theology*, Vol. I. Harper, 1962.

Vorster, W. S. (ed.): *Reconciliation and Construction: Creative Options for a Rapidly Changing South Africa*. UNISA, 1986.

Walzer, Michael: *Exodus and Revolution*. Basic Books, 1985.

Wink, Walter: *Naming the Powers: The Language of Power in the New Testament (The Powers: Vol.I)*. Fortress, 1984.

Wink, Walter: *Unmasking the Powers: The Invisible Forces That Determine Human Existence (The Powers: Vol.II)*. Fortress, 1986.

Wink, Walter: *Violence and Nonviolence in South Africa: Jesus' Third Way*. New Society Pub. (Philadelphia), 1987.

Index